Items should be returned on or before the last date shown below. Items not already requested by other borrowers may be renewed in person, in writing or by telephone. To renew, please quote the number on the barcode label. To renew online a PIN is required. This can be requested at your local library.
Renew online @ **www.dublincitypubliclibraries.ie**
Fines charged for overdue items will include postage incurred in recovery. Damage to or loss of items will be charged to the borrower.

**Leabharlanna Poiblí Chathair Bhaile Átha Cliath**
**Dublin City Public Libraries**

Dublin City
Baile Átha Cliath

Central Library, Henry St.
An Lárleabharlann, Sráid Anraí
Tel: 8734333

| Date Due | Date Due | Date Due |
|---|---|---|
|  |  |  |

# The Vibrant House

Irish Writing and Domestic Space

Rhona Richman Kenneally
and Lucy McDiarmid

EDITORS

FOUR COURTS PRESS

Typeset in 12pt on 15pt AdobeCaslonPro
by Carrigboy Typesetting Services for
FOUR COURTS PRESS LTD
7 Malpas Street, Dublin 8, Ireland
www.fourcourtspress.ie
*and in North America for*
FOUR COURTS PRESS
c/o ISBS, 920 NE 58th Avenue, Suite 300, Portland, OR 97213

A catalogue record for this title is available
from the British Library.

ISBN 978-1-84682-648-1

Printed in England
by TJ International, Padstow, Cornwall.

# Contents

## Their house

# Illustrations

*(pages 79–104)*

**Rhona Richman Kenneally**

Dorothea Lange, 'Kenneally's (house interior)'

**Eiléan Ní Chuilleanáin**

Honan Hostel and the Warden's House, University College Cork
Mosaic floor of Honan Chapel (detail from above)
Mosaic floor of Honan Chapel (detail of animals)
Mosaic floor of Honan Chapel (detail of serpent)
Window of St Gobnait, Honan Chapel

**Mary Morrissy**

Detail of the dining room of Mary Morrissy's family home
Artwork on the stairwell of Mary Morrissy's family home

**Colette Bryce**

Westend Park, Derry

**Macdara Woods**

Martinstown, Athboy, Co. Meath

**Howard Keeley**

Parlour of Hazelbrook House, Bunratty Folk Park
Farm Parlour, Ulster American Folk Park
Poole photographic collection: nursery sideboard


**Nicholas Grene**

Teach Synge, Inis Meáin
Scene from *Riders to the sea*, Druid Theatre, Dublin


**Lucy McDiarmid**

The *Asgard*
Mary Spring Rice and Molly Childers onboard the *Asgard*
Dublin residence of Kathleen and Tom Clarke at the time of the
 Easter Rising


**Angela Bourke**

The house Maeve Brennan grew up in: 48 Cherryfield Avenue,
 Ranelagh


**Adam Hanna**

Anne Heaney at the water pump on the Bellaghy family farm


**Tony Tracy**

Dublin streetscape in *Adam & Paul*

# Acknowledgments

As editors of *The vibrant house* we would like to express our deep appreciation to our contributors for entering into the spirit of this project – which was many years in the making – to bring to life the domestic spaces inhabited by themselves and by others. We are grateful for financial support from the Social Sciences and Humanities Research Council of Canada and the Office of the Vice President, Research & Graduate Studies and Faculty of Fine Arts of Concordia University, and for the funds granted to Lucy McDiarmid as the Marie Frazee-Baldassarre Professor of English at Montclair State University. We would like to thank Fionnuala Walsh for the research that she undertook on our behalf and for making the index. Sara Spike contributed to the success of this volume by managing the preparation of the final manuscript for submission to the press, and she was also an important collaborator with regard to the acquisition and preparation of images. Thanks go as well to Pata Macedo for her contribution to the design of the book, and to Martin Fanning and Sam Tranum at Four Courts Press for agreeing to publish this collection and taking it through the editorial process. On behalf of all those whose writing appears on these pages, we gratefully acknowledge the researchers, photographers, librarians and archivists, family members, friends and others who gave their support to each author, without which such scholarship would be impossible.

Grateful acknowledgement is made to Gallery Press for permission to reprint Vona Groarke's poems '3' and 'How to read a building', and to the Poetry Foundation for permission to reprint Colette Bryce's essay '*Omphalos*', originally published in *Poetry Magazine*.

# 3

## Vona Groarke

It is late. The night is required to fold itself up
into squares that get smaller and smaller
the more I notice them. I am learning
to pay attention to this narrow, straight-line house
that must have had all its corners by heart before
ever I came to fit my life snug under its eaves.

I could count the balustrade shadows as standing in
for decades, or for owners, in my stead, and know
it is not for me to believe they left nothing behind:
nothing in how a door will open or a door will close,
or a window lean into what the rowan tree has to say.
The banister's way with three hinged centuries
has more heat in it than it needs to have, even on this
July evening when the rooms at the top of the house
vouchsafe another summer day tomorrow.

I am the clean slate. I am off-white walls
and open windows, a garden planted from scratch.
I am floor-length curtains and bookcases,
rooms that listen nicely to each other.
I am door knobs and reading lamps, blue glass
bowls on window sills, family photographs,
corners with silence in them, that sly peace,
a contrivance to which my blue and white hours
and too much clean bed linen give the lie.

My house of uneven numbers,
of my children's hyphenated lives.
My house of small hours, of voices
a little quieter than they need to be.
Our summer is all in paragraphs,
everything supposedly given to light,
despite the slip in every corner
with a May date written on it

by ghosts who listen to everything,
but cannot make sense of it; who gather
in their arms what light the house holds,
pooling it in doorways so none of us
will ever have to step out into dark;
who fret the dog every now and then and,
to make up for it, ruffle lavender in its pots
so the scent slips in the back door; who play
noughts and crosses in the trellis shadow
and don't care who loses, who wins.

# 'I am off-white walls': exploring and theorizing domestic space

## Rhona Richman Kenneally

> I am the clean slate. I am off-white walls
> and open windows, a garden planted from scratch.
> I am floor-length curtains and bookcases,
> rooms that listen nicely to each other.
> I am door knobs and reading lamps, blue glass
> bowls on window sills, family photographs,
> corners with silence in them, that sly peace,
> a contrivance to which my blue and white hours
> and too much clean bed linen give the lie.

This is the middle stanza from '3', one of two poems by Vona Groarke that appear in this volume on Irish domestic space. Evident in this stanza is the presentation of the house as a metaphor to underline the relationship between the speaker-occupant and the house itself. The speaker in this stanza *is*, we are told, a living and breathing version of what is conventionally thought of as inanimate architecture – walls, rooms, corners – including the contents of that architecture, such as curtains, bookcases and door knobs. In this sense, Groarke's poem communicates the intimate bond between the house and this member of the household and his or her fellow (former) human beings, the 'ghosts' who proprietorially 'gather/ in their arms what light the house holds, / pooling it in doorways so none of us / will ever have to step out into dark'.

But another way of interpreting the stanza flows from what seems like an implicit suggestion from Groarke – that the domestic space depicted here possesses sufficient power and influence to warrant its own voice. That is, the speaking 'I' can also be understood as the house itself, with its rooms that 'listen nicely to each other' and 'vouchsafe another summer day tomorrow', anthropomorphized to highlight the significance of the contrapuntal conditions and activities it generates among the living (and nonliving) constituents of this built environment. With powerful language, the house in this poem invokes domestic space as a visual, material and spatial milieu that deserves to be acknowledged for its role as a transformative agent, fundamentally shaping the very beings of its occupants.

As my co-editor Lucy McDiarmid and I suggest, home as metaphor, symbol or synecdoche is different from home, the *physical* material and spatial entity. This book brings attention to, teases out and also considers the merits of entwining these two conceptualizations. We do not claim that one is to be preferred over the other, or to be thought of as more legitimate, or accurate, or enlightening. We do suggest, however, given the centrality of language and literature (and word-based histories) in Irish studies – evidenced, for example, by the preponderance of courses in these disciplines in Irish-studies university programs – that an interrogation of spatiality and materiality is not as often foregrounded in curricula and publications, and must therefore be intentionally singled out as worthwhile.

Yet such an approach does have significant representation in Irish studies. Scholars in disciplines centrally engaged in materiality and spatiality, such as anthropology, folk-life studies, geography, architecture and design, who are trained in how to think about matter (and sometimes in how to create it), use evidence gathered through sustained direct and indirect engagement with extant buildings and artifacts, including photos, maps, drawings and other image-based as well as text-based primary sources. E. Estyn Evans,

Kevin Danaher and Henry Glassie are a formidable triumvirate whose collective oeuvre abundantly repays careful and repeated scrutiny.[1] Claudia Kinmonth's studies of Irish furniture and of rural interiors as represented in art also set important precedents, as do Elizabeth FitzPatrick and James Kelly's edited collection *Domestic life in Ireland* and the five-volume *Art and architecture of Ireland* edited by Andrew Carpenter.[2] An influential landmark from the discipline of geography, the *Atlas of the Irish rural landscape* appeared in 1997 and was expanded and reissued in 2011; it spurred a succession of works on a similar theme.[3] Approaches to Irish material culture and the natural and built environment have also been pursued by literary and cultural critics who have generated important scholarship that demonstrates the efficacy of looking at things and spaces as contributors to the evolution of Irish culture and society.[4]

1 See E. Estyn Evans, *Irish folk ways* (London, 1957); Kevin Danaher, *Ireland's vernacular architecture* (Cork, 1975); Kevin Danaher, *Hearth and stool and all!: Irish rural households* (Cork, 1985); Henry H. Glassie, *Passing the time in Ballymenone: culture and history of an Ulster community* (Philadelphia, 1982). 2 Claudia Kinmonth, *Irish country furniture, 1700– 1950* (New Haven, CT, 1995); Claudia Kinmonth, *Irish rural interiors in art* (New Haven, CT, 2006); Elizabeth FitzPatrick and James Kelly (eds), *Domestic life in Ireland*, proceedings of the Royal Irish Academy (Dublin, 2011); Andrew Carpenter (ed.), *Art and architecture of Ireland*, 5 vols (New Haven, CT, 2014). See also Linda King and Elaine Sisson (eds), *Ireland, design and visual culture: negotiating modernity, 1922–1992* (Cork, 2011); Rhona Richman Kenneally, 'Cooking at the hearth: the "Irish cottage" and women's lived experience' in Oona Frawley (ed.), *Memory Ireland, ii: Diaspora and memory practices* (Syracuse, NY, 2012), pp 224–41; Rhona Richman Kenneally, 'The elusive landscape of history: food and empowerment in Sebastian Barry's "Annie Dunne"' in Máirtín Mac Con Iomaire and Eamon Maher (eds), '*Tickling the palate': gastronomy in Irish literature and culture* (New York, 2014), pp 79– 98; Rhona Richman Kenneally, 'Tastes of home in mid-twentieth-century Ireland: food, design, and the refrigerator', *Food and Foodways*, 23 (2015), 80–123; Rhona Richman Kenneally, 'Towards a new domestic architecture: homes, kitchens and food in rural Ireland during the long 1950s' in Elizabeth FitzPatrick and James Kelly (eds), *Food and drink in Ireland* (Dublin, 2016), pp 325–47; Rhona Richman Kenneally, 'Memory as food performance: the cookbooks of Maura Laverty' in Michael Kenneally and Margaret Kelleher (eds), *Ireland and Quebec: multidisciplinary perspectives on history, culture and society* (Dublin, 2016), pp 166–82. 3 F.H.A. Aalen et al. (eds), *Atlas of the Irish rural landscape* (Toronto, 1997; 2nd ed., Toronto, 2011). Examples of subsequent work along the same lines include John Crowley et al. (eds), *Atlas of the great Irish famine* (Cork, 2012); Jim Mac Laughlin and Séan Beattie (eds), *An historical, environmental and cultural atlas of County Donegal* (Cork, 2013). 4 See, for example, Adele M. Dalsimer, *Visualizing Ireland* (London, 1993); Malcolm Kelsall, *Literary representations of the Irish country house* (Basingstoke, 2003); Vera Kreilkamp (ed.), *Rural Ireland: the inside story* (Boston, 2012), which includes essays by three

Each of these analytical strategies, originating from distinct but nevertheless related domains of scholarship, raises critical issues about Irish material culture, the built environment and, more specifically, Irish domestic space.

Scholars embedded in materiality and spatiality studies work from the premise that architecture and material culture deserve careful analysis in their own right, because they are elements of the wider built and natural environment that constitutes our physical world. From this perspective, space can be understood as more than a passive backdrop for human activity, more than a 'collection of preexisting points set out in a fixed geometry, a container, as it were', as Karen Barad asserts.[5] Instead, a house, for example, can be studied as a universe in flux, its characteristics continually constituted and reconstituted through the dynamic interactions among the people who occupy it, and the material culture and energies such as wind or light that coexist within and around it. In this conceptual framework, physical matter (what we typically call *things* or *objects* and habitually treat as inanimate) is profitably conceptualized as 'vibrant', as Jane Bennett argues, because of the 'curious ability of inanimate things to animate, to act, to produce effects dramatic and subtle'.[6] Hence 'off-white walls' can produce effects dramatic and subtle on those who come in contact with them. A wall does not simply bisect a space into two segments; it segregates or separates, and thus requires individuals who wish to circulate through the full space to go around, climb over, squeeze under or cut out a hole to enable passage. This ability of architecture – and also its contents, including, in the case of '3', 'reading lamps, blue glass / bowls on window sills' – to affect the behaviour and experiences of individuals who interact with it has

art historians, a designer and an archaeologist; Lucy McDiarmid (ed.), 'Irish secular relics', *Textual Practice*, 16:2 (2002); Lucy McDiarmid, *Poets and the peacock dinner: the literary history of a meal* (Oxford, 2015); Lucy McDiarmid, *At home in the revolution: what women said and did in 1916* (Dublin, 2015); Paige Reynolds (ed.), 'Irish things', *Éire-Ireland*, 46:1/2 (2011); Gerry Smyth, *Space and the Irish cultural imagination* (Basingstoke, 2001); Fintan O'Toole, *A history of Ireland in 100 objects* (Dublin, 2013) and http://www.100 objects.ie, accessed 19 June 2017. **5** Karen Barad, *Meeting the universe halfway: quantum physics and the entanglement of matter and meaning* (Durham, NC, 2007), p. 180. **6** Jane Bennett, *Vibrant matter: a political ecology of things* (Durham, NC, 2010), p. 6.

both intentional and unintentional repercussions, not to mention attendant cognitive, sensory and emotional implications for the humans involved. In the discourse of the spatial turn, then, even something as seemingly humble as a spring-loaded door-closer has been deemed, in Bruno Latour's canonical text, a 'highly social actor that deserves careful consideration'.[7]

The agential capabilities of Irish domestic space, when observed through this lens, soon become apparent. The relative inaccessibility of the upper floor of a Victorian two-storey house (a common typology in Ireland) constitutes, by virtue of its design, a filter to restrict access by strangers to more private spaces – such as bedrooms – located upstairs. It also compromises those with limited mobility, who must then rely on others for assistance to reach the upper level, and those, such as servants, who may have heavy loads to carry, whose lower social status is consequently reinforced vis-à-vis the home-owners' unconstrained movement. We invite readers of this collection to consider the idea that a house itself is 'vibrant', has this kind of agency, owing to its material and spatial properties – its design, materials, contents, geometry and distribution, capacity to hold or repel atmospheric conditions such as warmth or light, and contextual relationship with landscape or resources. Through its material and spatial particularities, a house co-determines, in tandem with its human inhabitants, the interactions, experiences and thought processes of its human (and nonhuman) residents. Such was the essential reasoning behind the title of this volume.

In the memoirs and essays that comprise this collection, the literary and the material/spatial, resonating in juxtaposition with each other, affirm two points. One is that the study of Irish domestic space justifies careful consideration of literary and other text-based primary sources as a means of determining how that architecture and its contents anchor 'home' as a concept or idea – for example, home as a seat of identity-formation, or of nation. The other is that, extrapolating to the wider sphere of Irish studies, interrogating how

7 Bruno Latour [Jim Johnson], 'Mixing humans with non-humans: sociology of a door-closer', *Social Problems*, 35 (1988), 298–310.

individual homes are described and analyzed in Irish literature can contribute in significant ways to a growing body of evidence of the social, economic and environmental qualities and impacts of Ireland's domestic spaces over time.[8]

### *The vibrant house*: structure and contents

As editors of *The vibrant house*, Lucy McDiarmid and I represent the disciplines of Irish literature, and architecture and design studies, respectively, and the genesis of this book springs from our discussions about how what each of us thinks and understands about domestic space can be enriched by the other's insights and experience. The expertise of the contributors to *The vibrant house* is vested in the areas of Irish literature, folklore, theatre and film. Each piece of writing offers a distinctive way to approach the physicality and materiality of home through language and narrative.[9] The sequence of these contributions begins, as does this introduction, with Vona Groarke's '3'. It ends with another of her poems, 'How to read a building', whose placement is an invitation for readers, having explored the other contents in the collection, to consider their own strategies for studying the built environment. The provocation of the poem's first word – 'Don't' – stimulates additional layers of contemplation.

Groarke's poems bracket the book's two main sections of writings. The first, 'Our house', consists of memoirs by five distinguished contemporary Irish writers. The second, 'Their house', illustrates various approaches for interrogating Irish domestic space, authored

---

8 For examples of Irish spatial studies that explore how domestic space supports or inspires initiatives that serve (or undermine) the individual or community, and how it reflects or fosters the efficient and sustainable use of resources, see, for example, Glassie, *Passing the time*; Mary Benson, 'Contemporary apartment living: living above place?' in Mary P. Corcoran and Perry Share (eds), *Belongings: shaping identity in modern Ireland* (Dublin, 2008), pp 117–28; Caitriona Clear, *Women of the house: women's household work in Ireland, 1922–1961: discourses, experiences, memories* (Dublin, 2000); K.C. Kearns, *Dublin tenement life: an oral history* (Dublin, 1994); Royal Institute of the Architects of Ireland, *Building on the edge of Europe / Construire à la frange de l'Europe: a survey of contemporary architecture in*

by critics who have vicariously engaged with, rather than directly experienced, the homes in question.

## Our house

'Our house' begins with a reminiscence by the esteemed poet Eiléan Ní Chuilleanáin about homes of her childhood. These include Tulach Óg, a small one-storey house on the Model Farm Road in Cork and, after 1949, the official residence of the warden of the Honan Hostel at University College Cork (the family moved to the residence when Ní Chuilleanáin's father assumed that position).[10] Fascinating, here, is a comparison of how the activities of everyday life played out in the two homes. Through its architecture and material culture, the Honan residence co-generated, with its inhabitants, the daily performances that characterized the family's elevated social status as a result of the promotion. Whereas the Model Farm Road home was a 'permeable' place in which family members, visitors and staff moved with minimum restraint through the space, the residence, as was characteristic of more formal middle-class houses, was, in Ní Chuilleanáin's words, a 'place of hierarchies and borders and structured visibilities'.[11] It secluded servants and children from certain public spaces most of the time, and yet facilitated necessary aural trajectories to ensure the appropriate movement of the hired help across these distinct spheres. This remembrance is a trove for a scholar of the spatial turn, and it also adds socio-historical context to

*Ireland embracing history, town and country* (Dublin, 1996).   9 For the purposes of this essay, *house* and *home* will be used interchangeably – although it is true of course that *home* can also refer to one's homeland, or some other set of relations or affiliations. Harvey Perkins and David C. Thorns note that the 'terminological slippage' between the two words is 'a taken-for-granted part of social life and reinforced in a wide range of settings and situations'. Perkins and Thorns, *Place, identity and everyday life in a globalizing world* (Basingstoke, 2011), p. 74.   10 For a literary exploration of Ní Chuilleanáin's childhood experiences in Cork, see Thomas McCarthy, '"We could be in any city": Eiléan Ní Chuilleanáin and Cork', *Irish University Review*, 37:1 (2007), 230–43.   11 For studies of the typology of the Victorian house see, for example, Jane Hamlett, *Material relations: domestic interiors and middle-class families in England, 1850–1910* (Manchester, 2010); Andrea Kaston Tange, *Architectural identities: domesticity, literature and the Victorian middle classes* (Toronto, 2010).

that period, for example in identifying one household that availed of the services of Magdalen laundries.[12] For admirers of Ní Chuilleanáin's poetry, the memoir is a rich resource, especially since the residence was subsequently demolished and the main humanities building of University College Cork erected in its place, an edifice that will never again house 'a family of children to be kept out of sight'.

Mary Morrissy's childhood home remained in family hands until relatively recently, and its agency is captured in fascinating ways in terms of visual cues it provided for its inhabitants. With the important exception of a front cloakroom, the house was filled with artwork of various kinds, some of which may be seen in photographs that I took when I visited the house in 2012, and which appear in this collection, including on its cover. Morrissy carefully details the framed reproductions of Dutch masters juxtaposed with paintings by family members – all 'pictures' chosen by her father. Hanging in the house until its recent sale, they were part of an enculturation process that also included, according to her father's wishes, museum visits and art classes for Mary and her brothers. Together, architecture, material culture and parents worked to reinforce the family's religious, cultural and national values, with the house as a microcosm in which everyday activities played out this macrocosmic agenda. Recognition that the house served as an arena for such performances is what makes the placement of Pieter de Hooch's *Woman lacing her bodice beside a cradle* directly over a lounge chair in the dining room so remarkable. As is evident in my photo in this volume, the chair is situated next to an opening into another room to its right, just as de Hooch's painting draws viewers to a mother occupying a chair and, to her right, an opening and then a door. This replication of de Hooch's configuration (along with the fact that, in my photo, the chair in Morrissy's house is gendered feminine by the lacy antimacassar) seems to further infuse the painting's narrative in the space. It is fascinating to imagine whether this placement of the artwork – by

12 For information on the Magdalen laundries see, for example, Emilie Pine, 'Coming clean? remembering the Magdalen laundries' in Oona Frawley (ed.), *Memory Ireland*, i: *History and modernity* (Syracuse, NY, 2011), pp 151–71; James M. Smith, *Ireland's Magdalen laundries and the nation's architecture of containment* (Notre Dame, IN, 2007).

Morrissy's mother, after her father's death – and the resulting parallel layout was coincidental, or intentional.

In her memoir, Colette Bryce makes reference to another piece of decor with the power to hold the ongoing attention of the household in one of the two homes that she depicts. A hall mirror served as a kind of nonhuman collaborator for anyone leaving the house, to ensure that personal appearance fits public expectations. Bryce also recognizes the mirror as a useful signifier of her present-day retrospective gaze at 'nine children looking out'. Aligning in another way with Morrissy's residence, Bryce's dwellings also constituted a teaching environment of sorts, albeit one of a very different kind. Here, the educational focus was not the arts, but the circumstances of conflict in Northern Ireland during the 1970s. Not paintings, but tear gas and weapons were the instructive tools, brought into the household, not by a father committed to introducing his children to aesthetic and social discourses of the world beyond, but by soldiers asserting the will of political power. Yet whereas the two houses that Bryce describes were clearly penetrated by surrounding external strife, they nevertheless shaped her persona in empowering ways. Living in a street of terraced dwellings, she thinks of herself and her three youngest siblings as fundamentally interconnected, *'terraced children*, as opposed to detached or semi-detached'. Indeed, the street itself became a sheltering accommodation for herself and her young neighbours and, in Bryce's recollections, this solidarity between humans and architecture helped them gain courage in the face of 'tanks, or bombs, or balaclavaed men'.

Theo Dorgan's contribution is a memorable recollection of the act of recall, of himself as a boy, looking around, telling himself 'you must remember this, you will need to remember this, you will need to have remembered this'. Elements of this story are narrated in a kind of braille, a topography experienced by Dorgan himself through the body and thereby communicated to the mind and imagination. The up-and-down gradations in a dwelling that was built on the side of a hill, and which therefore could only be entered and exited by ascent and descent, are absorbed at different scales. These range from full human size – hills that demand 'the trudge upward, deep and satisfying in muscle and bone', or the 'vertiginous light-hearted downward plunge, giddy and flying free' – to the miniscule, whose subtly captured nuances include kitchen floor tiles that were 'never quite level' so that 'to reach the front door from the kitchen door with a coloured marble or a Dinky car … called for skilled propulsion of a high order'.

The origins and daily events of this respected poet's home-place also stimulate contemplation of matters of order and movement between humans and nonhumans in physical space, and their effect on the built environment itself. The Dorgans' family home owed its location and its construction to a collaboration between Theo's father and five other men, who bought a piece of land, divided it into six, and then 'worked as labourers on each other's houses, bonded by work as they were bonded by friendship'. These men came to this project having already been acquainted through co-membership in a hurling and football club. It is touching to imagine how the strategically positioned yet interdependent assemblage of team members on a playing field transformed itself into a dynamic orchestration of fellows-in-arms to erect a flank of six houses that would sit stable and immobilized by '[s]olid steps, poured concrete that has never shifted or cracked'.

If, according to Macdara Woods 'time itself is the Place, and the various situations and stage settings are incidental', it is through the places invoked in this essay that key elements of Woods' experiences over time are exposed to the reader. He observes that he felt familiar, from first encounter, with the spatial and material qualities of his farmhouse in Umbria (the first residence mentioned in the memoir), as a result of having spent much of his childhood on his grandmother's farm: 'I have been at home here [in the Italian farmhouse] from the beginning; I know instinctively how to inhabit it.'

Such interconnectedness of lived experiences over time is fascinating for many reasons, one being that it supports Gaston Bachelard's description of home as 'our first universe, the real cosmos in every sense of the word'.[13] Anthropologist Daniel Miller elaborates on this idea in his pivotal study *The comfort of things*, in which he writes that 'household material culture may express an order which ... seems equivalent to what one might term a social cosmology ... the order of things, values and relationships of a society'. Moreover, he notes, such a cosmology is 'holistic rather than fragmented', even if elements in it might be contradictory.[14] Water and fire are predominant features of the cosmology that Woods invokes, as was often the case in traditional Irish dwellings, especially before electrification and the installation of piping for indoor running water.[15] Thinking of home as a cosmology also offers a new perspective through which to understand Woods' reaction to his encounter, in a museum in France, with farmyard tools that brought him right back to his childhood. '[M]y hands automatically closed on phantom forms of them; I knew the making of them, their function and purpose,' he writes. Their place in his cosmology had already created the necessary associations.

Woods' recollections have a special appeal to the scholar of the spatial turn, even though they are, by his own admission, a product of 'life and memory come together with artifice'. Drawn from actual experience of the kitchen, the turf shed and the barn in one Meath farmhouse during the 1940s, they can be juxtaposed with other representations of the everyday domestic interactions between people, other living beings, things and spaces in rural Ireland. Such representations of rural life have ranged over the years from the idealistic fantasy of Eamon de Valera's 'cosy homesteads', to quantitative fieldwork that measures rooms and furniture in inches.[16] They encompass data from projects such the Schools' Folklore Scheme

13 Gaston Bachelard, *The poetics of space* (Boston, 1994), p. 4.   14 Daniel Miller, *The comfort of things* (Cambridge, 2008), p. 294.   15 See Richman Kenneally, 'Towards a new domestic architecture'.   16 The term 'cosy homesteads' appeared in a speech broadcast on national radio on St Patrick's Day, 1943, in which *Taoiseach* Eamon de Valera referred to 'The ideal Ireland ... that we dreamed of ... a land whose countryside would be bright with cosy homesteads, whose fields and villages would be joyous ... with the romping of sturdy children ... and the laughter of happy maidens, whose firesides would be forums for the wisdom of serene old age. The home, in short, of a people living the life that God desires that men should live.' Maurice Moynihan (ed.), *Speeches and statements by Eamon de Valera, 1917–73* (Dublin, 1980), p. 466.

undertaken in the late 1930s by the Irish Folklore Commission, and extant material culture housed at such institutions as the Museum of Country Life, the Bunratty Folk Park and the Ulster Folk Museum. Yet another resource is Dorothea Lange's 1954 photographic portrait of Co. Clare, one image of which may be seen in this collection.[17] Each has its own strengths and caveats, which is why a trans-disciplinary, triangulated approach to thinking about and studying domestic space is optimal. And while it is crucial to shed light on the entangled nature of this most iconic of Irish built environments, care must be taken also to devote the requisite attention to other Irish housing types in other kinds of communities. Irish geographer Ruth McManus (among other observers) notes:

> If we think for a minute of the images that we have of ourselves and the ways in which we tend to project Irish culture to other people, it becomes clear that these images are couched in terms of rural nostalgia. The thatched cottage with the turf fire somehow appears more Irish than the suburban semi-detached house, even though statistically we are far more likely to be living in suburbia than in a rural idyll reminiscent of de Valera's speeches.[18]

One of the merits of this collection, we believe, is that Woods' memoir sits side by side with those of the other contributors to 'Our house', who were urban dwellers, and also with the essays in the following section that add historical and other contextual dimensions.

17 National Folklore Collection, Ireland, University College Dublin, Schools' Folklore Scheme (1937–8), http://www.ucd.ie/irishfolklore/en/schoolsfolklorescheme1937-38, accessed 19 June 2017; Conrad M. Arensberg and Solon T. Kimball, *Family and community in Ireland* (Gloucester, MA, 1961); National Museum of Ireland, Country Life, http://www.museum.ie/country-life, accessed 15 July 2015; Shannon Heritage, Bunratty Folk Park, http://www.shannonheritage.com/BunrattyCastleAndFolkPark/BunrattyFolkPark, accessed 19 June 2017; Dorothea Lange, *Dorothea Lange's Ireland*, with Daniel Dixon and Gerry Mullins (Washington, DC, 1998). 18 Ruth McManus, 'Urban dreams – urban nightmares' in Jim Hourihane (ed.), *Engaging spaces, people, place and space from an Irish perspective* (Dublin, 2003), p. 33.

## Their house

The essays in the second section of this collection bring together a range of spatial and material sources to shed light on Irish domestic space. All explore writings that communicate essences about the domain of home and its links to individual, cultural and national affiliation.

Howard Keeley's essay uncovers significant reverberations between politics and literature, especially in post-Famine Ireland, to demonstrate how matters of housing were threaded through the discourse on Irish independence and the fostering of an Irish middle class. As Keeley observes, following the inception of the Land League, 'the domestic-material was crucial' to fuelling nationalist ideals. One debate was whether or not to foreground, in home rule rhetoric, promises to improve the quality of everyday life in Irish dwellings as a means to attract the widest degree of public support. Such a discourse is evidence of the centrality of Irish domestic space as a factor in home rule politics, not only symbolically, but also in terms of actual bricks and mortar (or, for that matter, stones and thatch).

Keeley's essay is innovative in its close reading of selected literary depictions of the middle-class Irish home. With reference to the work of Gerald Griffin, William Carleton and George Moore, and with special attention given to the 'Fenian polemicist' Charles Kickham and his best-selling novel *Knocknagow*, Keeley concentrates on one room, the parlour, to illustrate how that particular space was presented as influencing and reflecting contemporary ideologies. Katherine C. Grier, a scholar of material-culture studies, argues that Victorian middle-class rhetoric identified the parlour as a 'setting for important social events and to present the civilized façade of its occupants'. This was an outcome of 'a strain of deterministic thought', already developed by the 1830s, 'that assigned to the house's physical setting and details the power to shape human character ... This "domestic environmentalism" conflated moral guidance with the actual appearance and physical layout of the house and its contents.'[19]

19 Katherine C. Grier, *Culture & comfort: people, parlors, and upholstery, 1850–1930* (Rochester,

As Keeley argues, in the context of the Irish material he examines, '[t]he parlour becomes a prime synecdoche for the arriviste agricultural bourgeoisie that grew to dominance across Ireland over the nineteenth century'. That is, the parlour serves as a 'distinguishing space within aspirational farmer homesteads', one that 'actualizes the dedicated pursuit of better and secure housing'.

Nicholas Grene's essay is a welcome opportunity to explore the vibrancy of actual domestic space in turn-of-the-twentieth-century Ireland, its representation on the pages of J.M. Synge's plays and essays and its re-representation as physical, dramatized stage spaces.[20] There is a distinct 'our house' flavour to Synge's fictional dwellings: as Grene makes clear, Synge undertook fieldwork of his own in various parts of Ireland and thereby had the personal experience of living in an assortment of traditional Irish rural dwellings. As the inspiration for houses in Synge's plays and the theatre productions that brought them to life, these first-hand accounts can further heighten the impact of his literature for readers and critics. Grene refers to a bedroom Synge occupied and wrote about in *The Aran Islands*, which calls to mind various features of traditional Irish dwellings in Co. Clare studied in the 1930s by Conrad M. Arensberg and Solon T. Kimball.[21] And because this essay succeeds Howard Keeley's in our collection, we have an opportunity to consider

NY, 1988), p. 6.    **20** For examples of Grene's work on Synge, see Nicholas Grene, *Synge: a critical study of the plays* (Totowa, NJ, 1975); Nicholas Grene, *Home on the stage: domestic spaces in modern drama* (Cambridge, 2014); Nicholas Grene (ed.), *Interpreting Synge: essays from the Synge summer school, 1991–2000* (Dublin, 2000); J.M. Synge, *Travelling Ireland: essays, 1898–1908*, ed. Nicholas Grene (Dublin, 2009).    **21** It is instructive to compare the type of sanctuary space observed by Arensberg and Kimball to a room that Synge occupied in the Great Blasket, and which is described in his essay 'In West Kerry: the Blasket Islands'. The anthropomorphic qualities of this space are notable. When it was time for bed, Synge's hostess brought him into 'the room beyond the kitchen … Then she took off her apron, and fastened it up in the window as a blind, [and] laid another apron … on the wet earthen floor for me to stand on.' An 'old hairbrush' propped the window open, and an 'iron spoon' served to lift the latch of the door. The room had two beds, 'running from wall to wall, with a small space between them'; Synge got into one, his host occupied the second, and, later, the host's son joined the other two men by 'clambering very artfully over his father, and [stretching] out on the inner side of the bed'. Window, floor, door, beds, room, men – all become interconnected entities here. J.M. Synge, 'In West Kerry: the Blasket Islands' in *Travelling Ireland*, pp 141–2.

overlapping traits that characterize the west room and the parlour, to recognize that both anchored, albeit in different ways, heritage and class affiliation. This essay also, of course, invites comparisons with Macdara Woods' grandmother's house.

Grene's essay is a compelling analysis of two of Synge's plays, *Riders to the sea* and *The shadow of the glen*. The agency of their fictional houses is conveyed through the ways in which the characters who occupy them interact with these spaces. As Grene notes, in *Riders* Synge adds a window to the kitchen of the house he had slept in on Inishmaan, thus giving both its inhabitants and the audience 'the ability to peek out fearfully at the turbulent landscape outside'. Such turbulence is reinforced when the door half-closed by Nora shortly after her entrance is '*blown open by a gust of wind*'. Grene also offers wonderful points of entry into the adaptation of these houses for theatrical performances. For example, he describes director Garry Hynes' strategy to disregard one of Synge's stage directions for *Riders* in the 2005 DruidSynge cycle production. The resulting choreography reinforces 'the agony of the interior for Maurya and her daughters', achieved as a materially and spatially driven visceral exchange between the performers and the set itself.

Lucy McDiarmid's essay echoes Keeley's in signalling the degree to which activities and circumstances related to physical domestic space have driven Irish history. She writes that 'the GPO-centered, bullet-centered, dead-horse-centered narrative of the [Easter] Rising is incomplete', inasmuch as 'the notion, the discourse, and the actual space of home are fundamental to the story'. The focus in her case is on extraordinary examples of domesticity remodelled or renegotiated during the Irish revolutionary period in nonfiction writing – diaries, memoirs and letters by Mary Spring Rice, Kathleen Clarke, Geraldine Plunkett Dillon and Mary Louisa Hamilton Norway.

McDiarmid's contribution broadens assumptions about what constitutes domestic space and the functions of homemaking. Whereas most of the other contributions to this collection refer to home in terms of purpose-built, single-household, effectively long-term residential edifices – whether a middle-class house, a warden's residence meant to be inhabited for a period of years, or a traditional vernacular dwelling – in McDiarmid's essay, a boat and two hotel rooms, and, in a qualified way, the GPO itself, serve as reminders that the place where one lives might have been built for other purposes, be moveable as opposed to immoveable, ephemeral, temporary, devoid of privacy and/or easily subject to invasion from without. Home is also a politicized environment, as Alison Blunt and Robyn Dowling argue, 'closely bound up with, rather than separate from, wider power relations'; in short, home is 'a contested site shaped by different axes of power and over a range of scales'.[22] In McDiarmid's essay, home could be as unpredictable a site as the office safe in the GPO that protected the Norways' family possessions, 'hidden within the walls of an office in a public building, … nested within the seemingly protective layers of family, nation, and empire'.

McDiarmid's essay also draws attention to how powerful the imperatives can be to normalize social performances of domesticity even under anomalous circumstances, such as when a dwelling typology is not conventional, or when expectations of refuge and privacy within the supposed sanctity of homespace are not met. On the yacht that conveyed Mary Spring Rice and five others, weapons, humans and household materials intermingled; one had to 'turn the mattress right back off the guns … to be able to turn down the [washing] basin'. The ubiquity and banality of domestic rituals such as eating dinner were also at the heart of inspired evasive strategies by Kathleen Clarke when her Dublin home was raided by Free State troops in search of anti-treaty republicans during the Civil War.

Angela Bourke's essay focuses on 48 Cherryfield Avenue, Ranelagh, Dublin. This is the dwelling that author Maeve Brennan occupied from early childhood until 1934 (when she was 17), a house that was fictionalized in a substantial number of her short stories. Bourke has been pivotal in bringing Brennan's writing to the attention of a growing number of enthusiasts, by serving as both

22 Alison Blunt and Robyn Dowling, *Home* (London, 2006), p. 21; Alison Blunt, *Domicile and diaspora: Anglo-Indian women and the spatial politics of home* (Oxford, 2005), p. 4. For a comprehensive exploration of these themes, see, especially, the introduction and chapters 3 and 4 of Blunt and Dowling.

critic and biographer.[23] This expertise drives Bourke's astute cross-interpretations between the short stories and the actual architecture of the house and its neighbourhood, which open up productive points of entry for readers of Brennan's work to learn more about the ways in which the house framed and encompassed the thoughts and activities of her characters. Bourke anchors Brennan's 'imagination's home' of her fiction to its physical, still-existing counterpart by introducing salient details about the house's size, layout and materials, including its façade of breeze block masked 'with a render of grey cement, moulded to look like stone', as well as by exploring the socio-economic makeup of this neighbourhood of Dublin.

As Bourke reveals, in certain instances Brennan depicts number 48 and its particular spatial qualities as exhibiting agency that directly affects the well-being of its occupants. As a gendered workspace, the maintenance of which requires ongoing toil by the woman of the house, it encodes 'an excruciating complexity of social unease and marital tension'. The hall and stairs, in Brennan's 'most memorable' stories, funnel household members through a compressed area where they must merge on their paths to and from other parts of the residence; as a result, 'anger, uncertainty and misunderstanding swirl coldly', at (and also because of) these communal points of convergence. The abrupt expansion of inhabited space elicits the opposite emotional reaction in the short story 'The sofa', so that when an old piano is removed from a room to make space for the piece of furniture that gives the story its title, its absence 'makes the children, the dog and even the mother giddy'. In Brennan's narratives this house is more than simply setting: it is a kind of energy force that influences the ability of the characters to maintain their composure and autonomy.

23 See Angela Bourke, *Maeve Brennan: homesick at the* New Yorker (London, 2004). In addition to those by Bourke, works devoted to Maeve Brennan include *Maeve Brennan: a traveller in exile* (Araby Productions for RTÉ, 2004); a play by Emma Donoghue, *The talk of the town* (2012); Patricia Coughlan, 'The American wedding dress', a lecture at Montclair State University, Montclair, NJ, 19 Mar. 2015. An excerpt from Maeve Brennan's short story 'The springs of affection' appears in Angela Bourke et al. (eds), *The Field Day anthology of literature*, iv/v: *Irish women's writing and traditions* (New York, 2002), pp 1219–22.

Adam Hanna's essay sets up a thought-provoking comparison between the childhood domestic spaces engaged in the poetry and prose of Seamus Heaney and those threaded through the writings of Derek Mahon. Hanna proposes that the study of 'the agential qualities of the material world takes on special inflections when the material studied is that of an intimate, remembered space – the first house', a position built on Bennett's assertions about things that have 'trajectories, propensities or tendencies of their own'. So significant do Heaney's invocations of that first house seem in his oeuvre – they feature, as Hanna points out, in his Nobel Prize speech as well as in his last poem, in which Heaney once more brings up 'the power / I first felt come up through / Our cement floor long ago' – that it is as if Heaney's quest to convey the vibrant materiality of his home place with all the force, depth and reverence that it deserved, was a pivotal driver of his poetic achievement. Certainly, the recurring focus that he bestows on water, on the family well, pump and indeed the water bucket, seems to support this position.

Hanna builds his essay on a foundation of binaries – religious (Heaney of Catholic, Mahon of Protestant descent) and urban/rural (Heaney's family farm in Co. Derry; Mahon's brick semi-detached house in North Belfast) – inherent in the two writers' treatments of domestic space. The essay's extended attention to Mahon's mother's crockery and her Dresden figurines is compelling, for one thing because it reveals how these domestic treasures are sometimes acknowledged as 'sentient' and 'neurotic', and also because they contrast with Heaney's more vernacular, locally derived, rural reference points.

Given the location of Hanna's essay in the sequence of this collection, readers are given the opportunity to carry resonances of previously discussed subjects and themes into this study – one being Bryce's appropriation of Heaney's musings on the Greek word *omphalos* in her memoir. The 'cutlery and ornaments' that the mother of Mahon's remembered house 'kept gleaming' call to mind the effort that it took for homemakers in Maeve Brennan's households to maintain brasses at an acceptable level of polish, and underscore the point that domestic space is also gendered workspace whose circumstances are sometimes far from the idyllic, stereotypical assumptions of 'home sweet home'.

Sofas explored within the collection also prove surprising points of convergence. Already discussed are the titular sofa of one of Maeve Brennan's short stories and the larger, 'firmer' sofa that was purchased by Eiléan Ní Chuilleanáin's family for the more formal rooms of the residence at the Honan Hostel, which thereby helped convey a sense of grandeur. In Keeley's reading, that same sense of grandeur is conveyed by a sofa in the 'elegantly furnished parlour' that appears in a short story by William Carleton, challenging a character's self-confidence: '[W]ould it be right o' me to sit in it [the sofa]?' he asks. 'Maybe it's consecrated?' According to Keeley, the sofa was an essential element of the 'bourgeoisifying' middle-class Victorian home. And as we will see in Maureen O'Connor's essay, addressed below, a three-piece suite of furniture in 'dark-green tapestry' triggers but cannot fulfil the aspirations of the central character in Edna O'Brien's short story 'An outing'. The sofa from Mossbawn that Hanna identifies as Heaney's 'memory-weight' – both of his own childhood (when he and his siblings sat on it and pretended it was a train) and of the contemporaneous death-trains of the Nazi Kindertransport – may therefore be contexualized by these other interpretations of domestic seating in *The vibrant house* that stimulated emotional impulses such as intimidation and self-discipline. Through such juxtapositions, the complexity of a sofa's abilities to 'animate, to act, to produce effects dramatic and subtle' is convincingly demonstrated.

Maureen O'Connor displays nuanced expertise in space and place studies and object-oriented ontology in her unpacking of Edna O'Brien's fictional houses. Evident in this essay is an already-developed body of scholarship in Irish literature – by O'Connor as well as by others – that embeds vibrant materiality. Her ideas incorporate those of Bennett, and also Bill Brown's study of 'thing theory', the latter having particular resonance among many cultural theorists.[24] Hence

24 Bill Brown, 'Thing theory', *Critical Inquiry*, 28:1 (2001), 1–22.

the 'melancholy ornaments' signalled in the title of the essay, which opens with the assertion that '[t]hings matter in Edna O'Brien's fiction'. O'Connor's exploration of the 'uncanny domestic subjectivity' in the short story 'A rose in the heart' – the house, in O'Brien's depiction, having 'a strange lifelikeness as if it was not a house at all but a person observing and breathing' – draws a connection, O'Connor notes, to the 'watching, reproachful houses found in [Elizabeth] Bowen's fiction'. Within this collection, moreover, the house in 'A rose' also strongly recalls the 'rooms that listen nicely to each other' of Groarke's '3'.

O'Connor has published extensively on Edna O'Brien, and also co-edited two important collections of essays on the author.[25] In *The vibrant house*, her investigation of O'Brien's dwellings demonstrates the efficacy of critical engagement that pays attention to the agency of things, in order to assert O'Brien's significance in the Irish literary canon in response to critics who have denigrated her writing as 'frivolous, drearily preoccupied with doomed heterosexual romance'. O'Connor takes as her point of departure discussions by other critics of the 'sadomasochistic dynamic' discerned in the interpersonal relationships in O'Brien's domestic spaces, and then extends that dynamic to include interactions between the humans and the nonhuman contents of those built environments. O'Connor thereby illuminates 'a hidden history of small refusals' by women in O'Brien's fiction, who, in the context of the rigidly patriarchal world of mid- to late twentieth-century Ireland, put their faith in the power of certain household ornaments to liberate them of 'the evils of drudgery, poverty and domestic abuse'.

Tony Tracy brings his expertise in Irish film studies to bear in a telling analysis of the 2004 film *Adam & Paul*. In this film, 'home' consists for the most part as 'improvised domesticity' – a discarded

---

25 See Kathryn Laing, Sinéad Mooney and Maureen O'Connor (eds), *Edna O'Brien: new critical perspectives* (Dublin, 2006), some essays of which derive from a conference they co-organized at the National University of Ireland, Galway, in 2005. See also Lisa Colletta and Maureen O'Connor, *Wild colonial girl: essays on Edna O'Brien* (Madison, WI, 2006).

mattress slept on by the drug-addicted central characters at the beginning of the film, or a man inhabiting a sleeping bag on a Dublin street. (These improvisations ironically call to mind the simulated home-spaces of Mary Spring Rice, Kathleen Clarke and the others discussed by McDiarmid.) Indeed, Tracy argues that the only seemingly normal living space depicted in the film, that belonging to Janine and her infant, proves to be, for Adam and Paul, an elusive Bachelardian 'oneiric house, a house of dream memory'. Reminiscent of the recalcitrant domestic spaces of Edna O'Brien's homes, this built environment offers them a mere 'fleeting and barely registered experience of home', from which they are once more ejected.

As in the essays by McDiarmid and Keeley and the memoir by Bryce, the spaces and contents of *Adam & Paul* notably activate and reflect the political and social narrative of their moment. The vibrancy of architecture in this narrative is pronounced, as Tracy makes clear, one case being the notorious Ballymun flats, a 1960s Dublin high-rise housing project that, by the turn of the twenty-first century when Adam and Paul undertake their meanderings, has become derelict and dangerous to inhabit. Moreover, through-lines are established between domestic space and wider geographies of 'home' – in Dublin, Ireland and beyond – to reveal a more comprehensive spacio-political back story in operation. Tracy highlights connections between the bench assertively occupied and defended by a Bulgarian man, the widening of the physical boundaries of the European Union in 2004 and the subsequent differentiation between those who dwelled permanently or only temporarily inside the physical borders of Ireland. Widening the lens allows Tracy to conclude that *Adam & Paul* is ultimately an exploration of 'alienation in a contemporary European context', through a 'theme of homelessness' that underscores the characters' vulnerability.

\*\*\*

John Ruskin, who played a key role in defining Victorian aspirations regarding domestic space, wrote:

> this is the true nature of home—it is the place of Peace; the shelter, not only from all injury, but from all terror, doubt, and division. In so far as it is not this, it is not home; so far as the anxieties of the outer life penetrate into it, and the inconsistently-minded, unknown, unloved, or hostile society of the outer world is allowed by either husband or wife to cross the threshold, it ceases to be home; it is then only a part of that outer world which you have roofed over, and lighted fire in. But so far as it is a sacred place, a vestal temple, a temple of the hearth watched over by Household Gods ... so far as it is this, and roof and fire are types only of a nobler shade and light ... so far it vindicates the name, and fulfils the praise, of Home.[26]

How closely each of the vibrant houses engaged in this collection adheres to Ruskin's model of perfection is, as I have argued, at least in part a function of the dynamic interactions between humans and things, spaces and forces. For some of the dwellers – Seamus Heaney and Colette Bryce to name two – remembered domestic space has been empowering precisely because of interactions with that built environment, interactions that have enabled its inhabitants the better to respond to the exigencies of what lies both within and outside it. In other cases, such as the temporary shelters explored in Lucy McDiarmid's essay, unsettled yet nevertheless enduring practices of domesticity are negotiated as a compromise between the ideals and the realities of everyday existence. Out of such negotiations, we realize, can still come achievement (as a collaborator in the birth of a nation, for example), or at least a way to cobble together some semblance of self-expression or self-fulfilment.[27] But for many others,

**26** John Ruskin, *Sesame and lilies* (1865), p. 123.   **27** Similarly, Christina Quinlan has studied the ways in which women in certain Irish prisons recast their cells as home, layering, over the material culture of incarceration, 'bedside lockers and tabletops [that] have knitted or crochet covers', as well as beauty products, potted plants and fresh or dried or artificial flowers, plus 'Mass cards and memory cards to console the women and to honour their dead'.

there is minimal, or no, relief from hardship, and domestic space is indeed nothing more than 'a part of that outer world which you have roofed over, and lighted fire in' – if that. Synge's Nora Burke, O'Brien's mothers and daughters, and Adam and Paul are forced to navigate through material and spatial domestic conditions that betray or undermine well-being, safety or esteem either by oneself or by others. In these matters, literature, theatre and film imitate life, and constitute a crucial arena from which to reflect and perhaps even act on such injustices. Turning to Henry Glassie and what he has to say about materiality and spatiality, we can be inspired by his urgings to investigate landscape and, by extension, material culture and the built environment, as '[a] record of change and continuity, as well as unity and division … a vast, collective work in progress, a visible material text, legible to all who tarry and look'.[28] The social cosmologies of domestic space framed in this collection, composed of rooms, possessions, people, components of nature as well as landscapes, co-create complicated interrelationships that demand no less rigorous or imaginative attention to their ravelled, messy, noisy and ultimately unresolvable nature. To tarry and look, through literature as well as through the material world itself, is what we hope to inspire with this collection.

Quinlan, 'Discourse and identity: a study of women in prison in Ireland' (PhD, Dublin City University, 2006), p. 254. See also her fascinating photo essay, 'Home and belonging: a study of women in prison in Ireland' in Mary P. Corcoran and Perry Share (eds), *Belongings: shaping identity in modern Ireland* (Dublin, 2008), pp 129–35. **28** Henry Glassie, 'The Irish landscape' in Rhona Richman Kenneally (ed.), 'New visual, material, and spatial perspectives in Irish studies', *Canadian Journal of Irish Studies*, 38:1/2 (2014), 43.

# Our house

# A moving house

## Eiléan Ní Chuilleanáin

The main humanities building in University College Cork, the university where I studied and still visit, is a large cruciform block built on the site of the house, now demolished, which was the official residence of the warden of the Honan Hostel. The hostel itself was a monument to various shifting currents in Irish history. It was built beside the institution known as 'the College', one of the 'godless' Queen's Colleges founded in 1845, supposed to rescue the Irish at one stroke from ignorance and sectarianism, with distinguished professors and a rule forbidding institutional allegiance to any religious group. Thus it was differentiated at once from the Church of Ireland stronghold of Trinity College Dublin, founded in 1592, and presently from the Catholic University of J.H. Newman and G.M. Hopkins, founded in 1851, also in Dublin.

Not only Catholics resisted the non-sectarian ethos. The hostel had started life as Berkeley Hall, a residence for Protestant students attending the university. Resident Protestant students declined in numbers and the hall was closed, later taken over by the Franciscan order of friars (their students attended the college), who didn't last even as long as the Berkeleyans. In 1913 a rich lady, Isabella Honan, left her money to a Catholic clergyman, Sir John O'Connell, to spend on education. He bought and refurbished the hostel, which then became a residence for Catholic male students, and built a Catholic chapel, which still stands on the grounds. The house that had been the dean of residence's, and later the friary (books stamped The Friary, St Anthony's Hall, included a complete run of Dickens), in 1915 became the warden's house, and the warden for the first time was a layman. My father, who was a professor of Irish, was appointed warden in 1949.

Most of my parents' thirty years of marriage was spent in my father's native city. For fourteen of those twenty-three years in Cork, we – my parents, my younger sister and I, presently joined by our younger brother – lived in that now vanished house. When we moved in in 1949 I was almost 7. We came from a pleasant small one-storey house on the Model Farm Road with a largish garden to front and rear. My sister lamented the change but I remember no regrets. I had always wanted a house with stairs and this one had three impressive flights. As the eldest too I felt an obligation to be positive. What was different in the new house? Apart from the size of the rooms, their number and names – the telephone room, the onion room, the attics – the doors into the hostel itself, the twenty-three apple trees in the garden?

Our old house was owned by my parents. They had moved there before I was born, when it was new; they had created the garden and we knew when certain trees had been planted and why. Moving there, they had left the old suburb of the Douglas Road, where my aunts and, for their last couple of surviving years, my grandparents lived, and I know my mother was glad to escape from the rented house that was so near his family. Wartime petrol shortages may have reduced visiting somewhat too. But as children we liked our aunts' home – they had *stairs*.

They – the three lay aunts, there were three more in convents – also had rather more, even, than was then usual, of the standard religious impedimenta of the day – the holy water fonts, vividly coloured crucifixes, votive lights, plaster statues, souvenirs from Lourdes, a big painting of the crucifixion in the main bedroom and a large portrait of the Dublin ascetic Matt Talbot over the dining table. The house was called St Joseph's: my grandmother had had seven children in under ten years, and my mother said that her devotion to St Joseph, who had just one stepchild, was a form of contraception. In our house we had a few Dürer saints and one dark monochrome carved-wood crucifix; my mother would not tolerate plaster. No wonder I became obsessed with devotional artefacts.

Our house on the Model Farm Road was called Tulach Óg, after the coronation mound of the O'Neill kings. It remains in my memory as a permeable place. We ran in the garden and hurt our knees and ran indoors to be comforted. My mother rode out on her bicycle dangling her cello. Visitors, a gardener, a regular beggarman came and went. We had nightmares and rushed into our parents' bedroom in the dark and they told us how cold we felt. The cat, Killarney Jim, dragged a rat in from the garden, took refuge under the kitchen stove and dared anyone to take it from him. My father worked on his PhD on the dining-room table and I was sent in to make him clear it away so we could have our tea. I had no sense of any difference in ownership between the parts of the house, though there was a maid's room with a maid in it, later taken over by Miss O'Neill, the nurse, who was called Miss O'Neill to make the point that she was not a maid.

That point immediately became more evident when we moved to the warden's house. It was a place of hierarchies and borders and structured visibilities. Now my father was 'the Professor' or 'the Warden' and he had a study to prove it – originally with wallpaper faked to look like dark wood panelling, which my mother soon got rid of. Now there was a maid's room reached by the back stairs, which rose from the boiler room, paused at a corridor with, originally, two maids' rooms (one was the onion room, which became a music practice room later) and a mysterious door at the end, and then after a few more steps debouched outside the drawing-room door. Miss O'Neill had a room beside ours, reached by the main stairs. Mrs Cotter came in by the day.

Neither servants nor children were to be on show at untoward times. I never saw my mother or father downstairs in that house other than fully dressed, and we learned not to appear in nightclothes and when not to appear at all. When the bishop came, Miss O'Neill kept us upstairs, and the maid brought in tea to the dining room, where the governors, chaired by the bishop, sat around the table with my father and his big minute book. Under the carpet there was a bell push so the maid could be summoned discreetly. Or on an ordinary evening there might be a student or two or three waiting to see my father in the large hall outside his study. The doors of the hostel were locked at eleven each night and anyone who wanted to stay out later had to come and ask for a key. In the rooms upstairs the furniture that came from Tulach Óg looked small and was joined by bigger, firmer sofas and extra tables.

(An effect I am suddenly aware of looking back is a change of the patterns of language. In our old house there was what felt like an easy swinging back and forth between Irish and English. Now there were extra people and extra business was being done, in English. Irish became more of an aspiration and speaking it was something one was accused of doing, or not doing – there didn't seem to be a right way of handling it. Much of this of course was just the effect of time passing. We were reading more and there were more books in English. My mother was beginning to make a career as a writer in English after publishing a couple of books in Irish. We were moved from a school that was supposed to be Irish-speaking – my father couldn't take their atrocious grammar – to a convent school where Irish was a 'subject' not a medium. And similarly we as girls were becoming more self-conscious and recoiling from strange – young and often clumsy – male presences, not wanting to be seen at a disadvantage. But the house also played its part.)

The house had been a friary, it had been a Victorian dean's residence. It was of the same vintage as the convents we frequented when visiting the veiled aunts, and the same as our convent school. It registered vanished ideas about housekeeping (the bell board in the kitchen showing which bedroom had signalled) and still-active notions of the institutional roles and responsibilities of education, my father *in loco parentis*, and it broadcast a strong message about private and public spheres. Until we were old enough to have a latchkey, we children went in by the back door, through the cloakroom with the maid's bathroom, into the back of the hall. If you were a visitor you rang the front doorbell and the maid answered. There was an outside hall with a set of coloured glass panels which gave time for whoever was in the inner hall to whisk out of the way. There was a hard ornate chair in the inner hall, and the main stairs, but the hall then continued to the back of the house where you had no business unless invited to dinner.

Upstairs there was the drawing room where my mother sat and wrote every day from eleven to one – her greatest boast that she did not turn her head when the front doorbell rang. In a locked cupboard in that room was her collection of books banned by the censorship board, to which I was later to be gradually introduced. Also, the bottles of spirits and vermouth which might, in the housekeeping wisdom of the day, 'have been a temptation' to servants. In childhood I tried to construct the plan of house and hostel in my head, and the hardest part was the fact that the drawing room almost backed on to the room with the mysterious door – the door beyond the maid's room and on a level a few steps lower than the drawing room. It was locked too, because it led to the hostel storeroom, and every Monday morning my mother let herself in with her key, unlocked a door on the other side and admitted the hostel cook and kitchen maid to give out stores and menus for the week. Her privacy, which she needed to write, was hemmed in by those locked and censored spaces.

In the convents too there was a private life going on behind a hall door. As schoolgirls we glimpsed it the odd time, sent to deliver a message to a nun, admitted to a front hall that had a thus-far-and-no-further message written on the walls, and the one hard chair. Then a nun, whisking out of a parlour where she had been seeing an official visitor, or coming from the chapel, would have let down her black skirt so it flowed, whereas in the school it was worn tucked up short over a shortish grey petticoat. What a change in them – their gliding walk, their fresh looks – just because they were in one room and not another. And what was being concealed, what revealed? Were they letting on that four hundred children and teenagers were just sordid business to be concealed like the petticoat? Or were they concealing from us another, a more intense, life? And what was it like during the school holidays? In our house as in the convent, time and presences changed places.

A different sort of presence obtained in the stunningly beautiful Honan Chapel at the end of our garden. A rickety iron gate in the fence was wreathed in convolvulus, a weed the gardener couldn't control. Beyond that there was a vision in white local limestone, chastely carved to replicate the Romanesque twelfth-century Cormac's chapel on the Rock of Cashel. As my father's name was Cormac, this seemed most appropriate. While the college was not supposed to have any religious allegiance, the special pews for the president and the warden, and the special Masses on important days – though the chapel stood on the Honan land not the college's – made it clear that was a dead letter. Attending Mass in the chapel on ordinary Sundays was a privilege: you had to have an academic connection. The gate into the college was generally open; another gate onto the street was generally locked. A couple of pious ladies who lived on the street nearest to the gate were allowed in as a special favour on Sunday mornings and the gate was unlocked for them. One of them was the sister of a deceased warden, I remember.

The interior of the chapel was a surprise, full of amazing colours, after the cool white exterior – in the windows by Harry Clarke and Henry Healy, in the liturgically coded vestments, the enamelled altar vessels, and what my sister and I loved best of all, the mosaic floor which illustrated 'The song of the three children in the fiery furnace': '*Benedicite omnia opera domini domino*' ('All ye works of the Lord, bless the Lord'). So there was a mean-looking leopard sneaking up on a squirrel, there was a peacock and an eagle and a polar bear, lots of fish swimming in the river that flowed the length of the nave and a contorted sea serpent that I preferred not to look at. The windows, as we got older, received more attention. They were full of stories – St Gobnait setting her bees on the robbers (she is the patron saint of beekeepers) and the monks of St Nessan's monastery pretending to be washerwomen chatting in Latin and Greek to frighten away the learned monks of a rival monastic school who had challenged them.

Our house, like the convent school, like the space around the chapel, was a place where sacred and secular met, and the encounter was visible, even in an Ireland where normal life and Catholic religion often seemed coterminous. In spite of the visiting bishop and the Catholic foundation, in spite of the warden's special pew in the Honan Chapel, the secular was dominant. If there was no holy statue in the house, there was a mysterious document: the grant of arms to the hostel from the Ulster king of arms, framed in the study.[1] The marvellous vestments of the chapel were kept in our attic, but the chapel meant to my mother, and she passed it on to us, the flowering of Irish art with the work of the Dun Emer Guild (Kitty McCormack of the guild came to stay), of Harry Clarke, Sarah Purser's studio and Egan's of Cork.[2] My parents' republican background meant, in the 1950s, a commitment to making the Republic work, to the legal, the political and the practical. My father laboured over the accounts for the (Protestant) auditor. My mother opened the mysterious door into the storeroom and checked the supplies of jam and tinned fruit; she lifted the telephone, and a string of vans and messenger boys delivered fresh food and sheets and towels, dispatched by the merchants and Magdalen laundries of the city.

In term time, they ate with the students while we had meals with Miss O'Neill. In summer, we all ate together. The barriers dissolved; we played around the hostel grounds and ranged through the adjacent college, which was almost as deserted. We slept in a tent in the garden; we picked raspberries and my mother made loads of jam; we lined up the apples in rows in the attic and she made apple jelly from the windfalls.

Until I was eleven or so, the house was my way of understanding the world, its differences and boundaries, and how they were not always there. And even then, but more certainly every year in the later

---

1 'Vert, in the doorway of an Irish Church or, the figure of Saint Finbarr proper, on a chief of the second, on a pale azure, between two lions passant to the dexter and the sinister respectively of the first, three antique crowns gold and For Motto Go Cum Gloire de agus O nora na hEireann.' Quoted in Catriona Mulcahy, 'The Honan Hostel', *Honan Chapel and collection online*: http://honan.ucc.ie/essays.php?essayID=6, accessed 26 Feb. 2017.　2 See Elizabeth Wincott Heckett, 'The part played by women in the making of the Honan Chapel', *Honan Chapel and collection online*: http://honan.ucc.ie/essays.php?essayID=8, accessed 26 Feb. 2017.

decade that I lived there, I knew that we were submerged in history. The date 1884 over the front door of the house, the stamped name of the friary on the books, reminded us how things had changed, and my parents occasionally reminded us that we too would have to move on, out of a house that was not really ours. In 1963 they left for Rome, and a year later I moved to Oxford; my home left me before I could leave home, and I never lived in Cork after that. Even now, the clean bright corridors and the water dispensers and committee rooms of the new building are slightly shocking, because I know there is no longer a family of children to be kept out of sight, and there will never be again.

# Four paintings and a cloakroom

## Mary Morrissy

The smallest room in our house, apart from the lavatory, was the cloakroom – an oddly anachronistic name for the cell-like room off the hall where we children hung our coats and deposited our wellies, the adults their stricken umbrellas. The cloakroom was plumbed for water with a small handbasin, so the nineteenth-century appellation coupled with twentieth-century functionalism made it an oddly ill-defined space, sitting rather importantly at the front of the house, but with a frosted glass window suggesting the secrecy of a closet. Ours was a standard four-bedroom, semi-detached house, half red-brick – up to the first floor – and then pebble-dash to the eaves, a common model in the Dublin suburbs of the 1950s, for which my parents paid the princely sum of £3,000.

As well as being a functional room, the cloakroom was a place of punishment. Its door had a sliding bolt on the outside, so there was no escape for the hapless occupant. It was where we were sent to cool off – the 1960s equivalent of the naughty step beloved of present-day parenting gurus. When my harried mother wanted to separate the warring factions that developed among four siblings, the most offending child would be sent there. Aping our elders, we often locked one another in the cloakroom, exploring the exquisite torture of claustrophobia and the delicious machinations of blackmail. *What will you give me if I let you out?*

Perhaps that was why, when reading *Jane Eyre*, this was where I imagined the young orphaned Jane being sequestered in the opening pages of that novel. Our cloakroom could not be further removed from the dark, damask-draped 'red-room' that Charlotte Brontë described – 'a spare chamber, very seldom slept in' – where Mr Reed had breathed his last and which gave the red room its 'sense of dreary consecration'. There was no high, dark wardrobe in our cloakroom, no stately bed with massive pillars of mahogany, no ottoman. Instead, we had bare walls painted a neutral shade – cream, eggshell white, something nondescript. On the floor was an earth-hued lino – linoleum being a very modern and fashionable floor covering of the time. This was in an expressionist pattern, a mix of muddy green, rust red and daubs of white – think of Philip Guston's early abstract work and you have it. It is the only room in the house where the original lino has survived and still adorns the floor almost sixty years later. So as well as being modern and fashionable in its time, it has proved to be durable. (Alas no longer; since writing this essay, the cloakroom has been refurbished as a bathroom.)

What the cloakroom had in common with Brontë's red room was that it exhaled the deprivation of the cell – emphasized by its jailer-like lock – and the dreaded threat of abandonment. What if you were left there, trapped forever among the musty coats giving off their whiff of neglect? Who owned some of these coats – dark plastic macs, transparently horrible, thick tweed overcoats and giant menacing galoshes that seemed far too big for my father's size eight shoes? It was as if the cloakroom harboured secrets that were older than the house itself, and suggested ghostly presences of another era.

This was a room where you couldn't sit down, where there was nothing to fiddle or play with, making it the perfect place to ponder your wickedness, and after the allotted time (sooner rather than later) to express your remorse. Or if the offence merited it, it was where you calculated the odds of further punishment. Deferred penalty was the ultimate deterrent. *Wait till your father gets home* were words we grew to dread. Which, in our case, could mean a long wait. My father worked as a customs officer and was away for weeks at a time in far-flung outposts of the Republic on night shifts at border crossings and alcohol factories. But what made the cloakroom the ultimate prison was its lack of visual distraction. There were no paintings, or what we called pictures, on the wall. If you had been locked in the sitting room, you could contemplate *The virgin of the grapes* (Pierre Mignard, Musée de Louvre, 1640s) in its ornate gilt frame. Or you might have considered *Fabiola* (Jean-Jacques Henner, 1885) – versatile patron saint of divorcees, difficult marriages, victims of abuse, adultery and unfaithfulness, and widows. This was a rather boring picture to my childish eye, a Roman profile view of an aristocratic-looking female draped in a red veil against a black ground. As in the matter of punishment, my father was the final arbiter of the images on the walls.

My father died in 1970, when I was 13, so I never knew him as an adult. Born in London in 1910, the son of an Irish emigrant journeyman carpenter, my father returned to Co. Clare when he was 5 and grew up in a cottage outside Kilrush. It was a crowded house. There were four young children, his parents, plus two members of the extended family – his mother's sister Molly, and Aggie, a distant cousin (not the full shilling) – both of them single women who cleaned and cooked and provided the surrogate mothering that female relatives in Irish households of the time gave in return for their keep – or because it was their instinct. My father completed his secondary schooling and joined the civil service as a 'junior ex' after leaving school in the early 1930s. Politically, he was a devoted Dev man – a bust of the Long Fella sits on the sitting-room mantelpiece. He died in the run-up to the infamous Arms Trial, which was to tear his beloved Fianna Fáil apart. Just as well, my mother used to say, the result would have killed him anyway.

He was a man of his time, which, I constantly have to remind myself, was the Edwardian era. A distant father, as fathers were then, slow to anger but fierce in his authority. What I remember most clearly about him now, and recognized even as a child, was his passionate auto-didacticism. (His favourite catchphrase when his children showed evidence of intellectual pride was, 'Sure I only went to the hedge school.' Not literally true, of course, but revealing of an acute insecurity about his educational shortcomings.)

Above all, he wanted opportunities for his children that he had not enjoyed himself. Hence, music lessons – he came along to our first lessons on the piano with Mrs Wiener, a rather elderly and grim German lady who lived nearby, and plodded along with our scales and arpeggios until we left him far behind in the garden slopes and climbed the laddered rungs of the Royal Academy of Music grading system. He learned German in middle age – strangely using Hitler's speeches at the Nuremberg rallies to perfect his accent. I'm reminded of Sylvia Plath's poems about her Teutonic father. In this age of political correctness, it's hard to view this choice of learning aid as a purely linguistic decision.

My earliest memory of his interest in art was visiting Dublin's galleries. I remember being brought to the Municipal Gallery (now the Dublin City Gallery) to view the Hugh Lane bequest, which spent half the year in Dublin, the other in London. I have a mental image of myself as a small child, my hand in his, standing in front of Renoir's *Les parapluies* and thinking it the most beautiful and most blue confection I had ever seen. I identified, of course, with the coiffed and bonneted little girl in the right foreground of the painting, dressed in what seemed her Sunday best and clutching her spinning hoop and stick.

My father didn't view art as just a spectator sport. On Saturday mornings when he was at work – or else he would surely have joined in – he arranged for my brothers and me to have art lessons. We were tutored by a succession of students from the College of Art (one of them a brother of the leading Irish fashion designer Paul Costelloe) in watercolours, pen and ink, calligraphy and lino cuts, a veritable array of artistic skills that I can only imagine he longed to have himself.

I am now the age my father was when he died. Perhaps it is this fact that makes me realize the rich aesthetic legacy he has left – not just in the cultural opportunities he insisted upon, but in the images he chose to surround us with. These aesthetic choices live on. The same images he chose hang on the walls of our home to this very day. All around them, the house has been modernized – aluminium windows, central heating, numerous changes of wallpaper and decor – but the pictures remain as a legacy of both his taste and his cultural aspirations, a permanent exhibition, if you like, of which he is the ghostly curator.

Although I can say what these pictures have meant to me – these were my first images and informed my childhood – I have never considered before what they meant to *him* and what they might tell me about the man I never properly knew. On making my inventory, the first thing I can say is that he was a Vermeer man. Practically all of Vermeer's thirty-eight authenticated canvasses adorned our walls – *The little street, The milkmaid, The art of painting, Girl with a pearl earring, View of Delft*. These were print reproductions which, I discovered, my father had cut from art books and framed. It was an eerie experience to examine the backstage of these framed prints that I have spent so long looking at. There on the cardboard backing he'd carefully placed to support the prints was my father's handwriting, often in pencil, giving the title of the work, the artist's name and dates. As if he knew that one day someone would lift them down seeking out their provenance. And, in some way, his.

His interest in Dutch painting extended beyond Vermeer. There are reproductions of work by Pieter de Hooch and Gabriël Metsu, both contemporaries of Vermeer – and interestingly, much more successful in their time than he was. The Vermeer images are all small, arranged usually in clusters of four, and because of Vermeer's current ubiquity, probably of less interest than my father's other choices. That he loved Dutch painting seems beyond question. And while, to my mind, de Hooch and Metsu have neither the absolute conviction nor the exacting stillness of Vermeer, there is a quality in their work of rigorous but graceful control, qualities I associate with my father.

Reviewing the broad strokes of his preferences, two strands emerge: the Dutch School and religious themes. Sometimes they overlapped. Vermeer, who converted to Catholicism, painted a version of the parable of Martha and Mary (*Christ in the house of Martha and Mary*), which was part of my father's collection. The religious preoccupation is not surprising – either for the time, or for the man. My father was a very pious Catholic. He followed the exacting requirements of his faith to the letter. Weekly confession, nightly prayers, daily rosary. I remember him measuring out his food for the Lenten fast – 'one full meal and two collations' for forty days – using a weighing scales at the table. Religion was, at that time, not just a pervasive feature of our lives, but formed the basis of animated family discussions. 'The prodigal son' was a favourite hot topic at the dinner table – my mother warning darkly that there would be no fatted calf for any of us if we went off the rails. But she was equally exercised by the injustices of 'The workers in the vineyard'. Why, she questioned, should the workers who'd only arrived late in the day, get paid the same as those who'd toiled since early morning? Often these debates would be between my parents – my father favouring the more orthodox view. As a result, these seemed live issues to us as children. To be surrounded by a great deal of religious art was equally unremarkable. What is remarkable is that it was of such a high standard.

Where did this passion for art spring from? It seems unlikely that there were many pictures in my father's own home, a workman's cottage in Cappagh, Co. Clare. I have no way of knowing, since the house went out of the family on the death of my grandmother years before I was born. But my father's brother was a talented amateur artist throughout his life, and two of his watercolours graced our walls right beside the Vermeers – so there must have been a strong predisposition to visual culture in the family. My grandfather was a carpenter, which might explain the appreciation of fine craftsmanship among his sons, but it's hard to imagine that they would have had much exposure to great works of art growing up – apart, of course, from the images the church offered.

Whatever the reason for my father's passion, there is no doubting it. What is of more interest to me is the insight it might give me into his character. Looking around our house, I've chosen several works of his (so identified in my mind are they with him, it sometimes seems as if he painted them himself) mainly because they are works I loved as a child and/or they have excited my curiosity in middle age.

The first is a Dutch interior by Pieter de Hooch (1629–84). De Hooch's subject matter was the seventeenth-century Dutch domestic interior. *Woman lacing her bodice beside a cradle* dates from de Hooch's later career, some time in the 1660s, when he concentrated almost exclusively on depicting the comfortable middle classes in their own milieu – the domesticated safety of home. In this painting the mother is opening her bodice as a prelude to feeding the baby. (In companion pieces, de Hooch shows the same woman actually feeding the baby.) The unseen infant lies in the cradle beside her. As a child, I did not understand why the woman seemed to be in a state of undress – breastfeeding was not a common sight in the Dublin suburbs of the early 1960s. I had noticed, however, that the buttons of her skirt seemed to be undone – as if her flies were open – to reveal what looked to my eye like a nightie underneath. This gave the painting a slightly illicit charge. But that was a minor note. My real interest was in the child in the painting. Here was a little girl making for the open doorway through which a tantalizing sun crept, flooding the tiled floor and illuminating the back of the painting with an almost celestial light. There she is, like a moth drawn to a flame. The moment the painting captures seems full of imminence – the child taking advantage of her mother's preoccupation, something that must have chimed with my own desire for escape. There were details I noticed as a child without actually understanding them. It never struck me, for example, that the aperture behind the mother was a bed – in seventeenth-century Dutch homes, beds were often hidden in living room alcoves. I saw this as a chimney breast or a curtained-off cubbyhole. (Perhaps even their version of a cloakroom?) I remember being fascinated by the cradle – a basket on rockers which seemed plump and fat with the solid-looking hood construction suggesting a similarly stolid infant within. De Hooch's concern with light meant that certain details were highlighted. Even though my interest was in the narrative of the painting – will the little girl make it through the open door before being called back? – certain painterly effects caught my eye. The glistening warming pan (which I thought was some kind of giant frying pan), the high finish of the black knob for cloaks to hang from, the red cloak itself with the upturned hem and the sheen of the tiled floor all spoke of a very clean and polished house.

For a man who spent a lot of time away from home, perhaps it was these warm and reassuring depictions of a cultured home life that appealed to my father. He was a man who had come late to domesticity – he was a 40-year-old bachelor when he married (to my mother's 28). I know little about this pre-existence. Was he sowing his wild oats? If so, he spent twenty years doing it. And by the time we came along, he neither smoked nor drank. Which either suggests a blameless youth, or the exact opposite. Perhaps he thought he would never enjoy marriage and children and home; perhaps the de Hooch prints predate his marriage and represent a young man's yearning for the grace and harmony of an idealized middle-class household. Or were there echoes of his own childhood in those orderly Dutch homes? Aspiration or nostalgia?

On the other hand, *La sainte cène* ('*The Last Supper*') by Carlos Oswald couldn't be further removed from the stillness of those Dutch interiors. Born in Florence in 1882, Oswald lived and worked in Brazil, where he was known as 'the painter of light'. He opened the first engraving workshop in Rio de Janeiro and was a charismatic teacher and prodigious printmaker. Perhaps his biggest claim to fame is drawing up the designs for the Christ the Redeemer statue, executed by the French sculptor Paul Landowski, that dominates the Rio skyline. From the second decade of the twentieth century (he lived until 1971), Oswald specialized in religious commissions. One of these, *La sainte cène*, was widely disseminated by the Stehli Brothers in Zurich. It is one such print my father bought.

*La sainte cène* is a standard depiction of the Last Supper, a horizontal view of the table with the apostles gathered around. Unusually, the figure of Christ is not in the centre, but placed in profile at the extreme right. Oswald captures a dramatic moment – presumably when Jesus predicts he will be betrayed by someone in the company. Several of the apostles standing behind Jesus display expressions of horror, hands aloft in shock and denial. The supper takes place in a vaulted cellar sunk in mossy shadow; the only illumination within the painting is a candelabra on the table, its tapers throwing light on the side-view of Judas' face. It seems obvious to me now that Judas is the figure cloaked in purple with his back to viewer. He is gripping the table edge, white-knuckled with guilt. He has upset a goblet of wine, which seeps like a bloodstain on the disturbed white tablecloth in a clever foreshadowing of events. But as a child, I remember heated discussions (much like the ones about the parables) about this painting, prompted by my father. Which one did *we* think was Judas? I wondered about the apostle sitting at the opposite end of the table to Jesus, quietly removed from the action. Now I see it's more likely that he is one of the recording evangelists, but then I thought he looked shifty, rather than merely observant. He seemed less a detached witness than a spy, a devious plotter.

Whatever about the dramatis personae, Oswald's Last Supper is drama at its most intense. It's a whodunit – or who will do it – rather than a static depiction of a ceremonial ritual. This is what I loved – and still admire – about Oswald's work. Was it the same for my father? In comparison to the composure of de Hooch, Metsu and Vermeer, Oswald's treatment seems largely emotional, a painterly confrontation of a Big Moment rather than the Dutch concentration on the small moment, the domestic detail. In that, the Oswald seems a departure for my father. It may just have been the theme. After all, we had prints of the Annunciation. We had a crucifix. Perhaps he thought this another iconic Christian moment that needed recording. But why this one? I would choose it for that depiction of Judas – sweating, terrified and guilty. The eye immediately goes to him rather than to Jesus, who looks pained and long-suffering but not terribly interesting. The painter has used the novelist's trick, depending on the viewer's knowledge to see what the participants of the drama fail to see. What this painting did for me was to flesh out Judas – he was not the crass baddie of the gospels, but the stricken, haunted creature of Oswald's painting. I doubt if my devout Edwardian father saw it that way, but by choosing this print, he showed an avid appetite for the luridly theatrical, a side to him I never saw beyond his record collection, which included Abbey Theatre productions of Synge, O'Casey and Behan.

My final pick from my father's collection is a pair of paintings that have hung on the stairs for many years and which, as a child, I loathed. Nor have they grown on me in adulthood. In that, they represent a kind of failure of my father's project, if what he had hoped to do was to instil admiration for the images he surrounded us with. In keeping with the spirit of this artistic exercise, I thought I should not just choose paintings I liked, but paintings *he* did. It was hard, however, to work out the attraction of the pair of deer – two long, brown, gloomy oil paintings meant as companion pieces. What could have possessed him? They are competent works; the animals are faithfully reproduced, although the doe's hooves look suspiciously dainty to me and the landscape rather oddly miniaturized. The subject matter doesn't help. This kind of wildlife, with the distinct whiff of the taxidermist's studio, is deeply unfashionable to our twenty-first-century eyes, betraying a kind of fusty Victorian pastoralism.

Apart from some Irish landscapes, which I didn't include here because they were wedding gifts and therefore not voluntary choices, my father's taste seems to have run to people rather than places. In that, the deer also went against type. But, I reasoned, something about their execution must have excited his interest. When I fetched them down from the wall there were no identifying marks on the frames, no gallery tag, no helpful signposts from my father to guide me. What was it about these rather overstuffed-looking paintings that made him buy them? These, I noticed, were original canvases, not cut-outs from calendars or art books. I asked my mother. (My father might be the artistic curator, but my mother is the custodian of his collection.) Oh, she said airily, they were painted by your father's great-aunt. She was a nun. And that was as far as my mother's knowledge went. What else is there to know? Well, that she painted – large ambitious paintings, by the look of it, even though they might not appeal to current taste. It set me wondering about this woman's life, *her* place in the inherited aesthetic. I know nothing about her, bar the scant details a cousin provided and those the 1901 census throws up. Born Bridget Morrissey, she entered the Convent of Mercy, Strabane, Co. Tyrone, aged 24 in 1884 and died there forty-eight years later. Her religious name was Sister Mary Berchmans Joseph, in honour of the sixteenth-century Belgian saint, John Berchmans. (My father's only sister entered the same convent in the 1920s, which explains why she chose to travel so far to enter the religious life; there was a family connection.)

By trying to solve one artistic mystery, I had stumbled on another. A mystery, perhaps, but also some kind of explanation. Is this woman, Bridget Morrissey, the progenitor of the painterly impulse that has shown itself in four generations of my father's family – my uncle, my brother and nephew all paint – and which manifested itself in my father as a vigorous evangelism for painting? Maybe so. But the fact of her begs a whole new series of questions. Did she paint before entering the convent or was it a pastime she adopted in later life? Or did she forsake her painting when she entered religious life? Are there other paintings of hers hanging elsewhere? Would I like them better?

When I began my sleuthing expedition, I was hoping to come to know my father through his collection of favourite paintings. I did not expect to find a genealogical link to the mid-nineteenth century in the process. The unexpected legacy of my father's permanent exhibition is not that I have necessarily come to know him any better, but that I have been introduced to someone I didn't know at all. It seems, too, I was wrong about the cloakroom. It was not the site of ghosts in our house; no, the spirit of the nineteenth century was, all along, hanging on the walls.

# *Omphalos*

## Colette Bryce

I would begin with the Greek word, *omphalos*, meaning the navel, and hence the stone that marked the centre of the world, and repeat it, *omphalos, omphalos, omphalos*, until its blunt and falling music becomes the music of somebody pumping water at the pump outside our back door.

—Seamus Heaney, 'Mossbawn'

*Omphalos, omphalos, omphalos* ... The rhythm of the word that conjured up for Heaney the pump in his childhood yard – the Greek term for the centre of things – calls to mind the helicopters hovering over the cityscape of my childhood, a constant part of the soundtrack of growing up. The army would use the racket of propellers to drown out speeches at Free Derry Corner. So in my mind, the blades are related to words, in opposition to our words, slicing up sentences in the wind.

An emigrant's view might also hover, surveying the misty valley of a city, grids of streets punctuated by churches, before focusing in on a house. It's near the upper end of a terrace, the house where we lived. Looking back, I can rarely locate the 'I', a common experience in large families. Memories have a collective quality. Mine are often from the point of view of 'the wee ones', the four youngest siblings – two sisters, my brother and myself. Something happened and 'we' were excited; something else, and 'we' were scared. The 'big ones', the five eldest girls, were a slightly separate tribe.

So the house was part of a terrace, and 'I' was part of a sequence of children. Perhaps we can think of ourselves, siblings from large families, as *terraced children*, as opposed to detached or semi-detached. Do we share interior walls, psychologically? My sisters and I appear in a recent poem, 'hand in hand like paper dolls', walking to the infant school. Most of the neighbouring houses had children and the street was one of open doors, as we darted in and out of each other's homes.

Our street overlooked the Moor, a series of terraces that runs from the cathedral on the left to the city cemetery on the right. Below the Moor lay the valley of the Bogside, with its neat rows of roofs adorned with TV aerials and smoke. My mother had grown up in our house and the upstairs drawing room from her less chaotic childhood was now a dormitory of single beds. My grandmother lived with us until she died in 1967. That year, the electronics factory that loomed behind our houses closed, leaving hundreds of men unemployed. The area, as it might have looked in my mother's heyday, was beautifully drawn by Seamus Deane in his novel *Reading in the dark*. His characters inhabit a maze of rained-on terraces, rife with political intrigue. Where Deane's novel ends, my life begins, with the advent of the '70s.

In 1972, one week after Bloody Sunday, our windows are blown in by an explosion down in the Moor. There are house raids by paratroopers and later, after a shoot-out at the gable end, they fire rounds of tear gas. Because the window panes are gone, the rooms fill quickly and my mother ushers everyone out, forgetting in her panic the toddler asleep in her cot. A courageous neighbour, Pat Breslin, covers his face and dashes up the stairs.

We would lean over the fence as funerals slow-footed along the Moor to the cemetery, led by the priest in his black suit. Or peep from the vantage point of the top windows when rioting erupted below. One night we watched, fascinated, as Metal Mickey – the bomb disposal robot – advanced towards an abandoned Cortina. To my mother's generation, going 'over the Moor' was the euphemism for dying. Years later, when I read Emily Dickinson's poem 'Because I could not stop for Death', I pictured Death's carriage paused by the terraced houses in the Moor, an image hard to dislodge.

When I was ten, we moved down the street from number 17 to number 4. I remember a stand-up piano being wheeled along the pavement like a barrel organ. The new house was a mirror image of the old, only slightly larger. Like vital clues in a mystery, the departing family had left behind a globe of the earth in dusty halves, and a pair of antiquated binoculars. These objects provided my first and lasting impressions of our new world, as our furnishings filled the freshly painted rooms.

In Jungian dream analysis, a house can symbolize one's psyche or self, the various levels of consciousness. The contents of an attic may signify hidden aspects of our personalities, brought to our attention by the dreaming mind. Some poems, like dreams, seem to come from another level, slightly beyond what we know or remember. Often, we capture only fragments. And when a poem is written, like a fully remembered dream, its meaning can remain withheld for a long time.

My recent poems seem to want to examine that place, and time, more closely. The results are only glimpses, seen through doorways, sometimes held in mirrors. The mirror in our hallway was consulted by everyone leaving or entering by the front door – checking faces, fixing hair. Now, in the hall mirror, I can see nine children looking out. I'm stealing this image from a Mary Poppins story, where a small boy asks her to tell him what he looks like. 'Look in the mirror,' she says, surprised. 'But there are so many faces', he replies, 'I don't know which is mine!' When the British soldiers raided our house in the early hours of the morning, my mother would request that they stack their rifles under the hall table, so as not to scare the children. I imagine each man's face suspended for a brief moment in that hall mirror, as he bends to set down his gun.

So the house is central to my poetic world, in its mirrors and in both of its mirrored incarnations, number 17 and number 4. And the terraced street is a concertinaed expansion of the house, a sort of cliff of rooms in and out of which many children flit like swifts. The street overlooks the valley of the town, which rises again beyond the Rossville flats to meet the crown of medieval walls. The writing is on the walls, of course, the slogans of the day in white emulsion. The house stands in its historical moment, in a particular war, where *trouble* is the norm, and children are not afraid of tanks, or bombs, or balaclavaed men. A chopper hovers over the walls, dips, turns and veers away. Weirdly, it feels like the safest place in the world.

# Home is where you start from

## Theo Dorgan

I was a strange child, it seems to me now, because every memory of my family home that I call up comes with a subsidiary, interlocked, interwoven memory: me, looking around me, telling myself 'you must remember this, you will need to remember this, you will need to have remembered this'.

Perhaps everyone does this.

Perhaps not.

I did not live naively in that house, as I hope to make plain; the ways in which I was conscious in and of the house cannot be found separate from the stones and tiles, the windows and concrete, the physical aggregate that was home.

Like this, then: I am 10, standing midway up or down the front steps, a summer's morning, the hedge between us and Mahony's next door crisp and newly trimmed, and over the hedge, coming out of the heat haze in the valley stretching away and down from our house, the domes and spires and chimneys of the city are starting to come into focus. I am completely, simply, utterly inside myself. I sit down, cross-legged, the buckles on my new sandals scraping my bare calves. I smell dust from the warm concrete of the step, fresh-cut grass, the tang of exhaust fumes as a motorbike growls past. Gradually, I am filling up with all I am seeing and feeling and smelling, and I am aware of myself telling myself to remember all this, that I will want to have remembered this. And something else, too, something slight but certain that I can only describe as some faint, definite intimation of an older self reminding me that he, we, will need to have remembered this.

Thus me, at 10, at home.

I have always loved hills, the sudden slant of things, the trudge upward, deep and satisfying in muscle and bone, the vertiginous light-hearted downward plunge, giddy and flying free – and I have always loved flat places, vantages, rest places, ledges over the known and the unknown, but best of all is the quick alternation of one with the other. Now, revisiting myself, my undying childhood, I see all of this may have started from home.

My father and five of his friends bought a piece of land and divided it into six plots on which to build their houses to a simple, common design. Land on the side of a hill that meant steps up to each house from the road, Redemption Road, that fronted the plots. Each of those steps is a site of memory for me, each was a kind of landing stage, jetty or runway for flights of fancy, for jumping off, for sitting on in contented vacancy, places to pause on the way up from the gate or in an otherwise headlong flight downward.

Sometimes arrested by a sudden perception, more often rapt in thoughtful and absorbing play.

The six men worked as labourers on each other's houses, bonded by work as they were bonded by friendship and by their membership of a hurling and football club, Na Piarsaigh, of which some, my father included, were founders. Such solidarity, such matter-of-fact mutual support. The builder who managed the construction was known as The Happy Man, because, of course, he was famously not. Such was, and is, the Cork city of my birth, where nothing is what it seems but everything is perfectly understood.

Solid houses, the men cast the concrete blocks on site. Solid steps, poured concrete that has never shifted or cracked. Plain houses, pebble-dashed, metal window frames, wide sills.

Working men, making their play for some kind of permanence in a life where nothing could be taken for granted, where nothing was taken as given except the assurances of family, trust in friendship, work.

And so, my birthplace, the house where I grew up. You stepped through the gate from Redemption Road into a tiny space of packed earth, you turned right, took the first two small steps and turned left, a small sloping lawn between you and Mahony's to your left, a smooth-plastered wall to your right, supporting the raised, and also sloped, front lawn. How that wall held heat in summer, your hand running pleasurably along its lightly textured roughness as you climbed. Shallow steps, broad steps, the fan-shaped broad step where you turned to face the last four steps.

Before you, looming overhead, the modest-sized house that seemed not huge exactly but solid, substantial, the rose-draped pergola rooted in concrete planters each side of the front door. But we mostly used the kitchen door, along the gable, through the wooden gate where the round-topped high wall almost met the house, the wall parallel to the road below, fronted by grass, the outer perimeter of the private space behind.

A beaten-earth yard to the side of the house, then, high steps through the first terrace of back garden to the larger garden above, the steps flattening to a path. The washing line flanking this upper path, permanently burdened with its flags and pennants. Down again now. At the back of the house, a concreted yard, continuation of the path that ran around the semi-detached house, the yard ending in the wall dividing us from Twomey's next door. The kitchen window, then the dining room window, another arch of rambling roses facing that window. My shy romantic father, planting roses for his Rose, my mother. Back in the side yard, over against the wall dividing public front from private back, a lean-to shed – coal store, bicycle store, home to a glorious chaos of odds and ends, garden tools, paint tins … astonishing, how much miscellanea, how much of life's near-detritus, can be crammed into a shed, as everyone knows who has ever had a shed.

Our childhood fort, too, our vantage point, sprawled on the hot tarred-felt sloping roof overlooking the road and its passing parade – as, we imagined, mailed warriors or men of the 5th Cavalry kept watch from their parapets, sighting along the length of our hurleys, or side by side with our spears laid up alongside. No point bringing bows or arrows onto that roof; rising to use them we would be immediately exposed and vulnerable to the enemy without. That six inches of rounded coping on the front wall was the difference between death and life, our safety and our salvation.

And beside the shed, between shed and hedge, a narrow, secret passage that I would take care to keep open when it became my business to trim the thick privet that bordered the property on each side.

The property. How alien that word when applied to what we knew, in all its layered and clouded complexity, simply as home. First world, sufficient and minutely known. Steps and flat places, slopes and flat places. Our goings out and our comings in, our stoppings and startings, the sudden freedoms of two, three steps at a time, outward bound, the sudden tiredness of my mother, labouring up from the front gate, laden with shopping bags; my father stopping, his bike over his shoulder, to turn and look backwards at something that had caught his attention on the road below.

Leaving the house, that lovely airy freedom, the opening out into infinite possibility; coming home, that lovely folding around you of the familiar and known, climbing into the secure. Into a place so deeply and thoroughly known and studied it was, in truth, an extension of the self.

Coming home in autumn, school not long before begun, the crisp outside air meeting the warm inside fug as you open the back door. The larder to the right, never quite full, by a miracle it seems to me now never quite empty. And, ah, the red and yellow square tiles of the kitchen, carried out into the hall towards the pebble-glass front door with its four panels. Always (but perhaps I need to imagine this now) the smell of cooking. On the tiles, if you squatted down in the hall to roll a marble, the smell of Mansion House polish. How intriguing it always seemed, that the tiles were never quite level. Such a minute and exact knowledge I had once, of where a particular tile was faintly raised above the others, where another dipped, so that to reach the front door from the kitchen door with a coloured marble or a Dinky car with wobbly wheels called for skilled propulsion of a high order. Or, overmastered by a sudden black impatience, simple brute force –

and the inevitable following sense of disappointment with yourself. Always that doubling self, that voice whispering 'remember this, you will want to remember this'.

Dining room to the left with its never-quite-extinguished fire, always clothes drying on a clothes horse in front of it. One night it will catch fire and I will walk calmly into the room, fold it in on itself and walk through the kitchen to throw it out into the yard. My mother staring at me, myself amazed at this unexpected coolness, decisiveness; myself pondering, even as I'm doing it, how crisp and decisive and unafraid I'm being. Eldest son.

Beside the dining room, front of the house, the almost empty room we call simply the front room. Empty all through my childhood because on rainy days, when we have to play inside, better to do it in an empty room. Near shock, years later, mid-teens, to watch it being furnished.

The stairs. The fuse-board facing them almost unfindable, so many coats hung on the hooks in this shallow recess beside the front door. Changing a fuse for the first time, Dad still at work.

Eldest child, responsible from the start – easy enough to say responsible for what, to write out that catalogue if I choose – but there is also that sense, faint but sure, of being responsible *to* something, or someone.

I observe that this box of memory is in the hands of me aged 9 or 10. Well of course, but I have to go back to the dining room, the arch of rambling roses outside its broad window. To the right of the fire, the table with the wireless on it. I was that age, 10, when I first turned the set around to watch the valves heat up, to smell the particular dust that comes with old radios, their lit interiors. And, in the other alcove, the one nearest the window, the three shelves of books, *The Pears children's cyclopedia* with its engraved line illustrations, the set of Companion Book Club titles that my father, at some stage, collected. *The ascent of Everest*, *The phantom major* (the story of how David Stirling founded the SAS, a book that will come back to life for me, years later, when, in a London pub where I'm working as a summer barman by night, I come across Davy, twenty-stone Davy, an original

member) and so many others: *The surprise of Cremona, The epic voyage of the Seven Little Sisters, The lost world of the Kalahari* … I believe I could list them all if I put my mind to it, I believe this because when, at 10, I began to make my way through those books I was telling myself 'remember this, remember this'. And not just, I want you to understand, 'remember what is in this book'; I meant also 'remember yourself reading this book, remember how it felt, what thoughts it spurred, where you were sitting or standing or lying, what kind of day it was, what the paper felt like, the smell of the ink …'.

That was when I began to be twice in the world, or perhaps it would be more accurate to say that was the age when I began to notice my way of being twice – for I'm sure that, even then, I was remembering having always been like this.

Under the stairs in the hall was chaos, a kind of indoor twin to the jumble of the shed outside minus the bicycle and the coal. I remember watching my father screw the tops of jars to the underside of shelves in there, then screw the jars full of rusting nails, nuts, washers and bolts to the lids. I thought that was very clever indeed, may even, like Frank O'Connor observing his father, have thought there was hope for the old fella yet.

The stairs, down which we would jump in the evenings when we couldn't think of anything better to do, the trick being not to skull yourself on the slant bit of ceiling overhead that followed the angle of the stairs. I claim the record of eight steps, have a clear memory of banging my head any time I attempted nine. My brothers and sisters, the older ones anyway, may dispute my claim – and here they are now, crowding in, my seven brothers, my seven sisters, our lost Nuala buried in faraway Carrignavar. I will be 17 when the youngest is born – but I have not the time nor the space nor the energy here to take on the task, Herculean seems to fit the case, of describing the human ecology of that house, the turbulent whirlpool of feeding, clothing and educating us all, the to and fro of relationships, the ebb and flow of needs and troubles and elations small and great, the give and take that became, of necessity, what bound us together, the many miracles of watching distinct and individual personalities grow and evolve in that soviet of energies and cares. Three bedrooms, boys, girls, parents, one bathroom, one kitchen … and one wage to feed us all.

Even then, my 10-year-old fetch, only half the family yet born, was entranced by the blunt and fascinating question, how is all this being managed? Yet, without charity or handout, with the help of the blessed children's allowance, somehow managed it was.

I feel him drawing away from me now, that child I was, that child who has never left me, who doubles my steps through the world, watchful, thoughtful, matching me step for step, perpetually interested to see how this will all eventually pan out. He knows it will take a book, perhaps more than one book, to give anything like an accurate depiction of what that was like, to grow up as first child in so big and near-chaotic a family. He is severe, this boy I was, this boy still with me: they have each their own story, my brothers, my sisters, and at the heart of each story some moment, some feeling, some perception absolutely necessary to, uniquely meaningful to, them and them alone. Not my business here. He wants no distractions. I see this as I watch the words emerge here before me on this blue screen; he wants me to say one thing that will bring him guiltless ease.

He wants it said, I think, that he liked our house best – no, not best, but particularly – when it was empty. Ever a planner, he would decide from time to time, when the need for silence and space became pressing, that wandering away off into the garden by himself, or off on one of his solitary rambles through the high fields behind the house, was not exactly what he needed. He would decide he was sick, would effortlessly persuade our mother he needed a day off school. A day to wander slowly through the house, touching things, tracing the texture of things with his fingertips or with his cheek laid against a wall, a curtain. Once, taking the mirror off a dressing table, from an upstairs window he passed away an hour signalling Collins Barracks high on its hill across the valley, 'Help, I am being held prisoner …'. His disappointment at getting no answer from those soldiers, his doubt that the book on the windowsill was giving him the accurate Morse letters …

It was only play, of course, but curiously detached play. He didn't care if they answered or not – truth to tell he would probably have got the fright of his life if someone had answered, and besides, sober realist that he was, he knew that he would not have been able to decipher any answer that might have come. I knew it then, I see it now, plain as day, he was simply conducting an exercise for his own private amusement, signalling not so much to the barracks as to the void, the void inside himself in which he was more than happy to amuse himself, forever if need be.

Fortified and protected, of course, by being in sole possession of his known place.

For all that, was he happy, that boy in the house of his childhood? I was, sometimes, but even then I did not believe there was some necessary, absolute, relationship between 'home' and 'happy'. Even then I knew there was more to this mysterious business of being in the world than could be encompassed by 'happy'. To tell the truth, I thought happiness, as usually understood and meant, a slightly ridiculous concept and ambition.

Then, as now, all I ever wanted was to feel fully myself and at home in the world.

Home is where you start out into the world from; you are never truly completely there, and you never leave. But you do. You are always leaving, leaving … but somehow there is never a sure 'there' to leave.

I think he knew that, then, the boy I was who is here inside me now, alive here and now as absolutely as he ever was in the moment by moment of way back then. I know he knew that, because here inside me as I type, here in my hands, I feel his hands enclosed in mine, articulate in mine. I feel his mind in mine. I feel his mind intuiting this moment in the future, as I feel my mind nearly lose its moorings, summoning up the past, struggling, and failing again, to understand – and all we have to agree on is that house, that vivid and actual house neither he nor I can ever truly and fully live in, not then, not now, not ever again, not ever.

# Liturgies of fire and water

## Macdara Woods

It is half past nine at night, mid-August, hot and dark, and I can hear the combine harvesters at work on the neighbouring farms and see their lights moving up and down the hills. This is the region of Umbria in central Italy, landlocked, without a coastline, but enclosing a 158-square-kilometre lake, Trasimeno, Etruscan Tarsmina, where Hannibal destroyed a Roman army in June 217 BC. It is where I have been living – when I can – over the past thirty years. This summer of 2012 the whole of Europe south of the jet stream is spread out under a heatwave; there are major forest fires in Spain and Portugal, minor ones here, and drought, which is why the harvesters and tractors are working the hills after dark, sometimes throughout the night, in order to avoid the sun.

You cannot choose where you will be born, any more than you can choose your family, but we do have some say in where we live out our lives. And in the end, I believe, we discover that time itself is the Place, and the various situations and stage settings are incidental. There is a kind of shell we carry, unbroken, through the decades.

When I first arrived at this house, out in the country, on agricultural land, between Perugia and Città della Pieve, it was, in a way, a return to Co. Meath in Ireland in the 1940s. A return from one side of my own tranche of time – almost fifty years of it at that stage – back to the other, to my grandmother's farm, where it seems to me I spent most of my childhood. Although I know that I attended school in Dublin, and also lived there with my parents, and indeed stayed at times with my paternal grandparents, it doesn't feel like that. My Dublin childhood, increasingly as I grow older, becomes less real, more phantasmagoric – when it doesn't disappear into vague stretches of indefinable loss altogether.

I don't know how many years I spent on the farm in total, but in fact it might as well have been from the beginning of time itself – my father told me I had been conceived there in a field, so I had, arguably, arrived there from nothingness, from before time. Nor have I ever really left it.

About twenty years ago, while driving to this Umbrian house from Dublin, we stopped off to break our journey at a small local agricultural museum in the south of France, and there – to my astonishment – I saw the farmyard tools of my childhood hung up as exhibits on a white-painted display wall. No cutting-edge gallery in New York or Paris or London could have produced quite such a shocking rush of simultaneous recognition and distance. I did not register the names of the various instruments, but my hands automatically closed on phantom forms of them; I knew the making of them, their function and purpose.

So too with this house. I have been at home here from the beginning; I know instinctively how to inhabit it. My grandmother's house in Co. Meath was long and low and narrow, a single storey, the central space being the kitchen, with a big open fire and a crane for cooking, a hard stone floor, and bedrooms and other rooms opening off at either end. The only difference between that much-repeated Irish blueprint and the house here is that the Italian tradition has two storeys, the family living space up above, accessed by an exterior stone staircase, with the beasts housed in the area beneath. Aside from the steps and elevation and the relatively newly installed running water and indoor plumbing, everything else was the same – the central kitchen with open fire, the wide chimney, the black smoke-crusted crane and the rooms opening off at either end.

A plan as formal and functional, as tested and repeated, as Frederick II's mass-construction castles built all over the peninsula. As Norman motte and bailey translating into stone. As the old deserted dwellings all over Ireland, now going back into the soil and rock and bog they came from, with more dignity than the unfinished Celtic Tiger zombie estates alongside them. So much so that I was hard put to it to say which image of which house was superimposed on which. I wrote a three-stanza poem about it, of arrival and acquiescence, part of a sequence about the place, with the *dinnseanchas* of both landscapes and both traditions reaffirmed and restated, the townlands in Meath and Tavernelle di Panicale. The first and last stanzas read:

*Scorpions*

I built a castello of stones and mud
and great baulks of seasoned timber
with oak doors in the walls
and then I whitewashed the walls on the inside
put a fire-back and pots in the fire-place
a new-forged crane and hooks and chain
and in preparation for the siege ahead
I laid in logs and charcoal
onions and oil and garlic
and sides of bacon hanging from the beams
and then I sat back and waited
this whole peninsula was waiting
and I was European and waiting for the Barbarians
[...]

And in the end like dreams they came
black scorpions came down my walls to join me
finding recognition in the whites of my eyes
soot creatures from before my childhood
from that rain-streaked chimney space
black scorpions came down my whitewash walls
and I know the limits of this farmhouse hearth
what people occupied this place
my grandmother's bedroom stretching away
away from the house and the hill and the furze
my dead uncles standing like frozen horses
and the beasts that stamp and knock beneath
and I am European and waiting for the Barbarians

And indeed the overlapping points of contact were unmissable, intimate and mundane – bars of soap in the yard, sharp implements and whetstones shoved in under the eaves of the sheds, old kitchen knives rusted and battered beyond belief, kept for cutting vegetables, or scraping them, or cutting twine. The general-purpose bicycles, the pinafores, prayers for rain, the constant busyness of endless tasks within their seasons, gossip, enthusiastic recounting of bad news, once-a-week shaving, the ritual preparations for going in to the local town – at once a different dimension and a mere mile away. And all the extraordinary liturgy of water. Water standing around in large containers – in Meath these were water barrels to catch rain running off from the roof, used for washing and other such chores, in Italy half-barrels and tubs lined up beside the housing of the well.

There is a whole piece to be written about water in and around the traditional farmhouse. As I have said, my grandmother's house had no running water – this was before the rural electrification schemes had brought instant power and light to the unbroken primeval dark of the countryside. So all drinking water came from the well, a spring of clear cold water a field away from the house. Several times a day, hail, rain, sun or snow, someone would have to make the trip with two galvanized buckets, invariably – when it was my turn – with the precious water building up a swaying momentum, like soldiers marching in step across a bridge, until in the end, at least a third of the load would slop over the rims, either into my boots or simply be lost along the way, depending on the season of the year.

Liquids and fire were the essential elements of my childhood. Most immediately the open kitchen fire, as central to life as the sun itself. All the activity of the house began there, from the rekindling in the morning with small dry sods of turf placed on the still-burning embers covered up with ash the night before. Everything and everyone gravitated to the fire – clothes were dried beside it, boots were set on the hob (a ledge running along the wall above and behind it), a truckle or settle bed was positioned beside it, and last thing at night, before covering the embers again and retiring to bed, was a serving of stirabout with milk, a kind of thick porridge boiled in a pot hung on the crane with pot-hooks, eaten warm at night, and cold in the morning.

I don't think it is fanciful to say that my grandmother was on personal terms with the fire. She coaxed and cajoled and trimmed and protected it, kept an eye on it at all times. She had two shrouds set aside for her eventual use and she used to air these regularly in front of the fire when she had time to spare. And when the electric light finally arrived in the early '50s, replacing the paraffin-oil lamps and candles, she would turn it off on dark afternoons because, she said, it took power from the fire, making it look weak and dim.

Liquid was every bit as central an element as fire. Indeed, my grandmother married the two, as it were, placing a basin of water on her bedroom windowsill on Holy Saturday so that she could see the sun dancing, reflected on her ceiling on Easter Sunday morning. Water was discernibly present all the time, audible, visible, much more than it is now, because if you do not have running water in a house you must keep different sized containers of it in use throughout the day, constantly pouring from one container to another – into basins, into the kettle, into pots boiling on the fire, into teapots, into mugs, from buckets and crocks into buckets and crocks, and back into basins for washing things – so that when I think of my grandmother and my aunt Milly I see them, and hear them, against this backdrop of liquid dispensed. Like moving figures on a painted vase. Pouring from amphora to krater.

Not only water, either. Outside the front door of the house, beside the turf shed, as far removed from the other outbuildings as possible, was the dairy. A cool space, almost votive now that I look back on it, which housed the separator, the churn, crocks of cream and a hollow wooden table containing the salted side of bacon – from which smaller cuts would be taken and hung in the kitchen chimney space ready for use. But the bacon, for me, was a subsidiary matter, despite the ritual of slaughter and salting. The real magic lay in the separator and churn and the mystery of converting milk into golden, salted butter.

The separator itself was the stuff of alchemy. A machine about two feet high, with a handle, and when it was all assembled and ready to start, there were two spouts sticking out at either side from the top, like downward-pointing horns. The milk was poured into a further container on the top, the handle was turned and the two streams – of cream and skim milk – would issue from the horns, a judgment as irreversible as sheep and goats on the Last Day, left and right, the cream to be kept in cool glazed earthenware crocks and the skim milk to be taken in buckets and fed to the calves. The cream would then sit until being poured into the churn, which rested on spigots on a heavy frame so that it could revolve head over heels at the turning of another handle. The lid was fastened on with catches like those on a drumhead, the drum would revolve, the cream swishing around inside, the process stopped every so often so the operator could peep in through a glass eyehole in the lid, and then – suddenly as it seemed – there was the new entity, bright orange butter sitting in its buttermilk, yet another liquid to be dispensed further into yet another waiting receptacle. The fresh butter itself plunged into a further crock of water in the chain, on the way to being salted and shaped.

The geography of the house and buildings was simple: the house was bordered on three sides by yards, and on the fourth by a garden. The yard in front of the house was for a more formal approach, with a hedge and a white metal gate; at right angles was the stone turf shed and dairy separating it from the open fields. A wall, with a small one-person-at-a-time gate separated it at the other side from the upper yard, business end of the settlement, a space bounded by three sides of outbuildings. Nearest the house was the stable, from which at night you could hear the extraordinarily evocative sound of a metal-shod hoof occasionally stamping on the stone floor. Next to that, the cowshed, with mangers on either inside gable, where the milk cows were tied and milked and the stall-feds were fattened over the winter. And further along, the henhouse, which it was my job to close up securely at night against the fox. There was another fowl-house too, exclusively for turkeys – another cash-engendering enterprise traditionally the domain and property of the women, along with eggs, chickens, butter and pigs.

Outside the cowshed, on the other side of a kind of cobbled walkway, was the dunghill, or midden, with a drainage pit, onto which the huge quantity of ash from the always-burning fire was thrown, along with the soiled straw bedding from the stable, the cowshed and the pigsty.

On the other side of the dunghill was a raised area of natural rocky ground where major farm maintenance jobs could be done. On one occasion in particular I watched while about five men replaced the metal rim on a newly remade cartwheel. The wooden wheel itself was placed on its side, raised well off the ground on large stones, and then the great metal rim was heated in a fire to glowing red and quickly lifted by men with tongs and slipped over the wooden rim of the cartwheel while other men threw buckets of water over it at just the right moment and the curls of smoke and flame changed at once into clouds of hissing steam as the metal contracted and gripped and pulled the wooden structure of hub and spokes and inside rim as tightly together as was possible.

There was another building alongside this area, the 'new barn', which looked pretty old to me, and was really out of bounds because it contained all kinds of unguents and potions in unmarked bottles – nostrums for dosing sick animals along with rat poison and weedkiller and bluestone, red raddle, caustic soda and the thousand and one other substances potentially lethal for small boys. And beyond this building, at the furthest remove from the house, were the pigs – fat and comfortable-looking, pink and bristly, grunting and sleeping, and somehow the most companionable of all the farm animals. Hens, ducks and dogs, even horses and sheep and cows could move around more or less at will, but were so clearly other species, whereas the pigs in their house, lying down, conversing with one another, were conscious and aware in a human way, and somehow almost judgmental, like adults, especially when they took a good look at you before turning away.

Interesting as this upper yard was, my favourite area was the haggard at the back of the house. Totally enclosed, on one side by an impenetrable hedge, at the end of it by a river, on the third side by the house and the backs of the stable and cowshed, and on the fourth by yet another barn, this one with two storeys, and a wall and hedge, with a large gap for access of farm machinery. I know that it was a relatively small area, but to me as a child it was as vast as Asia, as hidden and mysterious. There were two big cocks of hay, at least twice the height of the house, an old rusting piece of machinery stamped Pierce-Arrow Wexford on the seat, hens, ducks and geese strolling unconcernedly and the little river at the end, overhung by sally trees, where I could make dams of mud and stones, and fashion dugout canoes by scraping out the pith from elder branches, and watch the water spiders, and sometimes make hopeless attempts at catching eels.

The most magical, as well as the most functional, place of all was the two-storey barn in the haggard. This was where the cleaned-out carcass of the newly killed pig was hung at the start of the curing process, and where we stored the wheat and oats which would get us through the winter. The meal was kept in large wooden bins, filled from a hopper above. And the sharp, dry, musty smell is with me as I write. Functional – and this is where the shock of the museum in the south of France is explained – in that the smaller farm implements and equipment that could fit indoors were kept here. Bradawls and awls, shears, block and tackle, shoemakers' lasts, packing needles in various sizes and a small anvil. All the items of harness were hung on the walls here, ready for fieldwork and for expeditions by dray or by trap. Horse collars, traces, hames, bellybands, straddle, bit and bridle, blinkers, reins, leather and wood and metal, all waiting at hand to be used, along with scythes, blades for the horse-drawn mowing machines, serrated, looking like sharks' teeth, slash-hooks and billhooks and hay-knives, graips, shovels, spades, hayforks, crowbars, a *sleán* for cutting turf, a surprising quantity of chains of all sizes, all on display, as it were, waiting to be used, but somehow – at this remove – invoking the kitchen in the castle of the Sleeping Beauty. The flames of the fire unmoving, the cook forever about to box the scullery boy's ear.

They wait, frozen, in my mind as I write this. Frozen as in that small agricultural museum. And this is where life and memory come together with artifice, and where it becomes difficult to say from my present 70-year-old perspective what that child of sixty-five and more years ago knew, registered, suspected. So recently come from nothingness, before time and I both could graft on layers of received meaning. I cannot think of Meath without sadness, at the memory of the sound of the curlew or now-vanished corncrake at night as I drifted to sleep, or the infrequent cars on the distant road humming their way up and down the gears, or the far away freedom of it all.

But this is not how it ends, because the one most palpably magical item of all is one I hesitate to mention. A memory at once so vivid and so troubling that I have often wondered how it might have strayed across from some other history altogether. There in the shadowy half-light of one side of the barn, stood a magnificent, glittering, dark-blue-painted, enamelled, inlaid-with-black-stripe carriage. With hard roof and doors in the side, huge black leaf-springs and slender elegant shafts, an item of rare quality and beauty, but – and this is what is so extraordinary – one that I never heard explained or even alluded to. To this day I know nothing of its provenance, or even if it had one. Like so much else since, I don't know where it came from, what it was doing there, or what may have happened to it subsequently. Nothing at all. Beyond that – even at this distance – I know that I believed that I saw it, sometimes more urgently than others, but always familiar, silent and huge among the dust motes.

# The vibrant house:
# a visual essay

More than a collection of illustrations, this visual essay forms an integral part of *The vibrant house*, conceived to complement and contextualize the themes found in the written works. Contributors were invited to provide discursive captions to accompany the images associated with their essays. These additions enrich connections that are already apparent between text and image, thereby stimulating new imaginings of the vibrancy and materiality of home.

## Rhona Richman Kenneally

 This image by American photographer Dorothea Lange was taken during her 1954 visit to Clare. Whereas the hearth is usually the focus of interior views of traditional Irish dwellings, this photo highlights another daily preoccupation, the conveyance of water, in buckets, from an outdoor well. (Following rural electrification over the next decade or so, running water would be standardized in rural Irish households.) Generally, it was women and children who fetched this elemental resource, an arduous task especially over long distances, even on a sunny day. What appear to be spills on the floor – spills that also suggest the weight of the vessels – and the gap between door and threshold, reinforce the embeddedness of this built environment in the surrounding landscape. (Photograph by Dorothea Lange, 'Kenneally's (house interior)', Dorothea Lange Collection, Oakland Museum of California, LNG54146.8)

## Eiléan Ní Chuilleanáin

This is an image of the Honan Hostel and the Warden's House before my time. It was on a prospectus giving information to incoming students – and of course their parents. It looks bare and institutional compared with my memory of how the place looked in the 1940s and '50s, when a Virginia creeper covered the walls and there was a little rose garden in front of our house, with a birdbath. Behind the hostel itself there were the students' tennis courts, and on the lawn nearest the viewer an enormous beech tree.

Our front door faces you and on your right is the big front door of the hostel. Years later I was told by a former inhabitant that they used to climb in using the pediment over the door to reach the window above. It looks very dangerous. The window beside our door is my father's study, the two above are the big drawing room and the ones above that are the children's bedrooms. The attic window is at the top; you can see how the ceiling sloped. (University College Cork Archives)

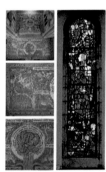

These are images from the Honan Chapel. The mosaics of the floor are by Ludwig Oppenheimer Ltd of Manchester. I tried not to look at the Leviathan, who is Celtically convoluted as a serpent but recognizable as a whale because he is spouting. His big teeth and his baleful eye frightened me. The animals on the left-hand side, especially the leopard, the squirrel and the birds – owls, parrot, eagle, geese – I know by heart, because we knelt in the pew just behind them. The aisle floor was a river full of fish. To look at works of art like these, weekly over years – that's what church art offers, and what a trip to a gallery can't hope to match. (Honan Chapel Trust)

The stained glass window is by Harry Clarke and shows St Gobnait as foundress holding her church; in the bottom panel she is setting her bees on men who attacked her convent. There are nineteen windows, some by Clarke and others by Sarah Purser. They are all beautiful, but this is the finest, I think. The depth of the blue, the severe outline of her face, the red of her hair and the dominating gesture of her hand I still find intoxicating. I used to try to stop on my way down the aisle to look at it but sometimes there was a hurrying crowd and I couldn't stop, and I remember the disappointment. (Honan Chapel Trust)

## Mary Morrissy

 Although my father was the curator of the 'permanent' collection, my mother was the custodian and frequently 'rotated' the pictures after his death. Thus *Woman lacing her bodice beside a cradle* (Pieter de Hooch) is hanging here in an alcove of the dining room (the institutional 'good' room beloved of the Irish middle classes) but it had also served time in several other locations – on the chimney breast in the kitchen and over the half-moon table in the hall. Beneath it is my mother's sewing machine and a rather ornate sewing box (a present to her from my father), plus an arrangement of artificial flowers. (My mother, though a keen gardener, was hopeless with indoor plants.) On the top right of the photograph, *The virgin of the grapes* (Pierre Mignard) is just visible in the next room. I don't recall this ever being in any other location. (Photograph by Rhona Richman Kenneally)

 The 'portrait' of *Fabiola* (Jean-Jacques Henner) – versatile patron saint of divorcees, difficult marriages, victims of abuse, adultery, unfaithfulness and widows – hangs at the foot of the stairs although it, too, was moved around. To the right is a gallery of framed family photographs that were my mother's domain and sprouted with the arrival of grandchildren. The open door on the right of the photograph – with the lock visible on the outside – leads into the cloakroom. (Photograph by Rhona Richman Kenneally)

## Colette Bryce

 Colette Bryce revisits her childhood street in 2010: 'When I was 10, we moved down the street from number 17 to number 4. I remember a stand-up piano being wheeled along the pavement like a barrel organ. The new house was a mirror image of the old, only slightly larger. Like vital clues in a mystery, the departing family had left behind a globe of the earth in dusty halves, and a pair of antiquated binoculars. These objects provided my first and lasting impressions of our new world'. (Photograph courtesy of Bev Robinson)

## Macdara Woods

 It is strange to look at this crumbling image from the first half of the last century, which survived long enough to be caught by my sister a few years ago. There is nothing vibrant here, not even the sheep – no voices, no people, no sounds of work or life. Like abandoned dwellings everywhere it has lost its context and its relevance. The figures who inhabited this home-place survive in memory imperfectly recorded: the flesh-and-blood young man who arrived from Cavan on a load of eels just after the Famine, the spinster lady who owned the farm at the time who fell in love with him and asked him in. My own great-great-grandfather, never to leave. *Record me. Record me. Write me down.* (Photograph by Siabhra Woods)

## Howard Keeley

 These images show some of the parlour in Hazelbrook House, constructed in 1898 and later rebuilt in the Bunratty Folk Park, Co. Clare. Invented in 1877, the phonograph by the window reflects the parlour's utility as a site of display. In Michael Banim's novel *Father Connell* (1842), Mary, a beggar girl, receives from Mrs Molloy, the housekeeper, a 'tour of discovery' of 'the [priest's] "nate" house'. The narrator explains, '[Mary] had been in the parlor … before, but under such circumstances, as only to have felt embarrassed with an overpowering sense of its importance. Now she dwelt, under Mrs Molloy's special instructions, on each article of furniture it contained.' Michael Banim, *Father Connell: a tale* (New York, 1888), pp 247–8. (Photographs by Rhona Richman Kenneally)

 A nineteenth-century Ulster farm parlour features in the Old World section of the Ulster American Folk Park, Omagh, Co. Tyrone. A rug covers a portion of the board flooring, and the wall to the left is boarded. Michael Banim's tale *Crohoore of the bill-hook* (1825) presents a 'boarded and well-furnished parlour at the back of the kitchen' (p. 4) – 'the state room of the [tenant] farmer's house', containing a 'corner cupboard … furnished with some substantial plate' (pp 13–15). In *The parlour novelist: works of fiction by the most celebrated authors* (Belfast, 1846). (Photograph by James Burke, used with permission of National Museums Northern Ireland)

From the National Library of Ireland's Poole Photographic Collection (*c.*1901–54), this image highlights a nursery. The room's sideboard manifests the aspirational heft associated with parlours. The artefact seems congruent with 'the mahogany desk and its brass handles' that in Kickham's *Knocknagow* (1883) a priest's housekeeper reveals to visitors by '[flinging] open the parlour door'. Charles J. Kickham, *Knocknagow; or, the homes of Tipperary* (13th ed. Dublin, 1887), p. 402. (Photograph by A.H. Poole, 'Poole's nursery', Poole Photographic Collection, National Library of Ireland, POOLEWP 0119)

## Nicholas Grene

Teach Synge, the home of the MacDonnchadha family on Inis Meáin, is where Synge stayed on his first visit to the islands in May 1898, and where Patrick Pearse stayed in August of that year. 'My room is at one end of the cottage, with a boarded floor and ceiling, and two windows opposite each other. Then there is the kitchen with earth floor and open rafters, and two doors opposite each other opening into the open air, but no windows. Beyond it there are two small rooms of half the width of the kitchen with one window apiece.' J.M. Synge, *The Aran Islands*. (Photograph by Cathy Hickey)

In this production of the final scene from the Druid Theatre production of *Riders to the sea*, the first of the six plays staged together as DruidSynge in 2005, the director Garry Hynes altered Synge's stage direction calling for a group of women to join in the mourning of the bereaved mother Maurya with the traditional keening lament. Instead Hynes had the women, black petticoats over their heads in lieu of shawls, turn their faces to the wall of the cottage and noiselessly beat their hands against it. (Photograph by Keith Pattison, courtesy of the Druid Theatre Company)

## Lucy McDiarmid

The *Asgard* was a wedding present from Dr and Mrs Hamilton Osgood of Boston to their daughter Molly and her husband Erskine Childers. It was Mary Spring Rice's idea to transport German guns for the Volunteers to Ireland in a private yacht, because it would be unlikely to attract military attention. On the return journey with the 900 rifles and ammunition, the *Asgard* sailed right through the middle of the British fleet. As subsequent events made clear, the fleet was preparing for war with Germany. The rifles were landed at Howth on 26 July 1914. (The Board of Trinity College Dublin)

Molly Childers (on left) and Mary Spring Rice on board the *Asgard*, July 1914. A box containing some of the rifles is clearly visible. Spring Rice kept a log of the voyage that records the challenge of housekeeping in the tight quarters on the yacht. So much of the log's attention is devoted to cooking, the positioning of mattresses and the quality of sleep that it is almost possible to forget the military object of the voyage. Childers' letters to Alice Stopford Green record the same kinds of details: 'Below decks we sleep, crawl over, sit on, eat on guns ... It is all gorgeous fun.' (Molly Childers, 'Letters from the *Asgard*', courtesy of the Board of Trinity College Dublin)

This house, at 31 Richmond Avenue in North Dublin, was the residence of Kathleen and Tom Clarke at the time of the Easter Rising. It was raided on 2 May by five officers with revolvers, who 'arranged themselves in a semi-circular form around the hall door'. An 'old lady' neighbour happened to be visiting, and in her 'old-fashioned bodice' Clarke had hidden the 'fairly large sum of money' that was part of the Volunteer Dependants Fund. Fortunately, as Clarke writes in her autobiography, the old lady's 'ample bust was not noticeably increased by the added bulk'. The soldiers tore the house apart searching for weapons but never searched the women themselves. (Kathleen Clarke, *Revolutionary woman*, photograph courtesy of Frank and Helen Litton)

## Angela Bourke

 The house Maeve Brennan grew up in: 48 Cherryfield Avenue, Ranelagh (2004). In her short stories, different families lead increasingly complex emotional lives in its rooms, hall, stairs and back garden; disappointed mothers tend pots of ferns behind the bay window downstairs: '... a small plain house in a row, faced from the other side of the terrace by a row of other houses just like it, all made alike of undistinguished gray stone with slate roofs and tiny front gardens protected by iron railings. It was a very ordinary house, a regulation uniform for the lives of certain families at a certain stage in their lives.' (Maeve Brennan, *The rose garden*, photograph by Angela Bourke)

## Adam Hanna

 Seamus Heaney's sister Anne with the pump at their family's farm. This pump appeared many times in his poetry, first in 'Persephone' (published 1966), and lastly in 'Quitting time' (published 2006). In 1978 Heaney began a radio piece: 'I would begin with the Greek word, *omphalos*, meaning the navel, and hence the stone that marked the centre of the world, and repeat it, *omphalos, omphalos, omphalos*, until its blunt and falling music becomes the music of somebody pumping water at the pump outside our back door ... There the pump stands, a slender, iron idol, snouted, helmeted, dressed down with a sweeping handle, painted a dark green and set on a concrete plinth, marking the centre of another world.' (Heaney, 'Mossbawn', photograph by Bobbie Hanvey, Bobbie Hanvey Photographic Archives, MS.2001.039, John J. Burns Library, Boston College, bh002893)

## Tony Tracy

 *Adam & Paul* recounts a day-long odyssey by two Dublin heroin addicts in search of a 'fix'. Reversing the familiar mytho-geography of Irish literature and film in which characters seek rebirth in the authentic and enduring setting of the western landscape, their journey takes them eastwards across the city towards death. The narrative is both bleak and blackly humorous, punctuated by a series of improvised, inhospitable and all-too-fleeting sites of repose – such as the bollard in this image – that serve to underline their exclusion from the consolations of home on both material and metaphysical levels. The image is illustrative both of the debilitating physical discomfort brought on by withdrawal as well the ways in which characters in the film (its protagonists as well as other homeless young men) seek to shape public spaces to private needs. (Irish Film Institute)

# Their house

# 'Flung open': walking into the parlour in Victorian Irish literature

## Howard Keeley

Addressing the nascent National Literary Society in 1892, Douglas Hyde, the son of a Church of Ireland rectory, urged the 'de-Anglicizing' of Ireland, not least by means of 'house to house visitations'.[1] By moving through and among the parlours of several literary houses, this essay will add to assessments of the place that better bourgeois housing occupied within the consciousness, identity and politics of Victorian, especially post-Famine, Ireland. In addition to offering a reasonable overview of the discourse, I will closely examine clerical, strong farmer, and bourgeoisifying peasant parlours in the bestselling Irish novel of Hyde's day, *Knocknagow; or, the homes of Tipperary* (1873), by the Fenian polemicist Charles Kickham – the 'one man alone', according to W.B. Yeats in his mid-twenties, who 'stands near' William Carleton as regards capturing 'Celtic humour'.[2]

Too often, critics of Irish literature privilege the dyad of big house and peasant cottage or cabin, effectively under-recognizing middle-class habitation. In fact, the domestic-material was crucial to the emergence of what, soon after the inception of the Land League, another Fenian, John Devoy, defensively deemed the 'best allies' of Irish nationalism, namely, 'a sturdy, well-fed, well-clad and *comfortably housed* agricultural population, giving employment to a correspondingly

---

1 Quoted in D. George Boyce, *Nationalism in Ireland* (2nd ed. London, 1991), p. 290.   2 W.B. Yeats (ed.), *Stories from Carleton, with an introduction by W.B. Yeats* (London, 1889), p. xvi.

comfortable class in the towns' (emphasis added).[3] Devoy was countering the notion – summarized in 1881 by Hugh Law, Ireland's attorney general – that 'the [Irish] people would become loyal to England, and oppose Irish independence, if they were in more comfortable circumstances'.[4] This was a recurrent concern for republican separatists as land politics increasingly won successes. R.V. Comerford for one holds that Home Rule, the quest for constitutional autonomy, lost out to material goals. This, I would argue, very much included the persuasion of the parlour, or small-h home rule. Comerford observes, 'in the early 1870s, as for long before and long after, popular Irish nationalism was a matter of the self-assertiveness of the Catholic community and of *a search for material benefits*, rather than a question of yearning for constitutional forms' (emphasis added).[5]

The parlour becomes a prime synecdoche for the arriviste agricultural bourgeoisie that grew to dominance across Ireland over the nineteenth century due to, among other things, electoral reform, the transition to ranch pastoralism ('corn to horn') and the Famine's near-evisceration of the peasantry through death and emigration. 'The real "peasant"', D. George Boyce explains, 'suffered ... the indignity of witnessing his very name, *peasant*, being appropriated by his pre-famine employers (and often, enemies) the tenant farmers' – a 'quirk of semantic alchemy', according to J.J. Lee.[6] In the introduction to his edited volume, *Representative Irish tales* (1891), Yeats approaches the latter coterie's literary efforts via an architectural metaphor. Having acknowledged that 'beside Maria Edgeworth's well-finished four-square house of the intelligence, Carleton raised

3 *Report of the trial of the queen, at the prosecution of the Rt. Hon. the attorney-general against Charles Stewart Parnell (et al.) for conspiracy in inciting tenants not to pay rents contracted for and deterring tenants from payment of rent, commencing Tuesday, December 28, 1880, and terminating Tuesday, January 25, 1881* (Dublin, 1881), p. 606. Paul Bew's 'rural bourgeoisie' and F.S.L. Lyons' 'shopocracy' are useful terms for the socio-economic groups Devoy has in mind. Paul Bew, *Land and the national question in Ireland, 1858–1882* (Dublin, 1978), p. 223; F.S.L. Lyons, *Ireland since the Famine* (London, 1971), p. 117. 4 *Report of the trial*, p. 605. 5 R.V. Comerford, *The Fenians in context: Irish politics and society, 1848–1882* (Dublin, 1985), p. 194. 6 Boyce, *Nationalism in Ireland*, p. 290; Joseph J. Lee, 'The ribbonmen' in T. Desmond Williams (ed.), *Secret societies in Ireland* (Dublin, 1973), pp 34–5.

his rough clay "rath" of humour and passion', he proceeds to identify a new middle:

> In Gerald Griffin ... and later on in Charles Kickham, I think I notice a new accent—not quite clear enough to be wholly distinct; the accent of a people who have not the recklessness of the landowning class, nor the violent passion of the peasantry, nor the good frankness of either, but who, possessing a sense of order and comeliness ... may yet give Ireland a literature ... The clerks, farmers' sons, and the like ... show an alertness to honor the words 'poet,' 'writer,' 'orator,' not commonly found in their class.[7]

Dating from the year of Catholic emancipation, Griffin's popular *The collegians; or, the colleen bawn, a tale of Garryowen* (1829) demonstrates awareness of the parlour as a distinguishing space within aspirational farmer homesteads. Consider, for example, how 'the Cottage' on 'one of [the] dairy-farms' associated with Daly – a 'wealthy middleman' with a 'national predilection' for studying 'works on Irish History' – contains not just a 'kitchen' (where a distinctly non-modern conversation about a 'fairy doctor' occurs), but also a 'little parlour'.[8] Therein, the woman of the house, 'Mrs. Frawley, the dairy-woman', stages an orderly, comely 'table decorated with a snow-white damask cloth, a cooler of the sweetest butter, a small cold ham, and an empty space ... destined for a roast duck or chickens'.[9] The dramatic promise of the 'empty space' could be read as the essence of bourgeoisifying tenant desire. Certainly, the parlour, more than any room, actualizes the dedicated pursuit of better and secure housing.

As even a cursory study of their propaganda confirms, the Land War and greater land campaign concerned themselves with houses as well as land, not least because, outside Ulster, Irish tenants had to construct, maintain and improve their homesteads under peculiar circumstances. Demanding, 'How long would the American people

---

7 W.B. Yeats (ed.), *Representative Irish tales* (Atlantic Highlands, NJ, 1979), pp 28, 31–2.
8 Gerald Griffin, *The collegians* (2nd ed. London, 1829), i, pp 16, 38, 225, 230, 232, 227.
9 Ibid., pp 227–8.

submit to such a law?' the American journalist Margaret F. Sullivan's *Ireland of today: the causes and aims of Irish agitation* (1881) incredulously reveals, 'The landlord would neither build a dwelling nor loan the tenant the money to build it … Was it then the property of the tenant? No; it belongs to the landlord … The labor of the tenant was perpetually confiscated.'[10] It is hardly surprising, therefore, that the savvy Charles Stewart Parnell regularly invoked the house alongside the farm, such as at the Westport, Co. Mayo, Land League meeting on 8 June 1879: 'You must show the landlords that you intend to hold a firm grip on your homesteads and lands.'[11] At Ennis, Co. Clare, on 19 September of that year, the crowd cheered when Parnell insisted that 'your determination to keep a firm grip on your homesteads' would influence the progress of 'the Land Bill of next session'.[12] However, a speech at the same gathering by T.D. Sullivan, publisher of *The Nation* newspaper, pushes closer to the domestic ideal whose apogee is the parlour. Sullivan admonished the audience:

> You have pitched your scale of living too low, and you have paid too much rent (hear, hear) … [Y]ou have been satisfied to live in bad houses … Resolve in your own minds that the first claim on the fruits of your industry is the support of yourselves, your wives, and your families in decency and comfort (hear, hear, and cheers).[13]

10 Margaret F. Sullivan, *Ireland of today: the causes and aims of Irish agitation* (Philadelphia, 1881), pp 144, 142. The Devon Commission (1843–5) heard from a certain 'esquire' with property in both England and Wexford: 'in England we have to do every thing for the tenants; the tenant walks into, may I say, a ready furnished house. The capital of the farmer in England and Ireland is very differently applied.' *Digest of evidence taken before her majesty's commissioners of inquiry into the state of the law and practice in respect to the occupation of land in Ireland* (Dublin, 1847), i, p. 152.  **11** Quoted in R. Barry O'Brien, *The life of Charles Stewart Parnell, 1846–1891* (London, 1898), i, p. 184. According to O'Brien, Parnell decided to attend the Westport meeting after a conversation with Kickham in which the Fenian denigrated the land question by holding that the Irish people 'would go to hell for it'. In a September 1865 editorial in the *Irish People* newspaper, Kickham declared, 'Our only hope is revolution.' Ibid., i, p. 83; quoted in Paul Bew, *Ireland: the politics of enmity, 1789–2006* (Oxford, 2007), p. 252.  **12** Quoted in *Report of the trial*, pp 140–1.  **13** Ibid., p. 143. Speaking in Westport, Co. Mayo, on 17 Oct. 1880, Land League official Thomas Brennan elicited cheers for declaring, 'I would wish to see the man that toils and tills God's earth with a comfortable home, and secure in the possession of that home.' Ibid., p. 342.

Sullivan's notion of pitching one's scale of living higher is useful when considering middle-class parlours in nineteenth-century Irish novels and other texts. Decade after decade, to think bigger was difficult, for the housing stock remained poor. Hoping to stimulate reform, the 1841 census emphasized that over three-quarters of Ireland's homesteads fell into the two lowest among four grades. The inferior stratum consisted of 'all mud cabins having only one room', while 'a better description of cottage, still built of mud, but varying from two to four rooms and windows' constituted a third-class dwelling.[14] 'Taking the average of the whole population', the Robert Peel-appointed Devon Commission's 1845 report about Irish land issues bewailed how 'in rural districts above forty-three per cent of families ... inhabit houses of the fourth class' – dwellings 'generally unfit for human habitation'.[15] Once unambiguously underway, the bourgeois or 'strong farmer' shift to the improved *domus* proved relatively speedy: one-tenth of rural families occupied fourth-class homes in 1861, but just a hundredth of them did fifty years later.[16] Scant wonder then that the parlour became a matter to grapple with, to observe and figure out.

In Kickham's *Knocknagow*, probably set in the 1850s, 'old Mrs. Hayes', housekeeper to a priest, Father Carroll, renders that room a kind of theatrical event, 'always watch[ing] the faces of visitors when she [flings] open the parlour door' of the presbytery to reveal a certain 'mahogany desk' with 'brass handles' (pp 404, 402).[17] In fact, her employer wants other and extra for what the narrator, in the style of a census-taker or surveyor, calls his 'thatched domicile' – 'a more modern article of furniture' to replace the desk, as well as 'the least bit of molding on the ceiling [and] hangings on the windows'

---

**14** *Report of the commissioners appointed to take the census for the year 1841* (Dublin, 1841), p. xiv. A second-class habitation was 'a good farm house, or in town, a house in a small street having from five to nine rooms and windows', while into the first class fell 'all houses of a better description than the preceding classes'. The census applied three assessment criteria: '1st, [the dwelling's] extent, as shown by the number of rooms; 2nd, its quality, as shown by the number of its windows; and 3rd, its solidity or durability, as shown by the materials of its walls and roof'. **15** *Digest of evidence*, p. 126. **16** Cormac Ó Gráda, *Ireland: a new economic history, 1780–1919* (Oxford, 1994), p. 241. **17** Charles J. Kickham, *Knocknagow; or, the homes of Tipperary* (13th ed. Dublin, 1887).

(pp 196, 402). Ultimately, having 'be[en] economical for a while', Carroll amasses 'ninety-three pounds', primarily towards 'the furnishing and fitting up of his cottage' (pp 402, 519). But the greater point to draw from the differences in aesthetic judgment between Hayes and Carroll is that, like many nineteenth-century Irish writers, Kickham presents no settled notion of what we might call middle-class Irish 'domiculture', a word coined around 1860.[18]

Over forty years before *Knocknagow*'s publication, the parlour tantalizes in 'Denis O'Shaughnessy going to Maynooth', Carleton's long short story about the title character's failed Catholic vocation, first published serially during 1831 in the proselytizing *Christian Examiner and Church of Ireland Magazine* and reprinted, with revisions, in the second series of *Traits and stories of the Irish peasantry* (1833),[19] from which I'll quote. Denis, his father Old Denis, and their parish priest Dr Finnerty journey to their bishop's residence, where the prelate's sibling, a lawyer, urges them to 'have the goodness to walk into the parlour … while I endeavour to soften my brother a little' in the matter of Denis' application to the Maynooth seminary. The visitors '[stand] for a moment to survey' the 'elegantly furnished' parlour, as if it were a vision of futurity (p. 308). But then Finnerty encourages Old Denis – 'a large man … but a small farmer … rent[ing] only eighteen acres of good land' (pp 237–8), that is, a not-too-shabby tenant[20] – to 'take a toss upon [the] sofa' to 'get a taste of ecclesiastical luxury', the bishop's 'ease and comfort' (p. 308). Old Denis has coached his intellectually prodigious son in rhetoric – a 'training for controversy' (p. 238) – so the reader is justified in seeking import in his expressions. By musing, 'would it be right o' me to sit in it [the sofa]? Maybe it's consecrated?' he effectively imparts holy significance to the parlour's defining artefact, thus affirming the

---

18 OED, s.v. 'domiculture': 'that which relates to household affairs; the art of housekeeping, cookery, etc.; domestic economy'.  19 William Carleton, *Traits and stories of the Irish peasantry*, 2nd series (London, 1877), p. 308.  20 Throwing a party *chez lui* in anticipation of his son's acceptance into Maynooth, Old Denis proves more than a peasant. In addition to 'a shouldher of mutton, a goose' and a pot of 'hung beef' at the domestic hearth, he maintains 'a tarin' fire down in the barn, where there's two geese more and two shouldhers of mutton – not to mention a great big puddin', an' lots of other things'. Bourgeois plenty,

centrality of the greater space to Ireland's domestic imaginary as early as the late-Georgian period. Once upon the sofa, Old Denis spontaneously exclaims, 'Oh, murdher!' an utterance readable as the death-notice of peasant habitation – a declaration of tentative entry into a new order. This interpretation gains force to the degree that the farmer's next, rapid-fire comments progress from the interrogative mode into sureness: 'Where am I at all? Docthur dear, am I in sight? Do you see the crown o' my head, good or bad? Oh, may I never sin, but that's great state!—Well to be sure!' (p. 308).

Introducing *Stories from Carleton* (1889), a book he edited for Walter Scott of London, Yeats asserted that the tales in *Traits and stories* 'began modern Irish literature',[21] and certainly the parlour sofa in 'Denis O'Shaughnessy' strongly suggests the better homestead's role in making Ireland modern, potentially even a 'great state'. Little astonishment attaches to Maria Edgeworth's report, in an 1811 letter to her father, that the drawing room in the earl of Longford's recently completed Gothic-revival Packenham Hall, near Edgeworthstown, contains a 'delightful abundance of sofas and cushions and chairs and tables of all sorts and sizes';[22] however, in 'Denis O'Shaughnessy' Carleton is figuratively enthroning no nobleman but a petty-bourgeois Irish Catholic farmer on a sofa: 'Do you see the crown?'

Arguably, 'The exile', from George Moore's short-story collection *The untilled field* (1903), is a reworking of 'Denis O'Shaughnessy'. Moore's writing style may be unembellished, but his protagonist, Peter Phelan, registers the elaborate when consulting with his parish priest in that man's parlour, noted as being 'on the left' of the presbytery's front door, the side of the goats per the judgment narrative in Matthew's gospel.[23] Observing Father Tom 'sitting reading in his mahogany armchair', Peter reads the piece of furniture: '[He] wondered if it were this very mahogany chair that had put the idea of being a priest into his head.' He next contrasts the cleric's

undoubtedly! Ibid., p. 297. **21** Yeats, *Stories from Carleton*, p. xiv. **22** Quoted in Knight of Glin and James Peill, *Irish furniture: woodwork and carving in Ireland from the earliest times to the Act of Union* (New Haven, CT, 2007), p. 192. **23** George Moore, *The untilled field* (London, 1903), p. 122. Matthew 25:33 records Jesus as declaring: '[H]e [the Son of Man] shall set the sheep on his right hand, but the goats on the left.'

parlour circumstances with the Phelans' place, which has 'only some stools and some plain wooden chairs', despite being 'the best house in the village'.[24] Parlour scrutiny and envy also surface in 'Some parishioners', the prior story in the collection. In the small-town home of one Annie Connex – whose name suggests the question 'any connection?' or the imperative 'only connect' – a neighbour apparently regrets failing to connect to and benefit from the agricultural embourgeoisement that the text highlights:

> She would never have a parlour, and this parlour had in it a mahogany table and grandfather's clock that would show you the moon on it just the same as it was in the sky, and there was a glass over the fire place.[25]

These items rather evoke the phrase '[a] little bourgeois comfort', all but spat out anent 'the moderns' – that is, his tenants demanding more – by the absentee landlord who narrates *Confessions of a young man* (1886), Moore's heavily autobiographical Künstlerroman.[26]

Connex's clock that can open up cosmic horizons and her mirror that can reveal and multiply the self – arguably, these items signal the parlour's transformational potential. The 'glass over the fire' would seem a bourgeois appropriation and mending of the 'cracked glass over the chimney piece', before which Sir Condy Rackrent shaves and cuts his face in Maria Edgeworth's *Castle Rackrent* (1800), even as the arriviste attorney Jason Quirk nears acquisition of 'all entirely' of the encumbered Rackrent estate.[27] Likely protesting too much, Edgeworth's narrator, Thady Quirk, criticizes his son Jason's bourgeois acquisitiveness, especially his participation in the seizure (in lieu of unpaid debts) of 'every thing at Castle Rackrent'. 'To his shame be it spoken,' Thady declares.[28]

During and after the Famine, of course, domestic materiality could become problematic due to another type of shame: survivor's

---

24 Moore, *Untilled field*, pp 122, 123.  25 Ibid., p. 71. The story makes much of 'a poultry lecture at the school house', an aid to farmers with middle-class aspirations.  26 George Moore, *Confessions of a young man* (New York, 1920), p. 142.  27 Maria Edgeworth, *Castle Rackrent: an Hibernian tale* (3rd ed. London, 1801), pp 118, 159.  28 Ibid., p. 130.

guilt – a shift of middle-class focus from rack-renting landlords to the disproportionately undone peasants. Perhaps we see this in the family called Kearney (meaning 'victorious'), the primary household in Kickham's *Knocknagow*, which enjoys domestic comfort, albeit without security of tenure. The patriarch 'Honest Maurice' is 'principal tenant' on a demesne (pp 496, 9), but the family under-utilizes its parlour (a room that the Film Company of Ireland's 1918 version of *Knocknagow* portrays as particularly well appointed). Is the family worried about being adjudged callously cavalier in a land familiar with hunger, poverty and their diseases, a country distressed by cabin-levelling and emigration? Having emplaced the Kearneys within the coterie 'Irish Catholics of the middle class', Kickham's unidentified narrator explains that 'instead of summoning the servants to prayers in the parlour', the 'general custom' among such households is assembling all beneath the roof 'to "say the Rosary" in the kitchen' (p. 35).

When the Kearney residence, Ballinaclash Cottage, a 'promiscuous collection of odds and ends of houses', becomes 'public property for some hours' during a religious Station, a significant division of domestic space occurs (pp 30, 34). 'By his own choice', the curate called Hannigan hears confessions, 'principally [from] women', in the kitchen, while his fellow cleric, O'Neill by name, bases himself in the parlour (p. 48). The narrator characterizes O'Neill as 'a very young man, with an air of refinement suggestive of drawing-rooms rather than of Irish cabins and farm-houses' (p. 47). By contrast, he celebrates Hannigan's 'manly figure' and 'homely, warm, Irish look', despite also acknowledging the perception of an English Protestant visitor – a participant observer with the telling name of Lowe – that Hannigan 'affect[s] the phraseology of the peasantry' (p. 47). Affected or not, peasant bias clearly asserts itself. Almost always, *Knocknagow* exudes an explicit expression of confident, bourgeois-material jouissance apropos of the two-storeyed, multi-bedroomed, box-bordered Ballinaclash Cottage. A species of domestic disharmony inheres as the kitchen eclipses the parlour of that 'nice place' and 'fine place' (pp 127, 297). Of course, the very term *cottage* seems a modesty topos, and the syllable *clash* suggests a conflicted state, with the likely Irish-language original *clais* having two disparate meanings – *furrow*, a seedbed, and *pit*, often used to denote a dump. The reader first encounters the place by means of uneasy rhetorical formulae. While Devoy's early 1880s speech proclaims the 'comfortably housed' state of the 'allies' of Irish nationalism, Kickham's early 1870s narrator opts for the litotes 'not uncomfortable' and adjective phrase 'commodious, if not handsome' when introducing the Kearney edifice (pp 9, 10).

Such descriptive scruple notwithstanding, that Maurice Kearney finds parlour status alluring, if not altogether graspable, seems evident in his choice of wife, a 'portly' woman who, because of marrying down, makes sure to render 'particularly conspicuous' during the Station a prestige heirloom alien to kitchen tables – her grand-mother's 'antique silver coffee-pot' (pp 16, 78). She exhibits 'reverential gentleness' when 'handl[ing]' the object, but that sacerdotal touch can stray into sensuality, '[h]er fingers ... sometimes play[ing] softly on the lid in a manner that cause[s] her husband visible anxiety' (pp 78–9). Maurice might prefer a less overt display of material fetish, and the larger proposition that this family harbours anxiety about parlours being built out of peasant exclusion may be argued vis-à-vis the remarkable scene in which the local physician, Dr Kiely, violates norms of politeness. He 'str[ides] into [the Kearney] parlour without even bowing to the ladies', intent on admonishing Maurice for accommodating his 'servants and workmen' in a filthy, ill-ventilated out-office, ripe for 'fever and pestilence' – a phrase that would not be out of place in Famine reportage (p. 484). While Maurice protests, Mrs Kearney promises reform; however, the novel undergoes appreciable warming towards the parlour once that space eases nearer the proletariat. A major secondary plot is efforts by Kiely's daughter, Grace, to add parlour grace to the domestic milieu of the principal peasant of the piece, Mat Donovan.

At least twice, *Knocknagow* is at pains to establish 'Mat the Thrasher' as the Platonic instance of his class: Lowe deems him 'a magnificent specimen of the Irish peasant', while Grace's eventual husband, the eldest Kearney son, Hugh, eulogizes Mat's thatched dwelling with freehold as a 'model peasant's cottage' (pp 26, 486). Unlike the stereotyping men, Grace recognizes that *peasant* no longer applies, Mat having evolved from thrashing into the new grazier-led economy. Citing his 'making money so fast as a cattle dealer', she encourages him to enhance his *domus* by adding 'a nicely furnished little parlour, with white curtains on the window, and some books' (pp 584, 452). Rather as Mrs Kearney's atavistic coffee pot excites ardour, the new parlour, Grace avers, will help Mat win the hand of Bessy Morris, the self-described grandchild of 'a respectable farmer [mother's father] and … a tradesman [father's father, a weaver]' (pp 318–19). A 'coquette' to the narrator, Bessy unapologetically practises the profession of dressmaking 'to earn as much as would make me independent' (pp 347, 313). For this paragon of modern female industriousness, Donovan extends his familial cottage by 'two rooms with good-sized windows'. One configures as a 'little boarded parlour', but the purpose of the second remains unstated, a coyness that rather suggests a connubial bedroom, prudent given Mat's mother's continuing presence in the house once he and Bessy wed (pp 605, 604). Mindful of Jacques Derrida's statement that architecture should yield 'places where desire can recognize itself, where it can live' (the conclusion of a 1986 interview with Eva Meyer), one recalls Mat's ample libido – 'always a play-boy', in the opinion of the local tailor (p. 166).[29]

In a sense, *Knocknagow* recognizes in the new Donovan parlour a place for itself – 'a bookshelf … with a goodly number of books arrayed on it'. Also distinguishing the space are 'papered walls and [an] American clock on the chimney piece' (pp 604, 486). The clock suggests a new temporality, and certainly the influence of foreign – especially American and English – artefacts and aesthetics upon the homesteads of Ireland's bourgeoisifying farmers was manifest as early as the 1830s. In *Rural houses of the north of Ireland* (1984), Alan Gailey explores how, in that decade, 'possession of a clock was a status symbol of considerable potency', with 'imported American mantel

---

**29** Quoted in Neil Leach (ed.), *Rethinking architecture: a reader in cultural theory* (London, 1997), p. 323.

clocks ... rapidly [coming] into favor at the expense of the local craft of longcase clockmaking' so that 'almost all local longcase clockmakers had disappeared by the 1840s'.[30] Free of European-type guild regulations, America, especially Connecticut, became globally dominant in the mass production of affordable clocks and watches, exhibiting such wares at the Crystal Palace exhibition of 1851. Constructing their clock cases from mahogany-veneered pine, enterprises like the Seth Thomas Company and the Barnes and Welch Company (founded in 1814 and 1831, respectively) exported millions of timepieces from 'the land of steady habits'.[31] Mat's favouring of an American product offers a material correlate to Yeats' notion of an internationalizing turn away from a distinctively Irish sensibility in literature – from the 'square-built power' of Carleton or Banim, either of whose 'heroines ... could only have been raised under Irish thatch'.[32] In an 1889 letter to Father Matthew Russell SJ, founder-editor of the *Irish Monthly* – written, significantly, from the pioneering Arts and Crafts garden suburb of Bedford Park, London – Yeats identifies in novels by Griffith and Kickham 'the tide beg[inning] to ebb' into 'the common sea of English fiction'.[33]

Nineteenth-century Irish timepieces could be distinctly Hibernian. Famously, the two Fermanagh Catholic brothers who established Donegan of Dame Street, Dublin, painted onto clock-face dials and carved into clock-case timber Romantic Ireland symbols – harps, round towers, shamrocks and the like. Mat's not purchasing such an item effectively diminishes his parlour's Irishness, a matter all the more notable because Kickham would likely have known of the funeral organized for John, the elder Donegan. In November 1862, around four thousand followed his cortege to O'Connell Circle, Glasnevin Cemetery.[34] However, the mere fact of a clock – any clock – renders the parlour as a forward-directed locus, suitable for Mat as a timetable-conscious railway traveller, a role

30 Alan Gailey, *Rural houses of the north of Ireland* (Edinburgh, 1984), p. 217.  31 Grace Pierpoint Fuller, *An introduction to the history of Connecticut as a manufacturing state* (Northhampton, MA, 1916), p. 22.  32 W.B. Yeats, *The Letters of W.B. Yeats*, ed. Allen Wade (London, 1954), p. 143.  33 Ibid.  34 Kevin Chellar and Carol Chellar, *300 years of Irish*

necessitated (as chapter 55 of *Knocknagow* underscores) by his cattle-dealing business. An ordnance survey memoir of 1832, part of an all-island project that did not progress much beyond Ulster, reveals how in Racavan parish, northeast of Ballymena, Co. Antrim, 'their great ambition is a clock … It is always termed "she" and there is … a carousal or merrymaking at the "setting up of her"'. But even in Co. Derry, less linen-prosperous than Antrim, a memoir writer could remark upon the 'general fondness for clocks', which 'may be heard striking in houses where there is hardly a chair to sit upon or a table to eat … food off'.[35] Arguably, such display was more feasible in Ulster, where the so-called tenant-right custom was supposed to guarantee fair rent, in addition to fixity of tenure and free sale (the 'three Fs'). By contrast, in his *In castle and cabin: talks in Ireland in 1887*, the America-based lawyer George Pellew quotes 'a clockmaker in Galway' to the effect that 'a farmer in the West of Ireland' is 'afraid to have a clock in his house, because if the agent came round and saw it, he would probably raise the rent'.[36]

Mat Donovan's 'freehould' frees him from such anxiety (p. 489), and, indeed, the necessity and efficacy of proprietorship is *Knocknagow*'s central point about land politics. But also critical is the fact that the Donovan parlour – a new, bourgeois alternative to the colonial castle-and-cabin dispensation – aligns Ireland with American-style modernity. This extends beyond the American clock, for we learn that the parlour and its sibling room are not the sum total of Mat's architectural initiatives. He also adds a 'barn, dairy, cow-house, and all other requisites' – a suite of 'out-offices', the narrator 'feel[s] bound to admit', that owes much to the generosity of Bessy Morris' father, an evictee whose emigration to the Great Lakes region yielded, in Mat's mother's words, 'carpets on his [American] flure' (pp 605, 378). While Dr Kiley may attribute 'the millions of money … sent from America' to 'the strength of the domestic affections' of the 'Irish peasant … a being of sentiment', Mat's parlour-anchored ensemble is fundamentally bourgeois (p. 486). As we have seen, Bessy is the

*timekeeping* (Dublin, 2010), p. 34.  **35** Quoted in Gailey, *Rural houses*, p. 217.  **36** George Pellew, *In castle and cabin; or, talks in Ireland in 1887* (New York, 1888), p. 158.

scion of tradespeople on the paternal side; in fact, her weaver grandfather, a veteran of 1798, gave Bessy's father 'three hundred pounds' to help win a strong farmer wife (p. 501). Hyde may have demanded the de-Anglicizing of Irish houses in 1892, but nineteen years earlier the physical-force nationalist Kickham was far from lamenting the Americanizing of their parlours.

A parlour whose range extends to carpeted Midwestern American floors is a good example of the capaciousness of significance available to nineteenth-century Irish authors that would inscribe parlours. Even within the single work *Knocknagow*, Charles Kickham has parlours serve multiple ends. One could usefully devote a houseful of paragraphs to such scenes as Father Hannigan's ejection of a problematic pair of 'gaunt' blind pipers from the parlour of a certain Ned Brophy – a 'snug farmer' with a 'good lase' – during the party to celebrate Ned's marriage to a well-dowried woman bent on 'secur[ing] … a husband, or rather a "nice place"' (pp 142, 228). Another significant occurrence is the retreat that a seminarian calling on Father Carroll beats through the parish priest's fanlight-distinguished (and, thus, likely Georgianized) green front door and into his parlour. The visitor feels bashful due to being 'survey[ed]' by 'ladies' with a 'field-glass, or telescope' from the terrace of a neighbouring big house. He '[sits] down by the [parlour] window', whose twelve panes offer some security, but also a way to gaze back, to break the aristocrats' spectatorial monopoly (p. 401). In addition, they cut him up in a proto-cubist fashion and, in a sense, proliferate his image; at the least, they render his 'slightly built' form more difficult for the Anglo-Irish elite to decipher and contain (p. 403). The multi-pane parlour window is distinctly middle class. In the mid-nineteenth century the wealthy often refurbished windows, especially lower-storey windows, with plate glass, an expensive product that permitted views uninterrupted by glazing bars; however, labourer housing generally featured the cheapest glazing option, namely, small (perhaps diamond-shaped) paned casement windows.[37]

37 The twelve-pane configuration emerged on better homesteads from the mid-eighteenth century as pane size increased and glazing bars narrowed. For a detailed discussion of the

Clearly, Kickham treats parlours in a sophisticated manner as his Ireland undergoes considerable and consequential socio-economic change.

Calling for 'rooms fit to be home in the fullest poetry of that name', Raymond Unwin and Barry Parker's Arts and Crafts treatise, *The art of building a home* (1901), would deem the parlour 'a false convention of respectability'; however, once established among the Irish bourgeoisie it long persisted as normative.[38] Discussing a 'typical' small-town shop-cum-homestead, the Harvard professor Conrad M. Arensberg's *The Irish countryman: an anthropological study* (1950) relates, 'Upstairs, a front room facing the street is transformed, by family portraits, an ornamental mantle and a piece or two of good mahogany, into a ceremonial parlour.'[39] The adjective 'ceremonial' perhaps speaks to a larger cognizance of the seriousness, even sacrosanctness, of the project of Irish remaking through the bourgeois homestead and the greater land campaign, whose 'rites' were parliamentary land acts, like the Wyndham and Birrell Acts (1903 and 1909, respectively). Parlours of the type Mat Donovan adds to his cottage have acute importance within Victorian Ireland's coming of age, and given the revolutionary change in proprietorship that land politics ultimately effected, one might even reckon them a world-historically special instance of what Unwin and Parker, when introducing their book, call 'the drama of our lives at home'.[40]

During its concluding paragraphs, *Knocknagow* traffics in domestic ceremony and drama, beginning with the married Mat Donovan's American clock. As it strikes eight, Mat rhetorically inquires of a visitor, Billy Heffernan, another peasant-made-good, 'Have you the flute?' (p. 628). The 'musical genius of Knocknagow', Heffernan answers by requesting that the Donovans 'come out to the kitchen', a reminder that, from the first, the new parlour had rendered his flute 'quite hoarse' (pp 44, 628, 605). In fact, when initially describing the completed parlour, the narrator acknowledges that

topic, see Nessa M. Roche, *The legacy of light: a history of Irish windows* (Dublin, 1999). **38** Raymond Unwin and Barry Parker, *The art of building a home: a collection of lectures and illustrations* (London, 1901), pp vi, 64. **39** Conrad M. Arensberg, *The Irish countryman: an anthropological study* (New York, 1950), p. 140. **40** Unwin and Parker, *Art of building*, p. vi.

'Old Mrs. Donovan … preferred the kitchen with its … old spinning wheel and straw-bottom chairs—as, indeed, did Mat himself, and Bessy, too' (p. 605). The final phrase is worth a second glance: appended to the sentence by a dash, it is choppy, with four commas and three unnecessary terms of insistence ('indeed', 'himself' and 'too'). One senses a narrator less than easy about the proposition that the peasant kitchen remains supreme. Certainly, within the last chapter, he has Hugh Kearney assert before Grace, originator of the idea of the Donovan parlour, that Mat's son 'will be ahead of his father—at least of what his father was in his early youth' (p. 626). Even Billy's kitchen flute-playing does not, in the end, unambiguously re-graft the novel onto peasant rootstock, onto aboriginal domesticity. The privilege of last words goes to the eldest Kearney sister, Mary, and her husband Arthur O'Connor (the sometime seminarian at the twelve-pane window, now a physician), and they fail to recognize the kitchen's distinctiveness from the parlour. 'An hour later' on from the American clock's chiming eight, the couple is journeying home from a Ballinaclash Cottage soirée. They hear Billy's music-making, but Mary assumes it to be an emanation of female singing from the open 'drawing-room windows' at Ballinaclash (p. 628). Here, a domestic endeavour on the part of what Grace calls 'the rustics' is taken as bourgeois (p. 291). Even when Mary realizes that the music 'is from Mat Donovan's' – declaring, 'I am much mistaken if it is not Billy Heffernan's old flute' – she makes no distinction between parlour and kitchen (p. 628). However, given her friendship with Grace, it seems probable that Mary assumes the parlour, made for the middle-class Bessy Morris, to be the performance venue.

Early in their courtship, Bessy, a chronic borrower of books from Mary, presents Mat with 'an elegant song book', a volume that likely ends up within the array of 'some books' Grace prescribes for Mat's parlour. To a degree, the volume may parallel Grace's signature book-possession, which Mat describes as a 'large' edition of Thomas Moore's *Irish melodies* 'wud the goold harp on the cover' (pp 584, 182). Moore's *Melodies* 'continued the literary program of the United

Irishmen',[41] and Bessy imparts to Grace 'the legend of Fionn Macool' (p. 584), source matter for 'The wine cup is circling' in the *Melodies*, a lyric whose third line invokes a 'trophied wall' and whose last reads, '"victory! victory!" – the Finian's cry'.[42] With such trophies as papered walls and an American clock, Mat's parlour amounts to a distinctive victory in modern Ireland's heave against what Michael Davitt deemed feudalism on the island. However ambivalently, the hard-line Fenian Kickham seems to understand the space as a kind of *omphalos* in the politicized quest for material betterment. Mat can do more than museumize Bessy's gift: his home improvements align with a programme in self-schooling that renders him, in Mary's words, 'a grave and thoughtful character, devoting all the time he can spare to reading' (p. 548). This educative impulse is anticipated in William Allingham's *Laurence Bloomfield in Ireland* (serialized in *Fraser's Magazine*, 1862–3), the 1864 Macmillan (London) book edition of which sported the subtitle *A modern poem*. Allingham's improving young peasant Neal Doran not only enhances or modernizes his parents' cottage by 'an added room', but also 'by degrees the common kitchen grace[s] / With many a touch of his superior taste'.[43] 'Neal's books' are enumerated among items – such as a 'well-fill'd dresser' and 'clean chairs and stools, a gaily-quilted bed' – that constitute 'comfort' and 'slow prosperity' chez Doran.[44] However, display on the order of the housekeeper Mrs Hayes' presentation of the parlour mahogany at Father Carroll's is absent, for although he 'praise[s]' the new 'gable-room' Neal's father forswears 'deal[ing] with [exterior] whitewash, lest the cottage lie / A target' for a rent hike.[45]

---

41 Mary Helen Thuente, *The harp re-strung: the United Irishmen and the rise of Irish literary nationalism* (Syracuse, 1994), p. 177. Thuente argues that Moore's 'popular middle-class songs' manifestly 'contradict the stereotype of him as a coward singing for his supper in English drawing rooms and fearing to offend his patrons'. Ibid., p. 196. In *Knocknagow*, two characters discuss the 'Fire worshipers' section of Moore's oriental romance *Lalla rookh* (1817), which laments the Muslim colonization of the Ghebers (Zoroastrians or Parsees) of 'Iran', acoustically suggestive of 'Erin'.   42 Thomas Moore, *The poetical works of Thomas Moore, collected by himself* (New York, 1853), iv, pp 101–2.   43 William Allingham, *Laurence Bloomfield in Ireland: a modern poem* (London, 1864), pp 79, 76.   44 Ibid., pp 74–5, 80.   45 Ibid., pp 79, 76, 75.

Mrs Hayes' peer and Bessy Morris' weaver grandfather, the former Croppy 'Old Phil' Morris, had removed his pike 'from the thatch for a manly fight' in the 1798 Rebellion, and he remains an unreconstructed physical-force nationalist, given to labelling 'the present generation ... a degenerate race' (pp 229, 217). However, even he acknowledges the centrality of house politics to the contemporary scene, cantankerously barking, 'Well I know that' when Hugh Kearney insists that a local landlord's levelling of twenty-two 'houses, *big* an' little' is 'a different thing' from the matters that animated the Vinegar Hill rebels (p. 229, emphasis added). While Hugh may be a 'capital builder' of 'castles in the air', some of them 'stately ... gorgeous and glittering', when the Kearneys confront possible eviction from their substantial house due to rent arrears, he proves himself other than a daydreaming epigone by emigrating to Australia, both to make money to repay an emergency loan and 'to have a[n antipodal] home for his father and mother and sisters, if they should require it' (pp 347, 558).

The '98 rebellion elevated the notion of an Irish republic, but *Knocknagow; or, the homes of Tipperary* resides within an ample canon of post-union Irish literature that tends, by contrast, to elevate bourgeoisifying homesteads. Such places progressed towards parlours with bookshelves for displaying 'elegant' books, with clocks, American or native, and with mahogany or 'more modern' desks, chairs and the like. In addition, they privileged slate roofs over thatch, however many warrior pikes the latter may have contained. Hugh's oneiric castles can, on occasion, puff up to 'stately' proportions, yet the state – or at least the national culture – beginning to emerge in his and Mat Donovan's Ireland lies beyond both castle and cabin, lies closer to the material particulars of complex parlours.

# Inside the house: Synge's stage spaces

## Nicholas Grene

At the end of *Riders to the sea*, the first play in the 2005 DruidSynge cycle production, the director Garry Hynes chose to alter Synge's prescribed scene.[1] The original stage directions call for a group of women mourners in the background '*keening softly and swaying themselves with a slow movement*' (iii, p. 23).[2] The keen was designed to continue as a choric background to the solo voice of Maurya's last great threnody: just before her final lines, '*the keen rises a little more loudly from the women, then sinks away*' (iii, p. 27). Instead of this, Hynes had the women, black petticoats over their heads in lieu of shawls, turn their faces to the wall of the cottage and noiselessly beat their hands against it. It was an inspired decision. It is difficult theatrically to manage the sound of the keen so as not to distract from Maurya's words; the traditional keen was itself a sort of chanted elegy for the dead, though often rendered as a wordless lament.[3] In Hynes' version, the women, with their heads covered, backs to the audience, recalled images of the Wailing Wall.[4] But most of all the

---

1 The full cycle of plays was first produced at the Galway Town Hall Theatre on 16 July 2005. For details, see http://www.druid.ie/druidsynge, accessed 4 Mar. 2017.  2 All quotations from Synge, except where otherwise noted, are taken from J.M. Synge, *Collected works*, i: *Poems*, ed. Robin Skelton (London, 1962); ii: *Prose*, ed. Alan Price (London, 1966); iii: *Plays 1*; iv: *Plays 2*, both ed. Ann Saddlemyer (London, 1968).  3 See Angela Bourke, 'Keening as theatre' in Nicholas Grene (ed.), *Interpreting Synge: essays from the Synge summer school, 1991–2000* (Dublin, 2000), pp 67–79.  4 The staging of this scene was devised by Hynes in collaboration with the choreographer David Bolger, with the mourning of Middle Eastern women in mind. They wanted something as strange to the audience as the keen would have been to Synge. Personal conversation with Garry Hynes, 29 Sept. 2010.

choreography of the female figures beating the cottage walls represented the agony of the interior for Maurya and her daughters that constitutes the action of the play.

In setting *Riders* inside the island cottage, Synge was using the dramaturgical form that was to become the hallmark of the Abbey play – the three flats that made up the realistically represented country kitchen, pub or shop that stood in for the life of a community and, by implication, the life of the nation. He wrote the play in the extraordinary summer of 1902 when he also wrote *The shadow of the glen*. Both *Riders* and *Shadow* were inspired by stories he had heard on Aran, and both used the one fixed interior setting – a domestic environment – in which women's lives were determined by the actions of men associated with a world without. The aim of this essay is to explore these two plays of Synge for the meanings dramatized in their stage spaces inside the house, in terms of both their original dramaturgy and later theatrical reconceptions like that of Garry Hynes in DruidSynge.

### Riders to the sea

The cottage in *Riders* is modelled more or less on the house in which Synge stayed on his visits to Inishmaan (1898–1901) – the home of Patrick McDonagh, 'postmaster and farmer', as the 1901 census return designates him, and his family.[5] Synge gives a quite detailed description of it in *The Aran Islands*, though anonymized as was his usual practice with his travel writings:

> My room is at one end of the cottage, with a boarded floor and ceiling, and two windows opposite each other. Then there is the kitchen with earth floor and open rafters, and two doors opposite each other opening into the open air, but no windows. Beyond it there are two small rooms of half the width of the kitchen with one window apiece. (ii, p. 58)

5 See http://www.census.nationalarchives.ie, accessed 4 Mar. 2017.

The McDonaghs were the most important family on the island. Their house, which also served as the post office for Inishmaan – a fact Synge never notes – was unusual in having the room with boarded floor and ceiling, a room let to other paying guests, including the young Patrick Pearse in the very year of Synge's first visit. It was also distinctive in having two other bedrooms off the central kitchen-living room. The norm for such traditional stone-built houses would have been three rooms rather than four, as Kevin Danaher points out: 'the vernacular form most frequently found in Ireland is that of the small farmhouse of three main apartments, the large kitchen-living room in the middle and a bedroom at each end'.[6] In such a layout, the single adults of each gender would have shared a bedroom. This, for instance, was the arrangement in the Great Blasket, where Synge slept in the one room with the other men of the house, in the same bed as Pádraig Ó Catháin, the so-called king of the island, and his son.[7] It is this pattern that Synge seems to have had in mind in imagining the cottage in *Riders*. When Nora comes in and asks where her mother is, Cathleen replies, 'She's lying down, God help her, and maybe sleeping, if she's able' (iii, p. 5). Maurya would be resting in the room she no doubt shares with her daughters Cathleen and Nora, while Michael and Bartley would have slept at the other end of the house. The only significant difference Synge makes to the McDonaghs' cottage (for obvious theatrical reasons) is to add a window to the kitchen, making it possible for the daughters to look at the weather and Bartley's progress down to the sea.

Synge was very aware of the women on Aran, both within and outside the environment of the houses in which they lived. There is a barely disguised erotic interest in the young women that surfaces, now in an aestheticized appreciation, now in his surprise at the lack of a similar preoccupation on the part of his male companions.[8] But it was the hard life of the older women that struck him most forcibly, and on which he comments repeatedly. 'On these islands', he remarks,

6 Kevin Danaher, *Ireland's traditional houses* (Dublin, 1993), p. 40.   7 See J.M. Synge, *Travelling Ireland: essays, 1898–1908*, ed. Nicholas Grene (Dublin, 2009), pp xxi, 140–2. 8 See, for example, ii, pp 76, 105.

'the women live only for their children' (ii, p. 92), and he elaborates on this later:

> The maternal feeling is so powerful on these islands that it gives a life of torment to the women. Their sons grow up to be banished as soon as they are of age, or to live here in continual danger on the sea; their daughters go away also, or are worn out in their youth with bearing children that grow up to harass them in their own turn a little later. (ii, p. 108)

Women on Aran in fact often worked outside the home, as Synge himself shows in *The Aran Islands*. Even in *Riders* Bartley gives his sisters instructions as he leaves: 'If the west wind holds with the last bit of the moon let you and Nora get up weed enough for another cock for the kelp' (iii, p. 9). But the emphasis in the play is on the domestic life of the women, their baking and spinning, and particularly on the virtually housebound old mother. In his account of the eviction he witnessed on Inishmaan, Synge is outraged by the plight of the woman of the house being driven 'from the hearth she had brooded on for thirty years' (ii, p. 89). That idea of the mother with her prolonged (double-meaning) brooding at the hearth is central to the conception of Maurya.

There are two struggles, two conflicts going on through the action of *Riders*, both near their end, both focused on the control of the house. One is Maurya's repeated, vain effort to keep her sons within the shelter of the home. In the clash between herself and Bartley as to whether he should go to the horse fair in Connemara, Bartley evades confrontation, busying himself with making up a rope halter to ride the mare down to the boat. (Synge comments with amazement in *The Aran Islands* on the willingness of the islanders to ride horses at full speed with only this sort of halter, without either bridle or saddle (ii, p. 79).) Bartley only responds captiously to his mother's objections on the side issue of whether the rope will be needed to lower Michael's body into the grave, and the likelihood of the body being found after nine days' fruitless search. He does not even try to answer the unanswerable question that Maurya launches at him: 'If it was a hundred horses, or a thousand horses you had itself, what is the price of a thousand horses against a son where there is one son only?' (iii, p. 9). In this skewed dialogue of the deaf, Maurya's final line before Bartley exits is not even addressed to him, but spoken *'turning round to the fire, and putting her shawl over her head'*: 'Isn't it a hard and cruel man won't hear a word from an old woman, and she holding him from the sea?' (iii, p. 11). The significance of the threshold, marking off the boundary between the dangerous space outside and the sheltered home in which Maurya strives in vain to keep her son, is emphasized by the momentary tableau as Bartley stands 'looking round in the door' (iii, p. 11) for the mother's blessing she refuses to give.

The mother tries to hold her men from the sea, to keep them within the house, and almost by definition she is bound to fail. Cathleen sums up the law of nature that makes Maurya's efforts futile: 'It's the life of a young man to be going on the sea, and who would listen to an old woman with one thing and she saying it over?' (iii, p. 11). Cathleen is Maurya's antagonist in the second struggle of the play, the struggle for control within the house itself, once again a struggle that the mother has all but lost before the play starts. Maurya's first line in the play, when she enters from the inner room, is a criticism of Cathleen's household economy: 'Isn't it turf enough you have for this day and evening?' (iii, p. 7). Maurya is unaware that Cathleen is climbing the ladder to the turf-loft not to fetch down more fuel for the fire, but to hide the bundle of clothes that may belong to the drowned Michael. Cathleen immediately responds to her mother's criticism with a justification of her use of the preciously conserved turf: 'There's a cake baking at the fire for a short space (*throwing down the turf*), and Bartley will want it when the tide turns if he goes to Connemara' (iii, p. 7). And they are off into another argument about whether Bartley will or will not go. Cathleen is the older daughter, who has taken over the running of the house, and the grudging resentment of Maurya, the superseded matriarch, is registered in little darts of denigration. When Bartley tells Cathleen 'if the jobber comes' (in his absence) 'you can sell the pig with the black feet if there is a good price going', Maurya snorts scornfully 'How would the like of her get a good price for a pig?' (iii, p. 9). It is noticeable that Maurya never once addresses Cathleen by name in the course of the action, reserving all her directed speech for the younger daughter Nora. As Maurya moves into the visionary trance in which she articulates the play's central tragic statement of mortal men as riders to the sea, from the point of view of the family she is coming to the end of her useful practical life. So when one of the men comments on how strange it is that Maurya, with all her experience of coffin making, should have forgotten to buy nails, Cathleen's laconic comment is 'It's getting old she is and broken' (iii, p. 25). The woman who has been at the centre of the house, managing and directing it, is now a powerless supernumerary.

The very situation of the house in *Riders* is one of exposure. We feel the force of this when shortly after Nora's entrance, '*the door which NORA half closed behind her is blown open by a gust of wind*' (iii, p. 5). The fragility of the shelter provided by the house is registered in the bulletin on the state of the weather she brings: 'Is the sea bad by the white rocks, Nora?' 'Middling bad, God help us. There's a great roaring in the west, and it's worse it'll be getting when the tide's turned to the wind' (iii, pp 5–7). The window that Synge added to the real-life layout of the McDonaghs' kitchen gives the women – and by extension the audience – the ability to peek out fearfully at the turbulent landscape outside. The direct threat of sea and sky is given its emotional correlative in the vulnerable exposure of Maurya, who has no more control over her sons than they do over the natural forces without. Synge, however, offsets the danger of sentimentalizing Maurya as *mater dolorosa* with his clear-eyed observation of the psychodynamics of the house. This is no dysfunctional family by whatever norms of function we care to judge it. Rather, rough communication or non-communication is a means of survival within the daily abrasions of household life under the pressures of intimacy and penury. So Maurya deals with the underlying power struggle between herself and Cathleen by means of harsh, deflected speech. Bartley evades his mother's pleas by nonresponse. And Maurya, most poignantly, and to her lasting regret, refuses the crucial last exchange of blessings as Bartley leaves. As a human tragedy, *Riders* gains depth and resonance as it dramatizes the management of anger within the house, as well as the impotent grief of the mother who tries to hold her sons from the sea.

## The shadow of the glen

'The last cottage at the head of a long glen in County Wicklow', where *Shadow* is set is a composite creation. The story of the man who pretends to be dead to catch his wife out in infidelity was a traditional folk tale which Synge heard from Pat Dirane, the *shanachie* of Inishmaan, on his first visit there in 1898. Told in the first person, as often with such stories, it ended with the narrator assisting the 'dead man' in the discovery and punishment of the adulterous couple in the bedroom. The tale comes to a dramatic end with the attack on the lover: 'The dead man hit him a blow with the stick so that the blood out of him leapt up and hit the gallery' (ii, p. 72). The folk tale is located in some unnamed place on the road from Galway to Dublin, but for the setting of his play Synge turned to a Wicklow locality he knew well from fishing and walking expeditions with his family. In particular, it seems to have been a visit to Glenmalure, described in the essay 'An autumn night in the hills', which provided him with one of the emotional germs of the play in its 'long glen'. The house in question belonged to the elderly, unmarried Harney brothers and sister and was in fact a very substantial building with seven or more rooms and many outbuildings.[9] But it was its isolated situation that struck Synge, and the loneliness of a woman in such a house with the men frequently away at their work in the hills.

Synge recast the Aran story of the pretend death to reflect that emotional plight, and reduced the size of the house to what sounds

9 See home of Michael Harney, Baravore (Knockrath, Wicklow), http://www.census.nationalarchives.ie, accessed 4 Mar. 2017. For a more detailed account of the source material, see Nicholas Grene, 'Synge and Wicklow' in Grene (ed.), *Interpreting Synge*, pp 33–7.

like a two-room cottage. At least, when Nora urges the Tramp to 'go into the little room and stretch yourself a short while on the bed' (iii, p. 45), it sounds very much as though this is the only other room besides the kitchen in which we see Dan Burke's body laid out. Dan is a relatively well-to-do farmer with 'a hundred sheep on the back hills' and a substantial sum of money in a stocking, which Michael Dara so systematically counts as potential dowry, but there is no sign of this in the play's setting. Instead, the constriction of Nora's life is all the more emphasized by the circumscribed living space. The forms of address that she and the Tramp exchange – 'lady of the house', 'stranger' – underline their social positions as settled woman and vagrant. While 'lady of the house' and 'master of the house' (used by the Tramp deferentially to Dan Burke at his first 'resurrection') are literal translations from the standard Irish *bean tí, fear tí*, their unfamiliarity in English and their frequent repetition in the dialogue foreground the opposition between the housed and the houseless.

There is in *Shadow*, as in *Riders*, a dramatized contrast between interior and exterior worlds, between the protected space of the dwelling place and the exposure of the spaces outside. It is there from the very opening of the play when the Tramp seeks shelter: 'it's a wild night, God help you, to be out in the rain falling' (iii, p. 33). Both Nora and the Tramp are aware of the terrors that lurk in the hills and might drive you mad like their common friend Patch Darcy, who ran 'up into the back hills with nothing on … but an old shirt, and [was] eaten by the crows' (iii, p. 37). The 'oppression of the hills', as Synge calls it in one of his Wicklow essays, is partly a fear of the supernatural, what Michael Dara calls things 'we'd be afeard to let our minds on when the mist is down' (iii, p. 51). It is also a perfectly reasonable awareness of the effects of the homeless life. Peggy Cavanagh is several times referred to as a cautionary example – 'Peggy Cavanagh, who had the lightest hand at milking a cow that wouldn't be easy, or turning a cake, and there she is now walking round on the roads, or sitting in a dirty old house, with no teeth in her mouth, and no sense, and no more hair than you'd see on a bit of a hill and they after burning the furze from it' (iii, p. 51). Against such terrors of the exterior, for Nora Burke the desolation of her life alone in the cottage is summed up in her description of the view from within:

> sitting, looking out from a door the like of that door, and seeing nothing but the mist rolling down the bog, and the mists again, and they rolling up the bog, and hearing nothing but the wind crying out in the bits of broken trees were left from the great storm, and the streams roaring with the rain. (iii, p. 49)

Nora's plight is almost the opposite of Maurya's in *Riders*. Maurya had 'six fine sons' and her torture is to see all of them in turn go out from the protection of her maternal house to the hostile natural world that is to take them from her. A key part of Nora's misery is her childlessness. She speaks enviously of 'Mary Brien who wasn't that height (*holding out her hand*), and I a fine girl growing up, and there she is now with two children, and another coming on her in three months or four' (iii, p. 51). (In the DruidSynge production, Catherine Walsh, playing Nora, underlined the point by placing her hand on her own slim stomach at this point.) For her, the only relief to the monotony of day after day 'sitting up here boiling food for himself, and food for the brood sow, and baking a cake when the night falls' (iii, p. 49), is conversation with men who may visit the house. She justifies herself in her final speech to Dan: 'what way would a woman live in a lonesome place the like of this place, and she not making a talk with the men passing?' (iii, p. 57). What Dan takes as evidence of infidelity – 'your fine times, all the talk you have of young men and old men' (iii, p. 53) – is no more than a basic need for companionship, ironically illustrated at the end by Dan's own willingness to sit and drink with Michael Dara, his would-be cuckolder.

Many critics have commented on the analogy between the situation of Synge's Nora and that of her more famous predecessor, the Nora of Henrik Ibsen's *A doll's house* (1879).[10] But the differences

10 See, for example, W.J. Mc Cormack, *Fool of the family: a life of J.M. Synge* (London, 2000), p. 160. Antoinette Quinn comments on the paradox that the Dublin production of *A doll's*

are as important as the similarities. The Helmers live in a well-appointed middle-class home reflecting Torvald's income as bank manager. When Nora chooses to leave, it is because she has come to recognize the unreality of her marriage and the roles played out within this doll's house ménage; she must go out into the world to try to find a more authentic self of her own. It remains unclear what she will do, but the woman who has repaid the loan she took out to fund her husband's life-saving trip abroad by legal copying work can no doubt find some way to support herself. The facts in Synge's play are very different. Nora's is no playacting doll's house home. She did not marry or stay with Dan Burke out of love, but out of the barest economic necessity: 'What way would I live and I an old woman if I didn't marry a man with a bit of a farm, and cows on it, and sheep on the back hills?' (iii, p. 49). She does not choose to leave the marital home – even after the appalling charade of Dan's mock death, she tries for a reconciliation with him. It is Dan who forces her out and affords no prospect of return: 'Let you walk out through that door, I'm telling you, and let you not be passing this way if it's hungry you are, or wanting a bed' (iii, p. 55). For the Burkes there can be no miraculously reconstructed marriage such as Torvald hopes for at the end of *A doll's house*.

Apropos of the controversy over the production of *Shadow*, Synge commented to his friend Stephen MacKenna: 'On the French stage the sex-element of life is given without the other ballancing [*sic*] elements; on the Irish stage the people ... want the other elements without sex. I restored the sex-element to its natural place, and the people were so surprised they saw the sex only.'[11] Like the controversy itself, this may seem a peculiar view of the play, as Synge seems to have gone out of his way to mute the sexual dimension of the story, certainly in comparison with his source. The wife in Pat Dirane's folk tale is caught in flagrante, enforcing the brutally misogynist moral: the 'dead man' was quite right to have 'two fine

*house* in June 1903 was utterly uncontroversial while the staging of *Shadow* in October of that year caused a furore. See Quinn, 'Staging the Irish peasant woman: Maud Gonne versus Synge' in Grene (ed.), *Interpreting Synge*, pp 127–8.  **11** J.M. Synge, *Collected letters*, i: *1871–1907*, ed. Ann Saddlemyer (Oxford, 1983), p. 74.

sticks ... to keep down his wife' (ii, p. 72). Dan acquires no such proof of Nora's unfaithfulness. There can be little doubt that she was fond of Patch Darcy; it is equally clear that there is a tacit understanding between herself and Michael Dara that they may marry in the event of Dan's death. But a consummated sexual relationship with either man seems highly unlikely. It is true that Nora does hint at Dan's impotence and her own frustration in a remark to the Tramp: 'he was always cold, every day since I knew him, – and every night, stranger' (iii, p. 35). And the Tramp, when inviting her to go with him, implies more satisfactory nights 'with no old fellow wheezing the like of a sick sheep close to your ear' (iii, p. 57). Nevertheless, the scandal was not caused by Nora's sexual behaviour as such, but by the very fact that she left the marital home in the company of a Tramp. However loveless a marriage might be, Arthur Griffith, the play's most vehement critic maintained, the true Irish country woman 'does not go off with the Tramp'.[12] The country cottage, key icon of the Irish nationalist imaginary, must be maintained as a bourgeois ideal of domesticity and fidelity.

The house, in fact, is virtually never a site of sexual satisfaction in Synge. From *When the moon has set*, his lamentable first attempt at an Ibsenian problem play, to his last unfinished tragedy, *Deirdre of the sorrows*, erotic fulfilment is always to be found in a flight from the interior. Even in the most eloquent love scene of *The playboy of the Western world*, Christy imagines his married bliss with Pegeen outdoors: 'astray in Erris when Good Friday's by, drinking a sup from a well, and making mighty kisses with our wetted mouths, or gaming in a gap of sunshine with yourself stretched back unto your necklace in the flowers of the earth' (iv, p. 149). Yeats in *The land of heart's desire*, or Yeats and Gregory in *Cathleen ni Houlihan*, could oppose a normative ordinary interior of love and marriage against the extraordinary call to a dangerous world without by the fairies or the symbolic old woman. In Synge, settled marriages are never anything but arranged bargains of house and property: Nora marrying Dan

12 *United Irishman*, 24 Oct. 1903.

Burke for his 'bit of a farm and sheep in the back hills', Pegeen bartered by Michael James for Shawn Keogh's 'drift of heifers and … blue bull from Sneem' (iv, p. 155), the rooms Conchubor has built for Deirdre 'with red gold upon the walls, and ceilings that are set with bronze' (iv, p. 259). Love, if it is to be found at all, must be sought outside the house.

## Reconceptions

Synge's plays, so unpopular in his lifetime, after his death suffered the alternative fate of becoming canon, the received classics of Ireland's national theatre. Constant revivals in tired productions made them appear the prototype of the identikit kitchen comedies or tragedies that became known as the generic 'Abbey play'. Where one-act plays such as *Riders* and *Shadow* had been the staple of the early repertoire of the theatre, when programmes were often created out of a combination of such short pieces, and curtain-raisers were still standard, it was hard to find a place for them in later practice dominated by the single full-length play. Even with the three-act works, such as the much-revived *Playboy*, there were difficulties associated with the shape and scale of the new Abbey Theatre of 1966. With its immensely high stage and its distanced auditorium, it was quite inhospitable to the dramaturgy of Synge – and other early Abbey plays – with their intimate spaces and closely observed poetic realism.

There were experiments with various sorts of alternative styles of staging to cope with this problem. For example, for the 1971 Synge centenary Abbey production of *Playboy*, director Colin George used a background of projected newspaper cuttings relating to the riots as a metatheatrical framing device to foreground the play's history. The *Riders*, in that same 1971 season, directed by Hugh Hunt, had a cutaway cottage interior on a stage all but dwarfed by cyclorama images of sea and sky. One of the most radical attempts to disrupt the naturalistic fourth wall convention was Patrick Mason's 1994 production of *Well* at the Abbey, which had pious processions of villagers entering behind the saint through the auditorium.[13] It has, however, been the Druid Theatre Company that has made the most sustained effort to reimagine Synge's work for the stage.

Druid has had a long-term investment in Synge from the first establishment of the company in Galway in 1975, so much so that Garry Hynes, the company's director, has referred to him as their 'house dramatist'.[14] Druid's early productions, culminating in the landmark 1982 staging, enforced rather than challenged Synge's realism. The Mayo shebeen of *Playboy* was designed in gritty period style, with an ad for Gold Flake cigarettes featuring the face of Edward VII juxtaposed with the icon of the Sacred Heart. Brid Brennan, as a scarcely literate Pegeen Mike, penned her opening letter slowly, tongue between teeth, scratching her head the while.[15] Returning to Synge twenty years later, Hynes had to find a different style to achieve her long-cherished project of staging all six of the plays in a single cycle. There was a sort of trial run for what was to become DruidSynge in 2004, with productions of *Playboy*, and of *Well* and *The tinker's wedding* as a double bill. For *Playboy*, Hynes went in the opposite direction from her early realist stagings, with a caricatural mode almost reminiscent of nineteenth-century *Punch* cartoons. An eclectic *Well*, ranging in period from medieval to the 1920s, featured a solid stone wall that had to be raised and lowered for acts I and III. For the full-scale production of the six-play cycle in 2005, Hynes had to clear the stage of such theatrical encumbrances and establish a unified design sufficiently open and flexible to encompass the full range of the work.

This she did with the help of Francis O'Connor's single set. Though re-dressed for each of the plays, the rectangular box set remained essentially the same: three high walls painted a dirty blue-green, one door at the back, two other doors to right and left, a

13 For these and other experimental stagings, see Nicholas Grene, 'Synge in performance' in P.J. Mathews (ed.), *Cambridge companion to J.M. Synge* (Cambridge, 2009), pp 154–6. 14 'Garry Hynes and Ann Saddlemyer in conversation', *DruidSynge*, 3 DVD set (RTÉ, Wildfire Films/Druid, 2007). 15 For fuller details see Nicholas Grene, 'Two London Playboys: before and after Druid' in Adrian Frazier (ed.), *Playboys of the Western world: production histories* (Dublin, 2004), pp 80–2.

window at one side, a high-up alcove in the back wall used to store a variety of objects needed for the different plays. A key design feature, however, was the stage covering of dark brown turf dust that allowed for the space to be alternatively interior or exterior. When it was an interior, it was the mud floor of a solid-appearing cottage or pub; when it was an exterior, it was the earth of a defined space of ground. So, the anxiously watched door through which the men carried the corpse of Bartley in *Riders* into the grief-stricken cottage became the door of the church from which the priest in *Tinker's wedding* looked out at his disreputable potential clients in their roadside encampment. The multiple casting of individual actors pointed to thematic contrasts and similarities between the plays. Marie Mullen, who had no less than five roles through the cycle, appeared first in *Riders* as the agonized old mother by the hearth, lamenting the tragic fate of her sons without. But she was seen next transformed into the scandalously anarchic Mary Byrne, mocking the orthodoxies of the settled life of marriage. *Shadow* opened the second half of the programme, with Catherine Walsh playing the melancholy Nora Burke trapped in the cottage-bound monotony of her miserable marriage to Dan Burke. In *Playboy*, which followed immediately after, she was Pegeen Mike, in an earlier version of that sort of situation: losing the only playboy of the Western world, she was left with nothing but the prospect of an equally joyless future in the shebeen with Shawn Keogh.

The production cycle was bookended by the two tragedies, *Riders* at the start and *Deirdre of the sorrows* at the end. The plays were bound together by a single prop – the 'white boards' that feature so prominently in *Riders* as the prospective coffin for Michael, ultimately to be used for Bartley. These remained on stage throughout to figure eventually in the scene of mass deaths at the end of *Deirdre*. For that scene, Hynes also brought back the black-covered keening women to repeat their ritual action of beating on the walls of the set. But by this point, that set itself had been transformed. For in the last act of *Deirdre*, suddenly the previously solid-seeming walls were pulled back; the doors fell off their hinges, the window frame collapsed. A space appeared between the walls and the edge of the stage, and into that space the white boards descended. After the killing of the sons of Usna, their bloodied dead bodies appeared in this gap right beside the boards.

It was a way of enforcing the catastrophic ending – not only the death of Naisi and his brothers and the suicide of Deirdre, but the destruction of the High King Conchubor's palace at Emain Macha that follows. And yet the shattered set also had a multiple metatheatrical effect. It pointed to the unfinished state of the play itself. Synge died before he could complete *Deirdre* to his own satisfaction. He left a request for his fellow Abbey directors to revise the text, but after much deliberation, Yeats and Gregory decided to leave it as they found it (iv, pp xxvii–viii). The entropy of the set might be read as a gesture to Synge's only partially successful final experiment in the epic style. The other plays were complete theatrical spectacles; this one was only a shell of what might have been finally achieved. At the same time, the declaration of the constructed and deconstructable stage design made manifest the constructed nature of all the plays. The whole cycle was viewed as the creation of a single theatrical imagination moving in stage space between the sheltering, entrapping interiors of the house and an outside world that might represent a liberating affirmation of life, but carried always with it the threat of death or an *unheimlich* uncanny.

There was always a certain literalism in Synge's theatrical imagination. He needed to start imagining his stage sets from places he knew, houses he had lived in or at least visited. So the McDonagh cottage on Inishmaan, in which he had stayed so often, provided the basis for the home of Maurya and her children in *Riders*. The folk tale of the man pretending to be dead to prove his wife's infidelity, which Synge had heard on Aran, only took on substance when he located it in the Harneys' Wicklow farmhouse in Glenmalure. He did not need to recreate these houses exactly, but modified them to the demands of his drama. The kitchen in *Riders* acquired a window to allow the women of the play to look out from within at the natural world in which their menfolk struggled with the forces of nature. The

Harneys' relatively large house was reduced down to a two-room cottage to enforce the claustrophobia of Nora's entrapment within it. Synge was determined that productions of his plays should be as authentic as possible, and his work was central to the peasant naturalism that became the distinctive idiom of the Abbey Theatre. But in the later twentieth century this sort of style came to seem old-fashioned and clunky, and new forms of theatrical realizations were needed to make Synge's stage spaces come alive again. What was so innovative about DruidSynge was that it took the traditional box set, which had always mimicked the real country cottage with fourth wall removed, and turned it into an avowed performance space. The stylized action of the mourning women in *Riders* and again in *Deirdre* beating against the walls introduced a strange ritual associated with a quite different culture in place of the ethnographically authentic keen. The flats of the set could enclose outside as well as inside space; the one turf-strewn stage could be alternatively the earth floor of the house or the ground outside it. And the self-dismantling of the set in the last stages of *Deirdre*, the final play in the series, reminded an audience of the constructed nature of the whole theatrical performance.

# Hairpins among the rifles: the domestic site in women's accounts of 1916

## Lucy McDiarmid

[I]t is terribly easy to lose one's possessions in the cabin; they drop between the mattresses into the rifles and disappear. There will be a lot of hairpins found among them when they are unloaded.

* * *

'Gordon' she said, 'You're ruining the guns with that coffee.'

—Mary Spring Rice, 'Diary of the *Asgard*', July 1914

Things were a bit crowded on the *Asgard* during the famous voyage that ran the guns to Howth. The weapons for a revolution, 900 rifles along with 29,000 rounds of ammunition, were packed and hidden in a 51-foot yacht on which seven people were living. Smelling of coffee and sprinkled with hairpins, the guns became part of the furniture. The domestic site was an armory. At one point, on 16 July off the coast of Devon, the *Asgard* sailed right through the middle of the British fleet: 'They seemed to be executing some night manoeuvres', noted Mary Spring Rice. 'There was one awful moment when a destroyer came very near.'[1] As subsequent events made clear,

---

1 Mary Spring Rice, 'Diary of the *Asgard*, July 1914' in F.X. Martin (ed.), *The Howth gun-running and the Kilcoole gun-running, 1914* (Dublin, 1964), p. 86. Some of the anecdotes in this essay also form parts of my book *At home in the revolution: what women said and did in*

the fleet was preparing for war with Germany.[2] It is highly unlikely that *their* guns were full of hairpins.

Like other Irish homes between 1914, when the guns were run to Howth and Kilcoole, and 1923, when the Civil War ended, the *Asgard* complicates any identification of the domestic site with definitions of privacy. Some of the best recent analyses of these terms occur in scholarly work on English materials. In *Private matters and public culture in post-Reformation England*, Lena Cowen Orlin identifies 'the private' with 'the household'. Her aim in the book is therefore 'a cultural history of the house: its notional structures, prescribed activities, prevailing aspirations, and persistent conflicts'. Her interest lies in the way 'post-Reformation men and women … conceptualized their private lives and … in their own awareness of how these conceptualizations both served and sometimes failed the community'.[3] In *Locating privacy in Tudor London*, Orlin extends her definition of what she now calls 'personal privacy' to 'interiority, atomization, spatial control, intimacy, urban anonymity, secrecy, withholding, solitude'.[4]

In this respect, the Irish home has always been different from the English home, at least since the beginning of colonial rule, because 'public' and 'private' have been differently located. As Carol Coulter has written, in late nineteenth-century Ireland,

> public and civic life was dominated by an outsider, who forcibly occupied that space … public space became alien for all the native inhabitants … The family, however, was different … It was an inviolate space, the one place where the occupier could not enter – at least, not without doing violence to his own

*1916* (Dublin, 2015). The arguments, the juxtaposition of anecdotes and most of the analysis, however, are original to this essay.   **2** From the account of Diarmaid Coffey, who sailed on the other gunrunning boat, the *Kelpie*: 'we had just sailed through the British fleet and … a destroyer had made for us as if to hold us up but had steamed away again. We had not paid much attention to the news from Europe and did not realize that what we had seen was the British fleet preparing for war under the guise of a review at Spithead.' Diarmaid Coffey, 'Guns for Kilcoole' in F.X. Martin (ed.), *The Howth gun-running and the Kilcoole gun-running, 1914* (Dublin, 1964), p. 121.   **3** Lena Cowen Orlin, *Private matters and public culture in post-Reformation England* (Ithaca, NY, 1994), p. 4.   **4** Lena Cowen Orlin, *Locating*

rhetoric on the sanctity of the family. Small wonder, therefore, that the family sometimes became the locus of resistance to the occupier.[5]

Coulter does not use the word 'house', but it is implied in that 'inviolate space' that 'the occupier could not enter', although of course the occupier did enter it often when its inhabitants were suspected of subversive activities. Even interior decoration could be revolutionary. As Lady Gregory writes, 'The chief ornament of many a cottage is the warrant for the arrest of a son of the house framed and hung up as a sort of diploma of honour.'[6]

Because the Irish home may function as the locus of a revolutionary subculture, the entire house, every inch of it, may be simultaneously 'private' (in any of Orlin's senses of 'intimacy' or 'solitude' or matters that are merely familial) and 'public' (in so far as it associates itself to the civic life of an emergent nation state), or what Nancy Fraser would call a 'counterpublic'.[7] Thus Orlin's brilliant analysis of the way architectural elements – doors, the long gallery, the corporate parlour, the closet, the party wall – constructed privacy in Tudor London does not fit the Irish home. Of course, the Irish landscape did have specially designed enclosed spaces to hide subversive activities: the priest hole, the hedge school and the Mass rock suggest a pervasive clandestine architecture of concealment.[8] But during the revolutionary years of the early twentieth century, the entire house was deemed a place of concealment by the authorities.

Writing about life on the *Asgard*, Mary Spring Rice (and to a lesser extent Molly Childers) uses a discourse of domesticity in a narrative of political engagement. The way she talks about the yacht's architectural features and the crowded space below deck epitomizes the way the deepest privacy, the most concealed space, may also be

*privacy in Tudor London* (Oxford, 2007), p. 1. **5** Carol Coulter, *The hidden tradition: feminism, women and nationalism in Ireland* (Cork, 1993), p. 10. **6** Lady Gregory, 'Felons of our land' in Lucy McDiarmid and Maureen Waters (eds), *Lady Gregory: selected writings* (London, 1995), p. 256. **7** Nancy Fraser, 'Rethinking the public sphere', *Social Text*, 25/26 (1990), 61. **8** Many English houses inhabited by Catholics during the Reformation also had priest holes.

the site in which matters of major political import are transpiring. Any analysis of the Irish 'home' during the Rising and the subsequent years of revolution and civil war must begin, then, in 1914, with a consideration of the unusual space in which Erskine and Molly Childers, Mary Spring Rice, and the others were cooking, eating, sleeping and washing on top of guns and ammunition. The most detailed accounts of the Irish home in this period are by women closely associated with the Rising's leaders, Kathleen Clarke and Geraldine Plunkett Dillon. A series of letters by Mary Louisa Hamilton Norway, whose husband was secretary to the Irish post office, shows how even an English woman's 'home' in Dublin became implicated in the revolution. What is conventionally considered the domestic site, where intimate personal routines and familial activities take place, may be equally defined as, and coextensive with, a military site – an armory, a front line, a lookout point – even when it is not hiding 900 rifles.

## Home afloat: Mary Spring Rice's 'Diary of the *Asgard*'

Mary Spring Rice's 'Diary of the *Asgard*' is a domocentric narrative; its frame is not the story of how the guns were run but of how a provisional home was constructed and reconstructed. As she tells it, the emphasis is not on ideology or revolution but on the maintenance of a domestic site under unusual and difficult circumstances: the guns invade their living space. The political narrative is subordinated to a continuing story of housekeeping. At the beginning, she and the others (Molly and Erskine Childers, their friend Gordan Shephard and two Gola Islanders, Charles Duggan and Pat McGinley) set up house on the *Asgard* and make order out of a 'fearful scene of confusion':

> In the midst of ropes, tinned foods, marline, and clothes just unpacked, we laboured to get things straightened out before our early start. I wearily pulled my clothes out of canvas bags and holdalls and stowed them as best I could, there was a fearsome

thunderstorm going on and it was breathlessly hot: however, I got to sleep at last. (pp 8–9)

The story ends in the evening of the day the guns were landed, as Spring Rice spends the night at Alice Stopford Green's niece's house in Dublin: 'I felt rather mean as I got into a glorious hot bath and thought of Molly and Erskine tired and worn out with everything upset, tossing about on the Irish Sea. But my bed was heavenly' (p. 97). The shape this frame gives the story of the gunrunning implies that the main subject was the practical aspects of house-keeping and domestic life. Throughout her diary Spring Rice emphasizes the instability of domestic arrangements on the *Asgard*, and so her arrival in a house with hot running water and a comfortable bed provides closure to the story.

Between these two moments, the focus of her narrative is on overcoming the difficulties in maintaining a home afloat. Not a word of patriotism appears, and it is not because she is being cautious: the guns feature prominently and explicitly in the diary, but so do food, cleanliness and the daily logistics of living on a yacht. 'One of my chief duties', she writes, 'was keeping the food hot for the late-comers, and as I sat close to the fo'castle door and the stove was just inside, it was quite handy' (p. 72). Spring Rice also records Molly Childers' response to the casual table manners of Gordon Shephard, the English crew member. At breakfast on 6 July Spring Rice 'heard a shriek from Molly – "He's pouring all the Golden Syrup on the bunk"' (p. 72).

Once the guns were loaded, the difficulties of housekeeping for seven people on a small yacht became even more complicated.[9] First 'we all fell to work doing the final cleaning of the saloon and cabin for the guns' (p. 78). Then 'We hastily hauled bags of clothes and mattresses and stowed them aft of the mizzen' (p. 79). Everyone except Molly (who was a semi-invalid and could not walk) laboured

9 The seven people included Erskine and Molly Childers, Mary Spring Rice, the Englishman Gordon Shephard, two Donegal fisherman, Patrick McGinley and Charles Duggan, and 'the lad from the Volunteer office' in Dublin, John Nolan.

to stow the rifles, while Molly 'put pieces of chocolate literally into our mouths as we worked' (p. 80). Then Spring Rice

> tumbled into the fo'castle, crawling over the guns in the saloon to get to it, and got the kettle on for hot drinks while the men were fixing the tow ropes. Down they came then and we all drank cocoa and beef-tea and then shifted down the mattresses and bags of clothes, which had been stowed aft of the mizzen, and lumped them down on the guns anyhow – we were too tired to settle them properly – and lay down just as the grey light of the dawn was breaking. I remember thinking how absurd it was to go to bed in daylight and then went off into a dead sleep. (p. 81)

The diary treats the packing of 900 rifles into small spaces on a yacht as all in a day's work. It is Spring Rice's jaunty, matter-of-fact, slightly amused tone that makes this collective activity seem simply like a more exciting form of furniture rearrangement. So much attention is devoted to pieces of chocolate, cocoa, beef tea, the positioning of mattresses and the quality of sleep that it is almost possible to forget that these seven people are running guns in the hope of arming the members of a paramilitary organization. Revolution is not only the unmentioned word; it does not appear to be on Spring Rice's mind.

With so much weaponry crowding the available space on the *Asgard*, personal ablutions and other daily routines like cooking and setting the table required improvisation:

> One has to turn the mattress right back off the guns in our cabin to be able to turn down the basin, so that one only does it when one really does feel too dirty to eat before washing [...]
> Fried eggs are very hard on rough days; they fly about the pan and get disintegrated. Awfully late at breakfast, and Mr Gordon was shaving in the saloon, while I propped up against the ammunition box in the doorway, was shoving in the breakfast things and trying to prevent them getting all mixed up with the shaving apparatus, as everything was shooting about the table. (p. 83)

The purpose of the trip, it seems, was to challenge Spring Rice's housekeeping skills and to test the limits of everyone's need for clear spatial boundaries. The 'ammunition box' that she refers to so lightly might as well have been a box of hurling sticks.

Spring Rice seems actually to enjoy the confusion of categories, but then, so did Molly. Molly Childers' letters to Alice Stopford Green emphasize, as Spring Rice's diary cannot, what a happy camper Spring Rice was: 'Mary a Spartan, helping with everything, cooking tea, wrestling with Primus lamps, Rippingill stove, etc. A heroine.' Like the voice in the diary, Spring Rice is 'cheery' as well as a '*great* companion'.[10] Childers also indicates the way the guns became furniture: 'Below decks we sleep, crawl over, sit on, eat on guns. Guns everywhere ... Our daily rub down in alcohol takes hours, one is so pitched about in the odd positions one has to take. It is all gorgeous fun and, joy of joys, Mary and I are up to it.'[11]

One boundary that was retained was that of gender. The women slept in the same tiny, stuffy cabin, attempting to retain a vestige of privacy. Sleeping on guns was not the problem ('I ... found my bed on top of the guns extraordinarily comfortable'); it was, as Spring Rice writes, 'sleeping in public':

> Molly and I decided it was altogether too hot to sleep with the cabin door shut and as it opened straight into the hatch and companion, it meant rather sleeping in public. The theory was that one put out the light and then no one could see in, but as it got light about 4 a.m. that rather broke down; however I don't really mind, compared to sleeping in a tug. (p. 71)

Privacy had to be specially constructed:

> The half-hour on deck before breakfast is very joyful after the stuffiness of dressing with the cabin door shut. I do as much dressing as possible with it open, but there were moments when it had to be shut. (p. 73)

**10** Molly Childers, 'Letters from the *Asgard*' in Martin (ed.), *The Howth gun-running*, p. 99.
**11** Childers, 'Letters', p. 103.

The cabin door had to be fixed permanently open so we had an arrangement of a dishcloth which could be hung across as a curtain when one was dressing, but it was too stuffy to keep it hung up at night and shut out the precious air that came down the companion. The worst was on a wet night when Molly insisted on shutting the companion hatch, not so much for herself as to keep the guns dry, and then the stuffiness was awful. (p. 83)

After breakfast I do a little washing behind the dishcloth in the cabin; then, if fine, the mattresses and blankets are given an airing on deck. (p. 84)

Molly's concern for the guns – that coffee and syrup not be spilled on them, that they be kept dry – is presented as a housewifely concern the way, say, protecting the finish on a cherry or mahogany table might be. The language remains the discourse of housekeeping and the labours of the two women are those of spirited sisterly housewives who find the whole enterprise jolly good fun. One word of patriotic sacrifice – sleeping in a stuffy cabin for Ireland, missing hot running water for Ireland – and the interest of the account would be different. The power of the 'Diary of the *Asgard*' comes from the utter absence of ideology and sentiment about the great unmentioned purpose of the voyage.

## At home in Fairview (north Dublin) and Limerick: Kathleen Clarke's *Revolutionary woman*

On the *Asgard*, the most private places, such as the little space behind the dishcloth where the women got dressed and undressed, were filled with the guns that would be used in the Rising two years later. It could be said both that the guns occupied domestic space and that ritual ablutions took place in an armory. Kathleen Clarke's situation in 1916, as described in her memoir *Revolutionary woman*, was different.[12] Her

12 Kathleen Clarke, *Revolutionary woman: an autobiography, 1878–1972*, ed. Helen Litton (Dublin, 1990).

house was not an armed camp, and when it was raided on 2 May, she was not doing anything subversive: she was working in the garden on the one hundred cauliflowers she had planted on the first day of the Rising (pp 78, 83). On that occasion and other similar ones, she responded by creating interiors within interiors, constructing new forms of seemingly domestic space in order to deceive the invading soldiers.

On 2 May 1916 the Rising was over, the rebels had surrendered and the leaders were in Kilmainhaim awaiting execution. Kathleen Clarke knew none of this. She was the wife of Tom Clarke, the oldest of the Rising's leaders, and the sister of Commandant Ned Daly, at 24 the youngest man to be executed, and she was waiting in great anxiety at home on Richmond Avenue, in Fairview, near the Drumcondra Road. An 'old lady friend' came by the house to find out what was happening, and while she was there, British soldiers arrived to raid the house. Clarke's house was of interest to the British military simply because she was a close relative of revolutionaries. Clarke heard and saw the soldiers marching up the avenue, and as they approached, she was trying to figure out what to do with 'a fairly large sum of money in the house, some of it receipts from the shop, and some of it money held in trust for the dependents' of people fighting in the Rising. The money was vulnerable not because it was a secret weapon or part of military plans: it was wealth that enemy soldiers would steal.

> [W]here was I to hide it? Time was short; any minute now they would be demanding admittance. Ah, sudden thought; I would give it to the old lady! She would scarcely be searched, even if I was. This was easier said than done. She was frightened, and I had to bully her into consenting. She was so terrified at the thought that she was quite helpless, and I was shaking with pent-up excitement. She had an old-fashioned bodice, buttoned from the neck down. I opened the buttons, put the money inside and rebuttoned it. Her ample bust was not noticeably increased by the added bulk.

The knock came at the hall door as the last button was buttoned. (p. 84)

Possibly aided in this inventive response by her youthful career as a seamstress in Limerick, Clarke invented a new 'interior space', one not visible, not part of the 'built environment', when her house was about to be invaded. The body, specifically the space between the guest's bodice and her 'ample bust', functioned as the safe interior that a domestic site might have been under other circumstances. Yet even that intimate space cannot be deemed altogether 'private'. The money was actually a 'fund', publicly collected, for dependents of executed men who considered themselves the government of a provisional Irish republic. Later Mrs Pearse, Mrs MacDonagh and Mrs Kent received £250 each, and other people other amounts. So the space the money occupied contained in a sense a national treasury: it was physically private but ontologically it participated in a political realm.

While four officers with revolvers tore apart Clarke's house in a search for weapons, a fifth armed guard stood watching over a room where Clarke, the 'old lady' and the maid Sarah (recently arrived from the Aran Islands and terrified at events she did not altogether understand) sat and waited for several hours. Under these circumstances Clarke asserted ownership of her home: 'In order to show them how little their actions disturbed me, I took up a Limerick lace handkerchief I had been making and worked on it throughout the raid.' It was 'a pure piece of bravado', she writes, but she was performing domesticity, and countering and defying the violence of the soldiers with an activity associated with women and the home. The single room where the women were held maintained the identity of the house as a home, while the rest of the house was treated as a secret armory. Clarke's handiwork on the lace, she writes, was 'very poor', but 'it seemed to have a soothing effect on the old lady and the maid' (p. 84).

The soldiers actually found something that Clarke heard them identify as 'a Mills bomb' (a form of hand grenade invented in 1915), but she purported never to have seen it before: 'I told him that if I had known it was there and what it was I would have taken good care not to notify the authorities, or leave it for him to find. He seemed very disconcerted at my reply' (p. 85). The three women were all arrested, but before she was taken off to Ship Street Barracks and locked up there, Clarke managed (with some difficulty) to have the other two women released.[13]

The construction of a second interior within a raided house is a common practice, and it was accomplished successfully by Kathleen Clarke's mother, Mrs Daly, when their house in Limerick was raided by Black and Tans.[14] The Tans were after an IRA man on the run but were unable to find him. Even Clarke herself did not know where in the house her sisters had hidden him; she was primarily worried about her mother, who was 'in bed, looking very frail and ill'. In fact, as she found out after the Auxiliaries left – a safe time after they left – the man was hidden in her mother's bed:

> All her life she had been accustomed to sleep on a feather bed, and when hair and spring mattresses came into fashion she got one, but would not be parted from her feather bed. She insisted on having it on top of the hair and spring mattress. Between the hair mattress and the feather bed, the man was stretched out. All the feathers were drawn to one side of the bed, and my mother lay on top of them. The bedclothes were drawn over all, and it looked just like an old lady in bed. Poor mother, what she must have suffered while the raiders were searching the room, not knowing but that any minute they might order her out of the bed to search it, find the man, and perhaps kill him before

13 Later that night Clarke was taken to Kilmainham jail, where she had a final meeting with her husband hours before his execution. 14 According to Maire Comerford, Alice Stopford Green also engaged in this practice at least once: 'When we were raided by the Auxiliaries after bedtime one night, I recall Mrs Green as she stood, in contemptuous silence, outside her bedroom door, at the top of the stairs. She was wearing one of her stiffest silk brocade gowns which hung straight from the shoulders. Her head was high, and her hands low, slightly joining in front. Fortunately I was the only one to notice something not quite normal about her figure. A whole file of the banned Republican bulletin was inside the gown. She could not have moved without something slipping; but then nobody dared ask her to move.' Maire Comerford, 'Alice Stopford Green' in Martin (ed.), *The Howth gun-running*, p. 24.

her. When we finally thought it safe to uncover him, he was nearly suffocated. (p. 181)

Like Molly Childers and Mary Spring Rice, Mrs Daly was lying on a mattress that was covering materiel. In a most intimate place, in her own bed at home, she was performing a military function, protecting a threatened member of a rebel army. She was a weak, terrified old lady in bed *pretending to be a weak, terrified old lady in bed*; she was 'performing' the domestic role she was truly living at that moment, and yet she was also simultaneously participating in a rebellion, interposing her own body between those of enemy soldiers. Her bed was a front line.

In a raid during the Civil War, one of Kathleen Clarke's children played a similar role, using his body to create an interior within an interior. Harry Boland, who was hiding at Kathleen Clarke's house, left it in a hurry when he saw Free State troops approaching. As he ran,

> He handed me a bundle of papers and told me to hide them until he came back … in a distracted way I kept saying, 'Where will I hide them?' The military were almost at the door when my youngest son, Emmet, said 'Put them here, Mama.' 'Here' was under his pullover. I said, 'It won't do, they would see the bulk and perhaps ill-treat you.' He said, 'They won't if I keep my arms like this on the table,' and there he sat all through the raid at the kitchen table, during a raid by Irishmen.
>
> I intended to appear very busy in the kitchen preparing dinner … They searched the kitchen, but took no notice of the little boy sitting at the table. (p. 199)

Emmet Clarke told Helen Litton, who edited Clarke's autobiography, that when the soldiers left, 'My mother came and relieved me of the load and found a secure place to hide them … She had brought in fresh plaice for all of us so that I had to eat the extra in case the soldiers would notice. For years after I did not like plaice' (p. 235). Like his grandmother in Limerick, young Emmet had to perform the role of a person in his own home doing something ordinary: he pretended to be a boy eating the dinner his mother gave him. Clarke herself also performed a domestic role, that of a mother feeding her children, as she was indeed doing at that moment. But as Emmet eats the plaice and as Clarke serves it, they are simultaneously participating in a civil war. Both of them defy the pro-treaty government while they perform homeyness.

## At home everywhere: Geraldine Plunkett Dillon's *All in the blood*

Geraldine Plunkett records having stuffed guncotton into a cushion once during a raid before the Rising, and on another occasion the gardener hid her christening mug in his hat so that British soldiers wouldn't get it.[15] But she did not spend much time creating hidden interiors. The Dublin houses she lived in were usually more overtly engaged in warfare: it was after all guncotton, not money or paper, that she was hiding. She was the sister and aide-de-camp of the 1916 leader Joseph Mary Plunkett, and because of her continuing involvement in republican activities, she was always presumed to be hiding guns or IRA men or plans for subversion of some sort, whether or not she actually was.

Even the site of Gerry Plunkett's wedding night was determined by military strategy. She married Tommy Dillon, her chemistry lecturer at UCD, the morning of Sunday 23 April, the day before the Rising began. She chose to get married at that particular time because, as she writes, 'the Rising would put an end to my world, nothing would be the same again and I was not going back to that hellhole of family life' (p. 221). Gerry and Tommy's Imperial Hotel room was selected because its windows looked directly onto Sackville Street opposite the GPO, where (as they knew) the Rising was due to begin the next day. Rory O'Connor, who had been best man in

15 Geraldine Plunkett Dillon, *All in the blood*, ed. Honor O Brolchain (Dublin, 2006), p. 234.

their wedding, went to the Imperial Hotel Sunday afternoon to tell them 'to look out from twelve o'clock the next day'. Gerry's final sentence for her Sunday entry is 'from now on we were sitting in the window, watching'. Her opening sentence for the next day is, 'From about ten o'clock on Easter Monday Tommy and I kept looking out the windows of our sitting-room in the hotel and from noon, on this beautiful day, we were sitting and watching through the open second-storey windows. It was breathless' (p. 222). Clearly, it wasn't a honeymoon; it was a vigil. As the memoir characterizes it, the hotel room was not so much a bedroom as a lookout point over the battlefield; its only important feature was its windows. The room at the Imperial, like the *Asgard*, served a double purpose. Just as the great unmentioned in Spring Rice's account of the *Asgard* is the future revolution for which the guns were run, so the great unmentioned in Plunkett Dillon's account of the day she got married is romance.

Geraldine and Joseph were two of the seven children of Count and Countess Plunkett, wealthy Catholics who owned a real-estate empire of sixty houses. All the Plunkett family's homes had military functions. Not only was the second-floor front bedroom at the Imperial a lookout, the Plunketts' primary house on Fitzwilliam Street was a warehouse for Howth rifles and the barn on their Larkfield property in Kimmage was a place for target practice. A twelve-acre rural estate in Kimmage that the countess pretended to own but had actually never paid for, Larkfield was an all-purpose domestic space – essentially a hotel with a transient population of Plunketts and their friends, where any number of activities could take place. It had a main house, cottages, a barn, a mill building and other houses already 'occupied' by two brothers who were bakers and a third who was a weaver; they came with the territory. The countess added cows (she thought she ordered three cows from Kerry, but she got eleven). Starting in January 1914 one battalion of the Volunteers was headquartered at Larkfield. Gradually the Volunteers began storing ammunition there and in the summer many of the Howth guns were kept at Larkfield. Tommy Dillon and Rory O'Connor founded the Larkfield Chemical Company there (intending to make aspirin).

Three hundred Irishmen from Liverpool and Glasgow, avoiding conscription, moved in, and by 1915 Larkfield was, in Gerry's words, 'effectively an armed camp'.[16] Michael Collins lived there briefly to help Gerry with the finances of the Plunkett family real estate. The famous 'Castle' document was printed at Larkfield. It was from Larkfield that George and Jack Plunkett left with their battalion for Liberty Hall.

At Larkfield the Plunketts had twelve personal acres with five or six houses to fill with friends and political sympathizers. The political instabilities of the time kept the Plunketts circulating themselves and their large extended family among their many Dublin houses. Just before, during and just after the Rising, all the Plunketts were in a state of continual motion. Gerry moved from Larkfield the day of her wedding to the Imperial Hotel for one night, and then she and Tommy put their bicycles on top of a car, left their luggage in the Imperial (where later it was entirely burned) and went to live in their new marital home, a Plunkett property on Belgrave Road. Joseph Plunkett had been staying in Miss Keough's nursing home in Mountjoy after surgery for his tuberculosis; the night before the Rising he moved to the Metropole Hotel on O'Connell Street, and for the rest of the week his domicile was, of course, the GPO. Gerry seems to have spent much of the Rising moving people from one house to another. At the time of her wedding, she writes, 'I moved Tommy's mother, Mrs. Dillon, from Edenvale Road to 13 Belgrave Road' (p. 221). Her sister Fiona moved from Larkfield to Fitzwilliam Street and then later to Oakley Road to stay with Muriel MacDonagh. After the Rising, Gerry moved Grace Gifford (who had married Joe in Kilmainhaim jail hours before his execution) to Larkfield; then when she was advised to let Larkfield, she 'moved Grace to Fitzwilliam St'. By October she 'had moved Muriel MacDonagh and her children from Oakley Road to Marlborough Road and Mimi [the sister who had been in America carrying a message to John Devoy] moved in with them' (pp 247, 250). During

16 For more detailed information about activities at Larkfield, see Ann Matthews, *The Kimmage garrison, 1916: making billy-can bombs at Larkfield* (Dublin, 2010), p. 193.

the Rising itself, two Dillons, Tommy's sister-in-law and her daughter, took refuge with Gerry and Tommy on Belgrave Road (p. 227).

After the surrender, the count and countess were arrested from their Fitzwilliam Street house and moved to Richmond Barracks; the countess was then moved to Mountjoy. It was Gerry who carried items from home to prison for them, as the countess was evidently trying to make Mountjoy into a home away from home. She wrote to Gerry,

> Bring a few eggs and flowers if there are any in the garden – my steel knitting needles are in the basket in the dining room and some more coarse cotton – some hairpins and a penny looking glass … Some MS paper would be a boon and a green book on dining room table 'Ancient Civilization'. (p. 239)

Countess Plunkett was a wealthy woman used to living comfortably. Naturally she thought of ways to make her cell nicer – interior decoration, for instance, fresh flowers, 'if there are any in the garden'. She also needed protein, an activity to keep her hands from being idle, accessories for hair and grooming, writing material and her final thought, a green-covered book on ancient civilization. Countess Plunkett's requests itemized the minimum necessary to reconstitute 'home' in prison. With the flowers, eggs, hairpins and the rest, if Gerry brought them, she could construct an inner domestic space within the domestic site manqué of her Mountjoy cell. Her requests are womanly, inclining to the decorative and the aesthetic, handiwork with a touch of high culture in the book. Just as Kathleen Clarke asserted domesticity by working on Limerick lace, so Countess Plunkett would make her cell homey by knitting and reading. Meanwhile, her actual home was robbed. When looters were caught with jewellery, the countess 'identified some jewels brought to her as her mother's diamonds' (p. 239).[17]

---

17 Count Plunkett's requests are more limited and do not suggest an attempt to recreate a domestic site. The count (in Richmond Barracks) asked for 'a change of linen (set of woolens, socks, shirt, collars, cuffs), brush and comb, toothbrush, sponge, towel and soap. Also a tin of condensed milk and 1lb butter, which I need and £1 in small silver' (p. 236).

## At home in the Royal Hibernian Hotel and the GPO: Mary Louisa Hamilton Norway's *The Sinn Féin rebellion as I saw it*

During the Black and Tan terror, the Dillons were living in Galway, where the various houses they lived in were often raided. Sometimes Tommy Dillon would escape out the back as the soldiers arrived; sometimes the whole family would run to stay with friends. The Dillons were nomadic, moving from site to site whenever they needed to do so. In this respect they were opposite to the Hamilton Norways, whose possessions and domestic site were fragmented and dispersed while (in 1916) they stayed in one place. Mary Louisa Hamilton Norway's account of the Rising shows how even the home of moderate home rulers – a family that was part of the governing British bureaucracy in Dublin – became defined in terms of its military function.[18]

Mary Norway's domestic history in the year before the Rising was already one of disruption. In 1912, when Arthur Hamilton Norway was appointed secretary to the post office for Ireland, the family (Mary, Arthur and two sons, Frederick and Nevil, later the novelist Nevil Shute) moved from Ealing, in London, to South Hill, a large house in Blackrock that 'opened up new country pleasures' for them – a pony, hay carts, greenhouses, rambling outdoors. But after Frederick was killed in Ypres in 1915, the Blackrock house, in Nevil's words, 'held so many memories of Fred for my mother and myself that it [was] better to get rid of it and start again'.[19] To escape the memories, the Norways moved to the Royal Hibernian Hotel on Dawson Street, just where Molesworth Street crosses it. The Royal Hibernian was then 'the most fashionable first class hotel in Dublin'.[20]

From that time on, at least so long as they lived in Ireland, the Norways' domestic space was fragmented. Their furniture was in

---

18 Mary Louisa Hamilton, *The Sinn Féin rebellion as I saw it*, republished in Keith Jeffrey (ed.), *The Sinn Féin rebellion as they saw it* (Dublin, 1999), pp 35–85.   19 Quoted in Jeffrey (ed.), *The Sinn Féin rebellion*, p. 18.   20 As quoted in Máirtín Mac Con Iomaire, 'Kenneth George Besson' in James McGuire and James Quin (eds), *Dictionary of Irish biography* (Cambridge, 2009), i, p. 505.

storage, their clothes and a few personal items remained with them in their room at the hotel, and their most treasured possessions – not only family jewellery, silver and other heirlooms, but most importantly, 'all our dear F.'s books, sword, and all his possessions, which we value more than anything else in the world' – were put in 'the safest place in Dublin', Hamilton's office. The 'silver, old engravings, and other valuables were stored in the great mahogany cupboards', and Fred's belongings and Mrs Norway's jewel case were locked in the safe that was built into the wall of Hamilton's office in the GPO on Sackville Street (p. 41). So they slept, ate and 'lived' in a provisional home, a place for transients, while their lares and penates were hidden away in a public building.

During Easter week, there were more such disruptions in the Norways' lives. As Arthur Norway says in *his* account of the Rising, with the exception of the telephone office in Dame Street, 'there was no Post Office, save the room which I had commandeered at the Hibernian Hotel, and the Telephone circuit, which I had appropriated'.[21] So the Royal Hibernian Hotel was not only their temporary home; its sitting room was Hamilton Norway's temporary office and, therefore, in this time of unstable spatial categories, an 'official' space. On the Friday night of Easter week, that temporary office, the hotel's sitting room, also became the Norways' safe-deposit box. There were so many snipers around and so many bullets flying that all the residents of the hotel were required to leave their rooms. Mrs Norway brought down the few valuables she had left in her room – '[Fred's] miniature and the presentation portrait of him, my despatch case with his letters, my fur coat, hat and boots' – and stored them in the sitting room, which had now become, by default, the new 'safest place in Dublin' (p. 58). All the residents of the hotel were crowded into the lounge, where most of them spent the night, although the Norways 'crept' back up to their room.

Although the Norways did not live in the GPO (unless you count the week when the Royal Hibernian Hotel functioned as both their

21 Arthur Hamilton Norway, 'Irish experiences in war' in Jeffrey (ed.), *The Sinn Féin rebellion*, p. 117.

home and the GPO), Hamilton Norway had put a certain amount of time and energy into reconstructing it, and they both felt a vested interest in its new elegance:

> When we came here H. was scandalised at the condition of the G.P.O. The whole frontage was given up to sorting offices, and the public office was in a side street, a miserable, dirty little place, that would have been a disgrace to a small country town.
>
> H. found that plans had been drawn up and passed for the complete reconstruction of the interior […]
>
> So H. *hustled*, and the work was completed and opened to the public six weeks ago.
>
> It was really beautiful. The roof was a large glass dome, with elaborate plaster work, beautiful white pillars, mosaic floor, counters all of red teak wood, and bright brass fittings everywhere – a public building of which any great city might be proud; and in six weeks all that is left is a smoking heap of ashes! (p. 67)

The rebels had commandeered this building not because of its interior decoration, of course, but because it was strategically central. They could not have known (or cared) that a tiny part of the building was one of the scattered fragments of the Norways' domestic site.

Joyce says of Mrs Kearney in 'A mother', that she thought her husband 'as secure and fixed as the General Post Office'. The reverse could be said of Mrs Norway: she thought the General Post Office 'as secure and fixed' as her husband. He was in charge of it, he had redecorated it, and after the Great War began, by his order it had a guard of soldiers ready 'to shoot to stop' any 'unidentified person' heading towards the instrument room. The safe that Mrs Norway considered so 'safe', a miniature site hidden within the walls of an office in a public building, was nested within the seemingly protective layers of family, nation and empire. She maintained a kind of faith even when, on Friday of Easter week, she thought the fire had destroyed everything. She was pleased that 'When the rebels took possession they demanded the keys from the man who had them in charge. He quietly handed over the keys, having first abstracted the keys of H's room!' (p. 55)

Mrs Norway's domestic life was so fragmented spatially that she could not keep track of her possessions. They were dispersed to so many cases, boxes and buildings that she could not remember what was where, and her access to them seems always to have been at several removes and mediated by someone else. On Sunday after the surrender, she discovered, to her immense relief, that some of the valuables she feared were in the GPO were in fact in the hotel, in another case:

> When we came back from Italy in March, H. brought back from the office my large despatch-case in which I keep all [Fred's] letters. I did not remember what else was in it, so I investigated and found my necklet with jewelled cross and the pink topaz set ... also the large old paste buckle ... But, best of all, there were the three little handkerchiefs F. sent me from Armentières with my initial worked on them; for these I was grieving more than for anything, and when I found them the relief was so great I sat with them in my hand and cried. (p. 62)

The pathos here and in so many places in Mrs Norway's letters comes from her apparent lack of agency: the possessions that mean the most to her seem to disappear and reappear almost as if of their own volition.

That 'safest place in Dublin' was ground zero of a surprise revolution, and when Mrs Norway believes there is nothing left of the things she had stored in the safe, she writes, 'I think I am past caring about any possessions now. F. and all his precious things are gone. Nothing else seems worth considering' (p. 77). But on 20 May 1916, as she watches the excavations of her husband's office, some of those things emerge. A Mr Noblett, Hamilton's trusted employee, shows her 'a great lump of molten glass', which she realizes must have been 'the cut-glass bottles in the large rosewood and brass-bound dressing-case in which I had packed all my jewellery'. Then,

When I went down again in the afternoon Noblett produced three little brooches that F. had given me on various birthdays when a wee boy. He always went out with his own sixpence, and nearly always returned with a brooch, which I used to wear with great pride. One, a Swastika brooch, he gave me when he was at Margate after that terrible illness, and he used to go on the pier in his bath-chair. The blue enamel on it was intact in several places; the other two were intact in form, but charred and black, with the pins burnt off. But how glad I was to see them again! (p. 78)

This vignette of the mourning mother rejoicing over the return of her dead son's childhood birthday presents to her, rejoicing in the ruins of a building where a rebellion has just taken place, forms an image that is startling because of its juxtapositions. Its peculiar power comes, I think, from juxtapositions of scale – the small brooches and the vast vacant shell of the GPO, the tiny moment of personal memory and the large forces of national history. It comes also, of course, from each side's obliviousness: Mrs Norway was as unaware of the rebels' griefs and joys as they were of hers. And what of the building itself? For this brief time, it is no longer a rebel bastion; it is not yet restored as a working post office, nor is it yet restored as a monument to Irish nationalist struggles. Enclosing as it does the relics of Frederick Norway, as well as the ashes of whatever items the rebels left there, the entire building has become, in effect, a giant reliquary.

The last 'find' from the excavations that Norway mentions is another kind of reliquary, a rich and complex emblem. Near the end of her final letter, Norway says,

Noblett gave me to-day one of Princess Mary's gift boxes that had been sent to me by a soldier at the front; except for being black instead of bright brass, it was absolutely uninjured – the medallion in the centre, and the inscription, date, etc. perfect. The Christmas card inside and the Queen's letter were just black charred paper, but you could see the M. and the crown above it on the card. (pp 79–80)

The idea for this box came from the seventeen-year-old Princess Mary, who thought that 'everyone wearing the King's uniform and serving overseas' in 1914 should receive a Christmas present 'from the nation'. It was funded by public subscription and contained – variously – tobacco, a pipe, a lighter, cigarettes, chocolate and a Christmas card from the Queen wishing the sailors and soldiers a 'victorious new year'.[22]

A gendered reading of this box might see it as a sign of the young Mary's emergent maternal feelings: she contributes to the male territorial war by sending sweets and pleasures to the men who may die for the nation. Her female nurturing instinct finds a place alongside the male killer instinct. An imperialist reading would see the survival of the box 'uninjured' as a miracle, a sign of the empire's ability to withstand the assaults of its enemies. An anti-imperialist reading might see it, with the benefit of hindsight, as a miniature of the GPO, a charred box, a blackened shell, its structure intact but its contents ruined. For Mrs Norway, it offered one final possession that her home away from home had protected.

\* \* \*

Looking at spaces that are architecturally private but functionally military offers a useful way of considering the Rising. It was a time when the boundaries of all enclosed spaces, not just those of the home, were disrupted and changed, and when substitutions and improvisations meant that spatial categories were unstable. Mary Louisa Norway tells the story of a man who moved his bed from the bedroom to his attic, placing it right under the trapdoor to the roof, so that if the rebel soldiers on the roof tried to enter, they would fall on top of him (p. 51). Meals were cooked and confessions heard in

22 See, for example, https://www.yorkcastlemuseum.org.uk/collections/collections-highlights/princess-marys-1914-christmas-gift, accessed 24 Mar. 2017.

the GPO; the rosary was said and people slept in the Jacob's Biscuits factory.[23] While the Volunteers occupied the GPO, postal functions continued, to a limited extent, in a room at the Royal Hibernian Hotel; after the surrender, the mail was sorted at a skating rink behind the Rotunda. General Maxwell ate his midday dinners in the provost's dining room, and as Elsie Mahaffy, another 1916 diarist, writes, 'The Provost's house became an inn.'[24] The emphasis on home and on domestic space in all these women's accounts is consistent with that larger vision of unstable spatial categories in the built environment. It also shows that the GPO-centred, bullet-centred, dead-horse-centred narrative of the Rising is incomplete, and that the notion, the discourse and the actual space of home are fundamental to the story.

---

**23** Maire Nic Shiubhlaigh, *The splendid years* (Dublin, 1955), pp 175–6. **24** TCD, MARL, MS 2074, Mahaffy, 'The Irish rebellion'.

# The house that never blew up: Maeve Brennan's Dublin home

## Angela Bourke

In Maeve Brennan's celebrated posthumous collection *The springs of affection* (*SA* hereafter), almost all the action takes place in the same small terraced house in Ranelagh, on Dublin's south side.[1] Even 'The devil in us', set in a grim convent boarding school, implies that house by separation from it. Three different families enact piercing, exquisite dramas in the same setting of doors, walls, stairs, windows, furniture, sunlight, shadows and daily activities, all evoked in meticulous, tactile detail.

Like those in *The rose garden* (*RG*), these stories originally appeared in the *New Yorker*, where Brennan was a staff writer for some thirty years from 1949.[2] 'The beginning of a long story' appeared in the magazine on 4 February 1961, but she may have written it much earlier, before the stories of the Brennans, the Derdons and the Bagots.[3] It tells of a different family, with three little girls, but no surname, in a small, cold, respectable row house in Dublin. Bridget, aged 4, is the youngest, and she can't be left alone in the bathroom, because its door has a glass panel that is pasted over on the inside with shiny translucent paper patterned in red and green diamonds, and because:

1 Maeve Brennan, *The springs of affection: stories of Dublin*, introduction by William Maxwell (New York, 1997). References below are to this American edition. *The springs of affection*, introduction by Anne Enright (Dublin, 2016), published just ahead of Brennan's centenary, has different pagination. 2 Maeve Brennan, *The rose garden* (Washington, DC, 2000). 3 For Brennan's life and discussion of her writings in their chronological contexts, see Angela Bourke, *Maeve Brennan: homesick at the* New Yorker (London, 2004).

she would tear the paper off, reaching up and tearing off little bits that she would lick and paste to her face so that she could run around the house saying, 'Look at me. Who am I? No, no, I am not Bridget. No, I am not a strange little woman. No, I am not the child next door. I am a bathroom window.' (*RG*, p. 212)

Brennan is describing 48 Cherryfield Avenue, Ranelagh, the house she lived in as a child. Her many depictions of this house recall Gaston Bachelard's meditation on the ways a childhood home becomes a lifelong reference point for the human imagination, his insistence that 'the house is one of the greatest powers of integration for the thoughts, memories and dreams of mankind'.[4]

According to John McGahern:

a writer writes out of his private world, and that is more or less shaped by the time one is twenty, twenty-one or twenty-two. Everything that happens to you changes you, but that private world is essentially shaped and one always works on that.[5]

Maeve Brennan wrote her stories in New York's glamorous post-Prohibition, post-war world of magazines and martinis, but the frugal family life she had known in Dublin until she was almost 18 was what shaped her private world.[6] In the autumn of 1934, after her father's sudden appointment to a diplomatic post in Washington, DC, she crossed the Atlantic with her mother and siblings to join him there. Constantly revisiting the past, her writing registers the shock of that deracination. Stories about the Brennans, Bagots and Derdons animate the modest Dublin interior in the early years of political independence just as James Joyce's writings did earlier for the city's streets and public spaces. Her superb depiction of the ways physical and social structures choreograph behaviour, thinking and

4 Gaston Bachelard, *The poetics of space*, trans. Maria Jolas (Boston, 1994), p. 6.  5 Rosa González, 'John McGahern' in Jacqueline Hurtley et al. (eds), *Ireland in writing: interviews with writers and academics* (Amsterdam, 1998), p. 42.  6 For the alternatives to domesticity that single women found in mid-twentieth-century New York, see Ann Peters, 'A traveler in residence: Maeve Brennan and the last days of New York', *Women's Studies Quarterly*, 33:3/4 (2005), 66–89.

power relations – what Pierre Bourdieu calls *habitus* – is perhaps her greatest gift to Irish literature and to our understanding of twentieth-century social history.[7]

Brennan lived in Cherryfield Avenue from late 1921, when she was almost five and the Anglo-Irish Treaty had just been signed in London, until she left Ireland. Her parents, Robert and Una Brennan, had both taken part in the 1916 Rising in Co. Wexford. Robert was in prison in England when his second daughter was born in January 1917. Taking the anti-treaty side in the new Irish Free State, he was often away from his family, on the run and earning little, during their first years in the house. From 1926, however, he played a leading role in setting up Eamon de Valera's Fianna Fáil party and especially its newspaper, the *Irish Press*. He was general manager there until February 1934, when de Valera, now head of the Free State government, appointed him secretary of the Irish legation in Washington. The following September, after Maeve had finished secondary school, and Paddy Morrissey, general secretary of Fianna Fáil, had agreed to buy their house, Una embarked for the US with her daughters – Emer, 23, 17-year-old Maeve and Derry, almost 16 – and their 6-year-old brother, Robert Patrick. Maeve would attend college in Washington and help her mother to entertain for the legation, before leaving home in her twenties. War in Europe kept her family in Washington longer than expected, but she had moved to New York for good.

\* \* \*

William Maxwell became Maeve Brennan's fiction editor at the *New Yorker*. He worked with many Irish writers, including Frank O'Connor and Mary Lavin, but once remarked privately that he thought Brennan was the best of them.[8] He wrote an introduction for *The springs of affection* in 1997, remembering her presence, her

---

7 Pierre Bourdieu, *The logic of practice*, trans. Richard Nice (Stanford, CA, 1990), pp 52–65.
8 Bourke, *Maeve Brennan*, p. 244.

preoccupations and the Dublin house he had never seen, which he called 'her imagination's home':

> It has a bow window and there is a tiny grass plot in front, a walled garden in back with flowers and a yellow laburnum. The front door leads into a narrow hall. Past the stairs, down three steps, is the kitchen. The front and back sitting-rooms are separated by folding doors. One room is heated by a coal-burning fireplace, the other by a gas fire. Upstairs there is linoleum on the floor of the back bedroom, none in the front one.[9]

He might have added that there was a beige carpet with a pattern of big pink roses on the floor of the front sitting room, for it appears in several of Brennan's stories about a family called Bagot. In one of these, the short, lyrical, more-or-less-happy 'The day we got our own back', a long spell of dry weather inspires Mrs Bagot to drag that carpet all the way through the house and lay it on the grass of the back garden, to brush and beat it clean without risk of grass stains, keeping the dog and the two children indoors out of mischief. Exhausted after that heavy work, she falls asleep upstairs with her younger daughter, and 7-year-old Lily goes quietly out to lie on the carpet.

Turning the house inside out sets Lily's imagination free. Indoors on the bare floor, she follows a precious penny down between the floorboards into the darkness and thinks she might get it back if the house blew up. In the garden, the carpet becomes magic and flies her away from all constraint, to Paris and to Spain. She has pestered her mother about the house blowing up, and getting the money back. Mrs Bagot has acknowledged that the house might blow up, but then told her firmly that it can't, because they are living in it. The carpet flies her safely back to the garden, and drowsily, the story ends, 'Never, never. That house never blew up' (*SA*, p. 239).

In 'The sofa', Lily is nine and it is winter. The old piano (mentioned in other stories, with ornaments arranged on top, but

---

9 William Maxwell, introduction in Brennan, *Springs of affection*, p. 7.

nobody playing) has been taken away to make space for a new, fat, beige sofa that will match the carpet's background. The absence of furniture makes the children, the dog and even the mother giddy. The sofa will face the fireplace, which has golden brown tiles and a brass fender with a filigree panel running all around its three sides, between bars that are flat, not round as in the back sitting room. At two in the afternoon, with the children at school, their mother sits in a low chair in the back room, waiting for the delivery. As in several other stories, the fire is already laid: 'paper, sticks of wood, lumps of coal, all in neat bumpy layers, ready to blaze up and spit sparks at the touch of a match'. This second fireplace has pale, greenish tiles, and a hearthrug, 'thin and fringed … woven in a dark Oriental pattern of red and green lines, circles, curlicues, and unfinished curves', laid on top of the 'diligently domestic red-green-and-brown linoleum', with its pattern of fleurs-de-lis (*SA*, pp 255–6).

The Brennans' new house, just ten years old when they moved in, should have meant independence and stability at last, in family life as in politics, but while the 1921 treaty established an Irish Free State, it also laid down the land border between it and the six northern counties that would remain in the United Kingdom. The lasting, bitter, political division that followed, between republicans like the Brennans and the 'Free Staters' who held power throughout the 1920s, would last for generations and immediately began to take its toll on personal happiness. For women like Una Brennan, idealistic activists relegated to domesticity by the relentlessly conservative men who now dominated both factions, the new regime brought only disillusionment.[10]

With the precision of intense emotion and geographical distance, Brennan's fiction recalls the domestic spaces she grew up in and the relationships they housed. Her best stories give epic proportions to small encounters between people who live at close quarters, their quiet desperation expressed as much in the spaces they move in and the surfaces they touch as in the words they speak. The rooms, stairs and hallway of the house her family lived in, its furniture and

10 Bourke, *Maeve Brennan*, pp 130–1.

fireplaces and small gardens front and back, become the settings not only for childhood dramas, but also for chilling descriptions of adult fury and frustration, confined explosively by the limitations of gentility, hope and fear. Her fictional characters often reflect that they have been kept in ignorance of some secret code, some 'ticket' that has been provided for other adults, but not for them.[11] Marriages contracted in happy optimism collapse when confined within the house's walls, and yet there is no escape. For her mother's generation, this was a political reality, copper-fastened by de Valera's constitution of 1937. Like her own life in hotels and rented rooms, Brennan's stories suggest that people would be happier, and might realize their dreams, if they never bought a house.

* * *

The sort of house Maeve Brennan wrote about and described in detail again and again was built in rows, or 'terraces', in towns and cities all over Ireland and Britain in the nineteenth century, first as a high-density response to the influx of workers from the countryside to jobs in mills and factories, then to accommodate a rising middle class. In Dublin, most terraced houses are of red brick, brought as ballast across the Irish Sea by the ships that carried Ireland's cattle to Britain. The smallest of these – flat-fronted, with two rooms downstairs and two above – open directly off the street, and originally housed manual labourers. Houses built for white-collar workers and the better-off are separated from the street by waist-high iron railings and front gardens; many have bay windows in front. Symmetrical side-by-side porches shelter pairs of front doors that open between glazed panels, under glazed transoms, into long narrow hallways. Two rooms open off one side of each hall, often with double doors between; a staircase lies straight ahead on the opposite side beyond them. Alongside it, the narrow passage may borrow space from the back room on its way to the kitchen, often two or three steps down,

11 Ibid., p. 204.

where the original tiled floors were laid directly on the earth. The largest of these houses, with two or three imposing storeys at the front and a right-angled 'return' at the back, could accommodate an extended family in considerable style. Many have an original attic room too, with its own staircase, and a skylight in the back of the pitched roof, where one or more resident servants once slept.

Ranelagh belonged to the nineteenth-century township of Rathmines, between the Grand Canal and the Dodder River, and the Brennans' house was one of the last of that narrow, vertical design.[12] Built in 1911, as the city expanded along its tram routes, its fabric was not red brick, but breeze block, made of coal cinders from the gasworks that supplied fuel for most of Dublin's cooking by then, and for much of its artificial light. The blocks, formerly used only for garden walls, were covered with a render of grey cement, moulded to look like stone. Modern homeowners have painted the fronts of these houses in ice-cream colours and shades of white, but Brennan's 'The beginning of a long story' tells how her family's house looked in the 1920s:

> a small plain house in a row, faced from the other side of the terrace by a row of other houses just like it, all made alike of undistinguished gray stone with slate roofs and tiny front gardens protected by iron railings. It was a very ordinary house, a regulation uniform for the lives of certain families at a certain stage in their lives. It was better than a workingman's house but not good enough for a successful man and his family to live in. It was a clerk's house, and the man who lived in it was a government clerk. (*RG*, pp 204–5)

With a little over 900 square feet of living space, this house held onto some features of the gentleman's residence. On the front door, the knocker, doorknob and letter box were plated with brass, like the fireplace fenders in the living rooms. The third bedroom was tiny and

12 The township of Rathmines and Rathgar became part of the city of Dublin under the Local Government (Dublin) Act of 1930, when its administration was taken over by Dublin City Council.

separate, intended to house a maid, who could be summoned from the kitchen by means of electric bell pushes on either side of the fireplace in the front sitting room. Thirty-eight of these houses had been built and occupied when the census of population was taken on 2 April 1911; twelve had live-in maids, most of them teenage girls. Eleven of the twelve maids were Roman Catholics, although only seven Catholic families lived on the street – a religious and class divide that further underlined its respectability.[13]

Maeve Brennan's family had no maid. Her mother did all the heavy housework, as the women do in her Dublin stories, but the design of their house dictated old-fashioned behaviours that were starting to feel oppressive, and at least to some people, ridiculous. Few houses were built in Dublin for twenty years after 1911. The war in Europe, the 'Troubles' and finally, a contested independence in the impoverished Free State, posed serious challenges to domestic life. When builders grew courageous again in the 1930s, instead of terraces punctuated by vertical windows, and door-cases reached by narrow garden paths, they built pairs of semi-detached houses with wide horizontal windows, their front doors as far from each other as possible. Gates wide enough to admit a car marked radical changes in the way people had learned to live.[14]

Like brass fenders, 'brasses' on front doors quickly tarnished to black, requiring regular vigorous rubbing with Brasso, whose classic metal bottle, with blue-and-white sunburst surrounding a scarlet label, has been familiar in households since the early twentieth century. Stair rods too were brass, holding down the strips of carpet that were essential if next-door neighbours were not to complain about echoing footsteps behind the party wall. Several of Brennan's stories mention the business of cleaning those rods, usually on Mondays. 'The beginning of a long story' recounts another tale about the irrepressible Bridget:

13 For digitized documents of the Irish census returns of 1901 and 1911, see http://www.census.national archives.ie/search, accessed 28 Feb. 2017.   14 For a discussion of the values represented by the British semi-detached house of the 1930s, and its design, which was enthusiastically adopted in Ireland, see Paul Oliver et al., *Dunroamin: the suburban semi and its enemies* (London, 1981).

There was dark-red carpet on the stairs, held in place by brass rods. The mother polished the brass rods every week, starting at the top and kneeling on every step on her way down. It was not a long way. One time she had taken all the rods out of the stairs and had taken them down to the kitchen to give them all a proper cleaning and Bridget had worked her way in under the carpet and had sat there on the bare stair, making a big lump under the carpet, and nobody could go up or come down. (*RG*, pp 205–6)

The older children are delighted with this escapade, but shining brass is code for an excruciating complexity of social unease and marital tension:

When the father heard the story, when he came home that evening, he laughed and said it served the mother right for working too hard and trying to do too much.

'If it isn't the brass rods on the stairs,' he said, 'it's the brasses on the front door. And if it isn't the brasses on the front door, it's something else. You'll wear yourself out.'

The mother replied that nothing made a house look as neglected as neglected brass. She added that it was very important to keep up the appearance of a place, especially here in Dublin, where the people were only looking for an excuse to look down on you. (*RG*, p. 208)

The father is not amused; he quickly becomes angry. Brennan's use of indirect speech for the mother suggests that her words were often repeated: as familiar to her children as the fleurs-de-lis on the 'diligently domestic' oilcloth in their back room.

In 'The day we got our own back', an autobiographical story about the Brennan family, we learn that when Free State soldiers raided the house on Cherryfield Avenue in search of Robert Brennan for the second time, in 1923:

My mother was getting along with her housework, and she had an apron tied around her waist. She had shined the brass rods that held our red stair carpet in place, and now she was polishing the oilcloth on the dining-room floor. (*SA*, pp 39–40)

Brennan writes about contentment and warmth in the rooms of the house and the back garden, but in her most memorable stories, anger, uncertainty and misunderstanding swirl coldly through the hall and up the stairs. Hall and stairs are areas of circulation – the places in the house that hold its functions and its occupants apart from one another, but where they must inevitably meet if anything is to move.

The front garden, on the other hand – 'the tiny plot of ground, hardly bigger than a tablecloth', where Brennan's timid Rose Derdon grew 'peonies, poppies and crocuses, and a diamond of frail new grass' (*SA*, p. 134) – is almost never occupied. Fully visible from the street, it is a zone that allows the public world to assess the social conformity of those within the house, even as it protects them from that world. Reinforcing the family's retreat from public spaces, the front sitting room in these stories, with its window so near the street, is rarely used, but a collection of ferns stands there, inside the starched white net curtains. Tended daily, this frail green barrier gives the mothers an excuse to observe what is going on, without displaying vulgar curiosity.[15]

In Brennan's devastating 'Family walls', Hubert Derdon turns his key in the lock of his front door, as he does at the same time every evening:

He felt in good health and good humor, and contented to be coming home after his day's work, and he was smiling as he stepped into the hall. There were red glass panels in the side frames of the front door, and he was always aware of the glass and always closed the door carefully. At the same instant that

---

15 See Irene Cieraad, 'Dutch windows: female virtue and female vice' in Irene Cieraad (ed.), *At home: an anthology of domestic spaces* (Syracuse, NY, 1999), pp 31–52.

he was hanging his raincoat on the rack, he looked down the hall and saw the kitchen door close quickly and quietly, but not quickly enough to prevent him seeing that Rose was down there. Her head was turned away from him as she closed the door. (*SA*, p. 172)

Older, better, terraced houses had patterns of leaded stained glass in their front doors and door surrounds. Closing the door so as not to risk damaging the red glass, Hubert has shown the same care for the modest fabric of his home as the wives do in all these stories. Now, however, trembling with anger, he goes into the back room, where he listens intently for sounds from below. He hears the kitchen door open, and Rose comes up the three steps to the room where he sits by the fire:

When Rose appeared in the doorway, Hubert felt such dislike that he smiled. He saw the confusion caused by the smile, and he saw her hand fasten on the doorknob as her hand always fastened on something – the back of a chair or her other hand – before she spoke. (*SA*, p. 174)

Hubert refuses to eat the food Rose has prepared – he has eaten his main meal in town at midday as usual – but later he finds that she has left him a tray:

There on the dining-room table, which they kept folded against the wall opposite the fireplace, she had left a tray. He went over and looked at it. Brown bread and a slice of ham. She had taken the time to shape the butter into curly balls. A tomato. Three chocolate biscuits. The teapot was at the fireplace, sitting inside the fender with the cozy over it. (*SA*, p. 190)

Brennan's stories deal much more with cleaning than with cooking or eating, but this is not the only one to mention the table folded by the wall. Drop-leaf, or gate-legged, dining tables were popular, and could be opened fully to seat six people when necessary.

The back room of a house like the one she describes was not large enough to accommodate a full-size table along with fireside chairs – and a fireside was the only comfortable place to sit in winter. It would be decades before Irish houses were built with central heating, and decades more before heating systems were retrofitted to houses like this one. All the main rooms in terraced houses had fireplaces, but most families lit only the kitchen fire in the morning, letting it die down later in the day. The fire in the back sitting room was lit in the late afternoon, and there the family sat together, leaving the front sitting room for special occasions, for children's piano practice or, as in Brennan's childhood home, for a display of ferns. In 'The beginning of a long story' it is winter, and the middle daughter, Johanna, is home from school with a cold:

> The mother had a fire going in the back bedroom for Johanna, who was in bed there, and the coal range was going all day in the kitchen, but the other rooms in the house were cold. The front sitting room was cold. The back sitting room, which they also called the dining room, was cold. The front bedroom, where the mother and father slept in their big brass bed, was cold. The bathroom, halfway up the stairs, was cold, and the little room they called the boxroom, next to the bathroom, was cold and felt damp. The narrow, linoleum-covered hall that led from the kitchen to the front door was like a dungeon, it was so cold. (*SA*, p. 205)

Brennan's Dublin stories tell us repeatedly that the kitchen of her childhood home was small and square, with a red tiled floor, a coal-fired range for heat and a gas stove for cooking. They never mention a refrigerator. Women bought fresh food daily and cooked it plainly, usually by boiling. They washed dishes and did laundry without the aid of machines, and if the weather was wet, hung clothes to dry in the heat from the kitchen range. In 'The beginning of a long story', 'The arms of the father's shirts hung down like streamers, stiff and dry, and brushed the mother's light-brown hair as she moved about the kitchen' (*RG*, p. 212).

Women ate in the kitchen with their children, and sometimes Rose and Hubert Derdon eat there together, but in general, men enter kitchens rarely. In larger houses, a door at the bottom of the steps from the hall led directly outdoors. Men never had to enter the kitchen in those houses.

Women went 'out the back' every day: in summer to tend the garden, watch over children and hang out laundry; in winter, whatever the weather, they went out to fetch fuel:

> They kept the coal and the firewood, together with her garden things, in a small wooden shed that was attached to the back of the house. Every day she carried in two scuttles of coal, one made of iron, for the kitchen stove, and one made of brass, for the sitting room. She sometimes wondered, when she lifted the coal, if Hubert had any idea how heavy it was. (*SA*, p. 159)

After fires had been lit, and had burned down, there were grates to be cleaned. Ash and cinders had to be removed to the dustbin in the back garden, and hearth tiles washed (*SA*, p. 169). Unlike older terraced houses, Cherryfield Avenue had no back lane or rear access, so the full dustbin had to be carried through the house every week for emptying by 'bin men' at the front. When coal was delivered, half a ton at a time, the coalmen carried it in sacks on their shoulders, through the hall and the corner of the kitchen to the shed, their faces, hands, boots and clothing black from its dust. The floors had to be cleaned after these operations – the porous red 'quarry' tiles washed and the hall linoleum polished again.

At the top of the hall stairs in a house like this, a small landing – barely big enough for Mrs Bagot's rough-haired white terrier, Bennie, to lie down – leads straight ahead to the 'boxroom' of Brennan's stories (*SA*, pp 223–4). The bathroom is beside it, tucked in next to the main part of the house, with its own window in the side of the return. The upper part of kitchen and bathroom doors was usually fitted with obscure glass, to allow some daylight into dark lobbies and landings. Translucent patterned paper, such as 4-year-old Bridget pasted to her forehead, imitated the stained glass used in grander homes; it was a low-cost way to achieve privacy. Larger houses have a full-size bedroom, or even two, above the kitchen, but few of those built before 1880 had a bathroom. The Public Health Act of 1878 provided for public sewerage and indoor sanitation, following similar legislation in England. It was introduced after the prince of Wales (later King Edward VII) contracted typhoid in Yorkshire in 1871. Owners of older houses sacrificed bedroom space to install bathrooms. Previously, they had washed in tin baths before the fire in a bedroom or kitchen, and used outdoor privies or 'earth closets', which 'night-soil' men emptied at intervals via a network of back lanes. At night, they used chamber pots, and the duties of a housemaid included emptying the pots into the privy.[16] Thirty years after bathrooms had become obligatory, the builder of Cherryfield Avenue economized on land by doing without back entrances.

From the return landing outside the bathroom door, a shorter flight of stairs doubles back to the upper floor of the main building, with doors to the front and back bedrooms. Brennan's fiction describes the back bedroom in detail: it was where she slept, with her sisters, and where the children sleep in most of her stories, sharing one big bed or using two small, narrow ones, sometimes with a cot. The exceptions are the stories of Rose and Hubert Derdon, whose cossetted son John has the big bedroom at the front, leaving his parents to share a brass bed, with a bolster and a patchwork quilt that Rose made as a schoolgirl, in the smaller back room, roughly eleven feet square.

This back bedroom has a big, rectangular sliding-sash window, the sill of which is only a foot above the floor. Small children can easily look out at the tennis players in the club that lies beyond their garden wall, and Rose, when she has been ill and sits in a chair, can lie back on cushions and watch the sky. The window has a roller blind for privacy, and curtains that the children's mother has sewed; in one story, a child's toy sewing machine stands on its inside ledge. Beside the window is a small table, 'all marked and stained with chalk and ink and putty and plasticine' (*SA*, p. 242). The wallpaper is cream-

**16** Mona Hearn, 'How Victorian families lived' in Mary E. Daly et al., *Dublin's Victorian houses* (Dublin, 1998), pp 83–4.

coloured, patterned with garlands of blue flowers that have faded by the time the children are old enough to notice. There is a chest of drawers with a small framed mirror on top and, of course, a fireplace.

The front bedroom has a fireplace too. That room spans the full width of the house, and boasts a three-sectioned bay window like the sitting room below it. It is the best room. A dressing table with drawers stands in the window recess; brushes, combs and mirrors are arranged on top of it, in front of the mirror. A big brass bed dominates the room, covered with an elaborate and precious patchwork quilt, which the children are not allowed to sit on, for fear of damaging it. The 'Long story' that began in the *New Yorker* in 1961 and continues throughout Maeve Brennan's 'Bagot' stories is about how a couple who have started out sharing this bed, and whose children have been born in it, come to sleep separately. The wife frets, placates and stays silent as the husband gradually detaches himself; eventually, he moves permanently into the cold, damp boxroom, to sleep in a small, lumpy bed alongside his books and maps and gramophone records. His wife continues to occupy the master bedroom, but is sometimes cold at night.

*** 

After the Brennans went to America, the next child to live in 48 Cherryfield Avenue was Eamon Morrissey, whose father, Paddy, bought it when they left. Born in 1943, Eamon was an only child. His mother was another Maeve, keenly aware of her literary namesake. She called her 'the great Maeve Brennan', buying the glossy *New Yorker* when it featured her stories for the extravagant pleasure of reading them in the rooms where they were set. She encouraged her son to read and admire them, but as he recalls in his one-man show, *Maeve's house*, 'I was young. I wanted to look out and discover the world, not experience what it was like to walk down the three steps from our hallway into the kitchen.'[17]

17 *Maeve's house*, written and performed by Eamon Morrissey, premiered on the Abbey Theatre's Peacock stage, Dublin, 24 Sept. 2013.

At the end of September 1966 Eamon Morrissey was a young actor in New York, travelling by subway from Brooklyn Heights to Broadway, to play Ned in Brian Friel's *Philadelphia, here I come!* He was somewhere under the East River, deep in the latest *New Yorker* in the clatter of the train, when the words on the page told of a man called Martin Bagot, coming home late, trying not to wake his household. The hairs on the back of his neck stood up, he recalls, as he read.

Martin Bagot 'let himself into the dim hall and hurried up the stairs without touching the banister, which creaked loudly in the silence of the night as it had done on the first day he and Delia walked into the house, when it was empty and full of hollow sounds' (*SA*, p. 227). Morrissey had known that banister all his life; knew too that no family called Bagot had ever lived in his family home. Fact and fiction merged, equally believable. Looking to the end of the story, he knew its author had to be Maeve Brennan; looking around at her adopted city, he resolved to contact her.

They met once, in the Russian Tea Room. More than forty years later, when his acting career was long established and Brennan's work had been revived, Morrissey turned that meeting, his epiphany, his own memories of home and his reading of her work and life into the one-man show that enthralled audiences at Dublin's Abbey Theatre in 2013. *Maeve's house* is named for his mother and for Brennan; he has since performed it in New York and Cork, with a revival in Dublin in 2014.[18]

Dublin's terraced houses grew shabby in the 1960s and 1970s as their occupants aged: young families preferred the new suburbs on the city's outskirts, with their well-lit, centrally heated, semi-detached homes. Old houses were carved into flats and bedsits for young workers and students, until traffic congestion, improved building techniques and a growing awareness of heritage made them attractive again – with modifications. When Maeve Brennan lived in Cherryfield Avenue, the boxroom looked out onto the roof of the shed, where the cats dozed in warm weather. This was where the privy was located in

18 Roy Greenslade, 'Morrissey on Maeve: how a house linked an author and an actor', *Guardian*, 2 Sept. 2014.

many older houses – the main reason why the kitchen of a terraced house was always dark, with a chimney, instead of a window, in its end wall. Mystifying in smaller, newer houses, this design quirk made sense in older, larger ones, where the kitchen had been the province of the maids. Servants were not encouraged to observe their employers' leisure, or, indeed, their visits to the privy. Instead of looking onto the garden, therefore, original kitchen windows in terraced houses look out on the narrow, paved yard beside the return. They face the high wall a few yards away that marks the edge of the property, and look up at the windows of their neighbours' bathrooms.

During the property boom of the early twenty-first century, many of the houses on Cherryfield Avenue changed hands for over a million euro. Most then underwent expensive makeovers, for young families, single people and couples without children. New owners were not prepared to act out the gentilities and separations dictated by their houses. They gravelled the front gardens, planting lavender and sculptural grasses. They built glazed, skylit, open-plan kitchen-living rooms across back gardens and paved what remained, installing outdoor seating, raised beds for planting, subtle lighting, gas barbecues and patio heaters. They opened up attic spaces with new stairs and skylights. Boxrooms made way for spa-style bathrooms, while extra bathrooms, tiny, but perfectly formed, found space in the corners of front bedrooms, or under the stairs.

Two architects from the UCD School of Architecture have documented these changes to the housing stock of Dublin's inner suburbs, noting that while employing an architect to design a house extension is a decision made by individuals, this happened on a scale that turned it into a common endeavour. They quote Bourdieu on the subject of *habitus*: 'Each agent, wittingly or unwittingly, is a producer and reproducer of objective meaning ... It is because subjects do not, strictly speaking, know what they are doing that what they do has more meaning than they know.'[19] Maeve Brennan's Dublin characters

19 Pierre Bourdieu, *Outline of a theory of practice* (Cambridge, 1977), p. 79, quoted in Michael Pike and Emmett Scanlon, '*Habitus*: a social anthropology of the contemporary house extension' in Elizabeth FitzPatrick and James Kelly (eds), *Domestic life in Ireland*, Proceedings of the Royal Irish Academy, section C, vol. 111 (Dublin, 2011), p. 336.

don't know what they are doing either, but her depiction of them brilliantly illuminates the gloomy interior of the Irish Free State's culture, its unhappy, frustrated women and its silences, hidden angers and power struggles.

# The vibrancy of first houses in the poetry of Seamus Heaney and Derek Mahon

## Adam Hanna

'My last things will be first things slipping from me,' wrote Seamus Heaney.[1] Like many people's 'first things', Heaney's could be found in his memories of his first house. Famously, the objects in and around the farmhouse that he lived in between his birth in 1939 and his going away to boarding school in 1951 lived on with remarkable clarity in his imagination. The water pump, the bucket, the butter churn, the sofa and many more objects from this place have become familiar items to the readers of his work. The preternatural vividness with which he remembered the construction, textures and temperatures of the 'first things' of this first house is apparent from a 2010 interview in which he described his very earliest memory:

> Well, my earliest memory is of my foot touching the ground of Mossbawn, the County Derry earth, or rather a floor laid above the earth. I was in a cot made by the local carpenter, and the bottom of the cot consisted of slats of timber, little smooth boards laid on kind of ledges. ... I remember lifting one or two of those boards and stepping off the bottom of the cot down onto the smooth, cool cement floor of the house. And I can still feel my little foot inside my old foot here.[2]

1 Seamus Heaney, 'Mint' in *Opened ground: poems, 1966–1996* (London, 1998), p. 396.
2 Heaney in conversation with Eleanor Wachtel, *Writers & Company*, CBC Radio, 25 May

Three years after giving this interview, Heaney recalled the sensory shock of this moment of initiation into the material world in 'In time', the last poem collected in his *New selected poems, 1988–2013* (2014). Dated twelve days before his death, this poem contains a recollection of 'the power / I first felt come up through / Our cement floor long ago'.[3] The presence of Heaney's very earliest memory in what must be one of his final poems invests his assertion that 'my last things will be first things slipping from me' with an uncanny air of prophecy.

Seamus Heaney's home in Mossbawn, where this memory was set, was thatched, whitewashed and screened from the road by alder trees and thorn hedges, and set in a townland that Heaney associated in his imagination with 'the much older Gaelic order of cattle herding and hill forts'.[4] Its pre-industrial aesthetic could not be more different from the first house of his friend and contemporary, the poet Derek Mahon. The house in which Mahon grew up, by contrast, was situated in north Belfast, one of many similar redbrick semi-detached dwellings that were built to house the industrial workers of the city. The deal table, cutlery and ornaments that his mother kept gleaming have repeatedly made their way into his work over the decades.

Many of Heaney's and Mahon's first memories are located in dwellings that are redolent of the binaries by which Northern Irish politics are constructed. Whereas Heaney's memories of his house are associated with what is rural, Roman Catholic and Irish, Mahon's remembered house can more readily be aligned with what is industrial, Protestant and British. Writing during years when such divisions were, at times, a matter of life and death, both poets repeatedly drew on the material qualities of their respective first houses as ways of understanding and representing their worlds.

This chapter will focus on the formative agency of houses and their material elements as inspirational stimuli in the poetry of Heaney and Mahon, exploring how, in the words of political theorist

2010, http://www.cbc.ca/radio/writersandcompany/seamus-heaney-interview-1.2790940, accessed 20 Mar. 2017.   3 Heaney, 'In time' in *New selected poems: 1988–2013* (London, 2014), p. 218.   4 Heaney, 'Something to write home about' in *Finders keepers: selected prose, 1971–2001* (London, 2002), p. 50.

Jane Bennett, things can have 'trajectories, propensities or tendencies of their own'.[5] The study of the agential qualities of the material world takes on special inflections when the material studied is that of an intimate, remembered space – the first house. One set of ideas through which to interpret memories of the first house are those of Gaston Bachelard. In his cornerstone work, *The poetics of space* (1954), one of the central ideas is that the first house creates sensory impressions that remain in the memories and bodies of their inhabitants, much as the 'little foot' with which Heaney touched the concrete floor of his house remained, as he said, within his 'old foot' decades later. Bachelard, illustrating his theory of the continued liveliness of the material of the first house in the minds and bodies of its former inhabitants, quotes the poet Rilke: 'I never saw this strange dwelling again. Indeed, as I see it now, the way it appeared to my child's eye, it is not a building, but is quite dissolved and distributed inside me: here one room, there another.'[6] Just as Rilke found that his life after leaving the first house could not be separated from the spaces he first experienced, Bachelard records how the internalization of the first house leads to an unconscious but continual back-and-forth between remembered domestic spaces and later sensory perceptions.

* * *

More than fifty years after Heaney's family left his first cottage, Mossbawn, he said in an interview 'I'm not away from that.'[7] And readers of his compendious collection of interviews with Dennis O'Driscoll are given a very sharp picture indeed of the house that Heaney, in spirit, never left.[8] The first thing a time-travelling visitor

---

5 Jane Bennett, *Vibrant matter: a political ecology of things* (Durham, 2010), p. viii. See also the provocative exploration of these ideas by Bruno Latour [Jim Johnson] in 'Mixing humans with non-humans: sociology of a door-closer', *Social Problems*, 35:3 (1988), 298–310. 6 Gaston Bachelard, *The poetics of space*, trans. Maria Jolas (Boston, 1994), p. 57. 7 Heaney in *Seamus Heaney in conversation with Karl Miller* (London, 2000), p. 29. 8 Dennis O'Driscoll, *Stepping stones: interviews with Seamus Heaney* (London, 2008). See, in particular, the 'Bearings' section, pp 1–60.

to the thatched and whitewashed Mossbawn of the mid-twentieth-century would notice would be the abundance of life it accommodated. Living in its three rooms were two parents, eventually nine children and an aunt. Cats and chickens lived with these twelve people; mice and rats could be heard skittering across the roof beams. A stable shared the same roof and behind the house were sheds that were built to house cows and pigs. Heaney described the sounds and smells of this cottage in an evocative line: 'Buttermilk and urine / the pantry, housed beasts, the listening bedroom'.[9] In his early poems that centre on these spaces, however, he gives some of his most focused attention to the material objects of the house rather than the humans and animals that lived there.

In spite of the relative poverty such cheek-by-jowl family existence indicates, in his early domestic poems Heaney often burnishes the material objects of Mossbawn with the lustre of rare and luminous materials. In 'Churning day' (his first collected poem in which the farmhouse at Mossbawn is visible), the gleaming and polished churns make butter curds 'like gilded gravel'; in his poem 'Thatcher', the craftsman who roofs his family's cottage 'left them gaping at his Midas touch'.[10] In two more poems, a nearby barn contains 'corn piled like grit of ivory' and a hole dug behind his house reveals 'the bronze riches of the gravel'.[11] Heaney conveys the significance of these seemingly banal objects through the intensity of his focus, achieving an alchemical transmutation of the material of the everyday.

Heaney's writing has transfigured as much as recorded the objects in this mid-century cottage. To take one notable example, the vibrant materiality of water in a bucket provided Heaney with one of his most significant symbols. In the 'Glanmore sonnets' (*Field work*, 1979), Heaney remembered how 'in the house, small ripples shook / Silently across our drinking water' in a bucket.[12] The bucket, a seemingly mundane object, is remembered as his point of induction

9 Heaney, 'Keeping going' in *Opened ground*, p. 401.   10 Heaney, 'Churning day', 'Thatcher' in *Opened ground*, pp 9, 20.   11 Heaney, 'The barn' in *Opened ground*, p. 7; Heaney, 'Mossbawn' in *Finders keepers*, p. 6.   12 Heaney, 'Glanmore sonnets IV' in *Opened ground*,

into the wondrous properties of water. When it was disturbed by vibrations from trains that ran over the line two fields behind the house, a sequence of concentric ripples would simultaneously seem to run both outwards from the middle of the bucket and back towards the same centre. From this small, easily overlooked domestic physical phenomenon, Heaney created a metaphor that enabled him to describe his understanding of poetry to the attendees of the Nobel banquet that accompanied his award in 1995. The truth that he intuited was that what lay at the origin could foreshadow what was at the furthest edge.

In his Nobel speech, as in many interviews, Heaney dwelt in detail on his first house, mentioning that the water in the bucket 'used to ripple delicately, concentrically, and in utter silence'.[13] His audience in Stockholm were prepared, then, when he raised the image of the bucket again later in the speech. By this time, however, its significance had widened greatly – the bucket had come to contain the essence of his entire aesthetic:

> poetry can make an order as true to the impact of external reality and as sensitive to the inner laws of the poet's being as the ripples that rippled in and rippled out across the water in that scullery bucket fifty years ago. ... I credit poetry, in other words, ... for making possible a fluid and restorative relationship between the mind's centre and its circumference.[14]

Heaney's use of the water bucket as an image that his audience could readily grasp is reminiscent of an attempt by an earlier Irish Nobel Prize winner, W.B. Yeats, to depict his own aesthetic in concrete terms. Yeats, in his high-modernist philosophical treatise, *A vision* (1925, revised 1937), schematized his vision of reality by using esoteric geometry. He represented objective and subjective forces as opposing, interpenetrating cones that he called 'gyres'.[15] Like Yeats'

p. 166.   13 Heaney, 'Crediting poetry' in *Opened ground*, p. 447.   14 Ibid., pp 449–50.
15 Margaret Mills Harper and Catherine E. Paul have produced modern editions of both versions with very helpful explanatory notes. See *A vision: the original 1925 version* in *The collected works of W.B. Yeats*, vol. 13 (New York, 2008); *A vision: the revised 1937 edition* in

turning, opposing gyres, Heaney's rippling bucket constitutes an attempt to illustrate in vivid, concrete form a pattern of action the poet apprehended in his own imagination. In both Yeats' turning gyres and Heaney's rippling bucket, contraries – the primary and the antithetical for Yeats, the centre and the circumference for Heaney – are harmonized and brought into confluence with each other. Heaney, unlike Yeats, however, draws on the material properties of an object from his first house rather than on esoteric geometry.

Accordingly, Heaney often invokes the rippling bucket in his poetry to signify responsiveness and communion. It is at the centre of his memory of peeling potatoes with his mother in the third poem of his sequence 'Clearances' (*The haw lantern*, 1987), written in memory of her. This poem records the harmony and understanding the two shared as the potato skins fell 'Gleaming in a bucket of clean water' between them.[16] Conversely, water icing over and therefore losing its fluidity portends dark times ahead: Heaney writes of a time when 'waterbuckets iced and frost / Hardened the quiet' in 'An Ulster twilight' (*Station Island*, 1984), a poem that records how the premonitory shadows of the Troubles fell as early as the 1950s.[17] Describing the material qualities of the first house in which he lived became for Heaney a means of communicating fundamental ideas. His earliest memory, of touching the floor with his foot, is not only present in his final poem. The same moment also appears in 'Squarings' (*Seeing things*, 1991), in which he remembers: 'I was four but I turned four hundred maybe / Encountering the ancient dampish feel / Of a clay floor. Maybe four thousand even'. This recollection ends with a thought on the consequences of the contact the poem describes: 'Out of that earth house I inherited / A stack of singular, cold memory-weights / To load me, hand and foot, in the scale of things'.[18] This seems on first reading like a reflection on the power of his origins to constrain him and hold him back, a vision of

*The collected works of W.B. Yeats*, vol. 14 (New York, 2015). A lucid exploration of Yeats' recondite 'system' can also be found in Terence Brown, *The life of W.B. Yeats: a critical biography* (Dublin, 2001). **16** Heaney, 'Clearances III' in *Opened ground*, p. 309. **17** Heaney, 'An Ulster twilight' in *Opened ground*, p. 38. **18** Heaney, 'Squarings xl' in *Opened*

his beginnings as a disabling and hobbling drag on his subsequent existence. However, a stack of weights is something associated with a set of scales, an object that for Heaney can signify a state of freedom and possibility. His poem 'Weighing in' (*The spirit level*, 1995), for example, vividly recalls the numinous significance of weights and balances in his imagination – on a weighbridge, 'everything trembled, flowed with give and take'.[19] The bridge in 'Weighing in', laden yet vibrant with latent energy, has affinities with the weighty memories that he inherited from his first house.

The sofa from Mossbawn, which Heaney remembered as standing beneath the front window, near the cot, is another of these 'memory-weights'. In 'A sofa in the forties' (*The spirit level*, 1995), Heaney describes sitting on this heavy object with his brothers and sisters, pretending they were on a train. By the time he remembers this game in the 1990s, his memory of it is shadowed by thoughts of the children who were taken to their deaths on the trains of the Nazi Kindertransport at around the same time as he was playing with his siblings. In this poem, the sofa has come to provide a tangible stimulus for less concrete ideas of tyranny and atrocity:

> Black leatherette and ornate gauntness of it
> Made it seem the sofa had achieved
>
> Flotation. Its castors on tip-toe,
> […]
>
> Potentially heavenbound, earthbound for sure,
> Among things that might add up or let you down.[20]

Alongside the air of funereal weightiness that hangs about this domestic object, the references to the sofa floating, being on tiptoe and being destined for heaven, all give the incongruous impression that it is straining for lift-off. At the same time, however, it is compelled by gravity to remain in its 'earthbound' spot, on the cement

ground, p. 384.   **19** Heaney, 'Weighing in' in *Opened ground*, p. 407.   **20** Heaney, 'A sofa in the forties' in *Opened ground*, p. 397.

floor of the kitchen of Mossbawn. In the way that it exists between two opposing possibilities, the sofa shares in the vibrancy of the water in the bucket. Similarly, in his poem 'The settle bed' (*Seeing things*, 1991), Heaney imagines lots of these heavy, archaic, 'Upright, rudimentary, unshiftably planked' pieces of furniture tumbling from the sky like rain. By imagining this fantastical fate for a weighty, inherited bed he shows that 'whatever is given // Can always be reimagined'.[21] At this point in his career when, as he recollected in 'Crediting poetry', he began to 'make space in [his] reckoning and imagining for the marvellous', he was reimagining the material properties of weighty domestic objects.[22]

Heaney returned to few objects from his first house as frequently as he did the pump that stood by the back door. During his lifetime, it passed from being a resource in daily use to being a souvenir from a former time: the pump was taken to the Heaneys' new residence, The Wood, when the family left Mossbawn in the early 1950s. It is no longer used to draw water, and now stands as an ornament in the flowerbed of the house, which is occupied by the poet's brother, Hugh Heaney. However, its portability is not what Heaney focuses on in his earliest representations of it. Rather, the pump is represented as a tall, faintly forbidding, cast-iron embodiment of an identity that is rooted in its locality, a totemic structure which 'staked and centred' the poet's imagination.[23] This is how Heaney presented it in his 1978 radio broadcast, later published in the essay 'Mossbawn':

> I would begin with the Greek word, *omphalos*, meaning the navel, and hence the stone that marked the centre of the world, and repeat it, *omphalos, omphalos, omphalos*, until its blunt and falling music becomes the music of someone pumping water at the pump outside our back door. [...] There the pump stands, a slender, iron idol, snouted, helmeted, dressed down with a sweeping handle, painted a dark green and set on a concrete plinth, marking the centre of another world.[24]

21 Heaney, 'The settle bed' in *Opened ground*, p. 345.  22 Heaney, 'Crediting poetry', p. 458.
23 Heaney, 'Mossbawn', p. 6.  24 Ibid., p. 3.

However, even in his description of this weighty iron object, there are more footloose energies at play. Heaney's incantation of the Greek word *omphalos* hints at a perspective that is wider than the domestic subject of the above passage might suggest. The poet views the remembered pump through his knowledge of ancient Greece, but also through the work of James Joyce. The *omphalos* with which the pump is associated appears in the first chapter of *Ulysses*: 'Billy Pitt had them [the Martello Towers] built, Buck Mulligan said, when the French were on the sea. But ours is the *omphalos*.'[25] In Heaney's poetry and prose the pump is not only rooted in the life of his remembered locality, but in Irish literature and, through its associations with Greek myth, in the inheritance of European cultural history. It has broadened in significance to become polyvalent, an object that Heaney simultaneously goes back to and goes beyond, remembering its physical particularity yet imbuing its material qualities with associations that take it very far from its home ground.

'Mossbawn' contains an account of the pump being put in place. In it, ideas of rootedness and the continuance of immemorial practices are at the fore, and there are no hints of the transience or threat with which he associates the pump elsewhere:

> I remember, too, men coming to sink the shaft of the pump and digging through that seam of sand down to the bronze riches of the gravel, that soon began to puddle with the spring water. That pump marked an original descent into earth, sand, gravel, water. It centred and staked the imagination, made its foundation the foundation of the *omphalos* itself.[26]

The words 'original', 'centred', 'staked' and the repeated word 'foundation' create a sense of permanence and continuity and, characteristically, there are mingled suggestions of antiquity and wealth under the surface of the land in the word 'bronze'.

While the radio piece emphasizes permanence, the end of the prose poem 'Sinking the shaft', by contrast, opens questions about

25 James Joyce, *Ulysses: a critical and synoptic edition*, ed. Hans Walter Gabler, 3 vols (London, 1984), i, p. 32.  26 Heaney, 'Mossbawn', p. 6.

whether the pump has been 'toppled'. Heaney published it three years earlier in his 1975 volume *Stations*, a collection of autobiographical, politically mindful poems, which was issued by a small Belfast press and has never been reprinted. As in the radio broadcast, the subject of 'Sinking the shaft' is the poet's memory of the pump being put in place:

> A stirabout, a gleam, a wet bronze puddled by their wellingtons. 'We're not a mile off it. Would you not come down?'
> Snouted, helmeted, the plunger like an active gizzard, the handle dressed to a clean swoop, set on a pediment inscribed by the points of their trowels. I suppose we thought it could never be toppled.[27]

Intriguingly, the pump in 'Sinking the shaft' seems to radiate a certain threat: it acquires an avian quality with words such as 'swoop' and 'gizzard', but the adjectives 'snouted' and 'helmeted' suggest it is a more intimidating imaginary presence. It is as if the poem and the memories it contains have been subtly imbued with the sense of menace which pervades the volume. In contrast with this latent air of threat, the words 'we thought it could never be toppled' have an elegiac feel, suggesting that the pump – for all its seeming permanence to the child Heaney – has since been uprooted.

The pump's potentially militaristic qualities have led to its significance being heavily contested by Heaney's critics. One of the most contentious debates has been over 'the invisible, untoppled omphalos' of 'The Toome road' (*Field work*, 1979), a poem which is narrated by a farmer from Heaney's district who watches and comments as a convoy of British armoured vehicles passes in front of him. The critical debate has centred on the standpoint towards contemporary politics indicated by the lines 'O charioteers, above your dormant guns, / It stands here still, stands vibrant as you pass, / The invisible, untoppled omphalos'.[28]

---

27 Heaney, 'Sinking the shaft' in *Stations* (Belfast, 1975), p. 8.  28 Heaney, 'The Toome road' in *Opened ground*, p. 150.

By the time this poem was published, the 'omphalos' had already been linked to the farmyard pump in Heaney's radio broadcast of the previous year. However, it also recalls the 'stone in the midst of all' in another poem evoking nationalism and the presence of the British military in Ireland – W.B. Yeats' 'Easter, 1916': 'Hearts with one purpose alone / Through summer and winter seem / Enchanted to a stone / To trouble the living stream'.[29] Whereas in Yeats' poem the 'stone' has been universally interpreted as representing the effects of militant nationalism, Heaney's critics have arrived at no similar clear-cut signification for the 'omphalos' in 'The Toome road'.[30] Neil Corcoran, Peter McDonald, James Simmons and Henry Hart have assigned varying significations to it, and it is indicative of Heaney's cultural importance that his mysterious references should lead to such intense critical debate.[31] For all the foreignness of the word 'omphalos', McDonald, Corcoran and Simmons have stressed its significance as a symbol of Irish nationalism. Corcoran interprets it as 'the navel-stone of nationalist Irish feeling, maintain[ing] a persistent, defiant opposition to the colonial power'.[32] Simmons, in a generally hostile article on Heaney's work, sees the 'omphalos' as associated with 'paramilitary nationalism'.[33] Hart, on the other hand, does not stress the potential of the image to symbolize nationalist resistance. Instead, he sees the 'omphalos' as representing a time and place 'where political and religious turmoil was eclipsed by pastoral calm and where beliefs were more certain, more stable'.[34] Peter McDonald has questioned Hart's interpretation, opining that 'there is a certain cracker-barrel innocence' about his reading of the poem.[35] However, Hart's more pastoral reading has been encouraged by Heaney's connections

29 W.B. Yeats, *Collected poems*, ed. Augustine Martin (London, 1992), p. 177. 30 In particular, the stone of 'Easter 1916' has been interpreted as relating to the effect of militant nationalism on the mind of Maud Gonne. See Brown, *Life of W.B. Yeats*, p. 231; R.F. Foster, *W.B. Yeats: a life*, ii: *The arch-poet, 1915–1939* (Oxford, 2003), p. 61. 31 Peter McDonald, *Mistaken identities: poetry and Northern Ireland* (Oxford, 1997), p. 52; Neil Corcoran, *The poetry of Seamus Heaney: a critical study* (London, 1998), p. 91; James Simmons, 'The trouble with Seamus Heaney' in Elmer Kennedy-Andrews (ed.), *Seamus Heaney: a collection of critical essays* (New York, 1992), p. 63; Henry Hart, *Seamus Heaney: poet of contrary progressions* (New York, 1993), p. 136. 32 Corcoran, *Seamus Heaney*, p. 91. 33 Simmons, 'Trouble with Seamus Heaney', p. 63. 34 Hart, *Seamus Heaney*, p. 136. 35 McDonald, *Mistaken identities*, p. 55.

between the word '*omphalos*' and the pump in the bucolic opening of the radio broadcast, quoted above.[36] Part of the reason Heaney's depictions of the pump have been so open to competing interpretations is because of his complex, changing responses to the material that forms it. His work responds to both the bucolic associations of the green-painted iron from which it is forged, and also to the more threatening and militaristic connotations of the same materials.

The pump appears in a handful of Heaney's other poems, but one of his most remarkable depictions of it is one of his last.[37] Heaney's penultimate volume of poetry, *District and circle* (2006), contains a poem in which the pump seems to be an elegiac symbol of his past. 'Quitting time' contains a description of the evening routine of a farmer who bears a strong resemblance to the poet's brother Hugh:

> The hosed-down chamfered concrete pleases him.
> He'll wait a while before he kills the light
> On the cleaned-up yard, its pails and farrowing crate,
> And the cast-iron pump immobile as a herm
> Upstanding elsewhere, in another time.[38]

The image of the farmer surveying his yard at the end of the working day invites comparison with Heaney himself surveying the long day of his own poetic career. The pump's presence here is mysterious, with the certainty of 'cast-iron' undercut by the assertion that it is 'upstanding elsewhere, in another time'. There is, of course, an ambiguity inherent in these lines: it could be the farmer who is 'Upstanding elsewhere, in another time' as he surveys the farm, recalling the past. Although it is no longer an '*omphalos*', the pump is still related to a classical stone that is obscure enough to need to be glossed for most modern readers. A 'herm' is 'a statue composed of a

---

36 The pump's associations with fixity and stability, which Hart identifies, have also been encouraged by the pump's appearance amid the seeming calm domesticity of the poem 'Sunlight' (*North*, 1975), collected in *Opened ground*, p. 93.   37 These other poems include 'A drink of water' (*Field work*, 1979) and 'Changes' (*Station Island*, 1984), collected in *Opened ground*, pp 151, 225.   38 Heaney, 'Quitting time' in *District and circle* (London, 2006), p. 69.

head, usually that of the god Hermes'. These were used as boundary markers and milestones in ancient Greece.[39] Rather than representing stability or hinting at military resistance, by 2006 the pump represented a limit, an ungainsayable marker post.

* * *

Vibrant objects from what he calls 'that first suburban house' also inhabit the imagination of Derek Mahon, who is of the same generation as Heaney and, like Heaney, was first recognized for his work in the cultural ferment that dovetailed with the political one in Belfast in the 1960s. He is, however, from a background that in some ways represents the flip-side of the Northern Irish culture with which Heaney is usually identified. Mahon's parents were Protestants who were engaged in industry – his father working in a shipyard, his mother, before her marriage, in a linen factory. Whereas Heaney went to a Catholic grammar school and Queen's University Belfast, Mahon went to a Protestant grammar school and on to Trinity College Dublin.

Mahon's first home was a red-brick semi-detached house behind a privet hedge and, as with Heaney, the objects found in it have been the starting points for some of his most significant explorations of life and art. In Mahon's poems, the porcelain, china and ceramic objects that he encountered in his childhood house – whether in the form of mugs and crockery or figurines – appear again and again. He values these objects as invoking a sense of form and polish: their coolness, smoothness and imperviousness to stains and the effects of the passage of time all seem to hold out for him an appealing model of what he might achieve with words. However, he repeatedly writes, too, of the susceptibility of these objects to violent acts.[40] These objects have taken on a suggestive role in his poetry owing to their contrasting qualities of immutability and vulnerability.

**39** *OED*, s. v. 'herm'.  **40** I have written briefly about the significance of ceramics in Mahon's work. See Adam Hanna, *Northern Irish poetry and domestic space* (Basingstoke, 2015), p. 94.

Dresden figurines appear in two of Mahon's poems, the backdrops for which are the domestic spaces that were ordered and maintained by his mother. Frequently taking the form of musicians or dancers in the clothes of the eighteenth century, these dainty ornaments seem the apotheosis of a certain ideal of domestic order. As such, a Dresden figurine is an appropriate hearth goddess for Mahon's 'Antrim road' (*An autumn wind*, 2010): 'I can still see that first suburban house, / whitewashed and tiny, tiny but at peace, / a "Dresden" figurine next to the clock / holding her skirt out as she reads a book'. In spite of this peaceable setting, a hint of future catastrophe enters the poem in its second half. In it, the poet imagines the hot glow of a 'fiery evening sun' filling the room.[41] This ominous image, in connection with Dresden figurines, evokes the firestorm that destroyed the city for which they are named in the years that Mahon lived in his 'first suburban house' in Belfast. The image of the fiery sun also recalls the fires caused by the blitz on Belfast during the Second World War and, more recently, by the Troubles.

In representing both intense heat and Dresden figurines, Mahon brings to mind the idea of the kiln in which these objects were fired. Of course, ideas of Germany and ovens in the Second World War have, like trains from the same time and place, very dark associations. For Mahon, as for Heaney, the world beyond the house is made imaginable through the material qualities of particular domestic things. Also like Heaney, Mahon is haunted by the idea that not so very long ago – around the time he was a child at home – some of the worst atrocities in human history were being perpetrated elsewhere in Europe. This later knowledge has come to reshape how both poets remember the objects that were in their houses in the 1940s. However, the solidity of remembered objects should not cause readers to think that memories of them are static entities. For both Heaney and Mahon, remembered domestic objects take on meanings and connotations that they could not possibly have had at the time the poets lived among them.

41 Mahon, 'Antrim road' in *An autumn wind* (Oldcastle, Co. Meath, 2010), p. 47.

The materialistic ethos of the post-war era is at the heart of 'A Bangor requiem' (*The yellow book*, 1997), another poem by Mahon in which Dresden figurines appear. In this elegy for his mother, Mahon writes of how these ornaments were expressive of an artistic sense that was susceptible to the actions of 'twisted ministers' and 'thick industrialists':

> with your wise monkeys and 'Dresden' figurines,
> your junk chinoiserie and coy pastoral scenes,
> you too were an artist, a rage-for-order freak
> setting against a man's aesthetic of cars and golf
> your ornaments and other breakable stuff.[42]

Mahon's description of his mother as a 'rage-for-order freak' has its origins in both his family memories and in literature. On the personal side, it reflects his impression, expressed in an interview, that his mother's 'obsessive' house-pride was the result of her giving up paid work outside the home.[43] On the literary side, it refers both to Wallace Stevens (the originator of the line 'Oh! Blessed rage for order') and to Mahon himself, who used the phrase in the title of one of his best-known poems, 'Rage for order', published in 1972.[44]

However, Mahon's attitude towards his mother's aesthetic is not one of straightforwardly celebratory affiliation. In an interview, he spoke about how the orderliness of the house in which he grew up would prompt a longing for disorder that would cause him 'occasionally to do deliberately infuriating things, such as knocking over a cup'.[45] This memory of a domestic object has a wider significance in relation to his work: his poetry is remarkable for the number of occasions on which porcelain, china or ceramic objects are destroyed or threatened with destruction.[46] The final stanza of the

---

42 Mahon, 'A Bangor requiem' in *New collected poems* (Loughcrew, Co. Meath, 2011), pp 226–7.   43 Hugh Haughton, *The poetry of Derek Mahon* (Oxford, 2007), p. 10.   44 Wallace Stevens, 'The idea of order at Key West' in *The collected poems* (New York, 1954), p. 130; Mahon, 'Rage for order' in *New collected poems*, p. 47.   45 Haughton, *Derek Mahon*, p. 10. 46 As well as the examples in the poems discussed in this chapter, there are others in 'The snow party' and 'The last of the fire kings' in *The snow party* (Oxford, 1975).

poem 'Courtyards in Delft' (*Courtyards in Delft*, 1981), which has been excised from most recent reprintings, contains just such a shattering of ceramics. The poem features a house that is partly an imagining of the Netherlands of the seventeenth century and partly a memory of Mahon's Belfast house in the 1940s and 1950s. The original version of the poem, after a description of the house's neatness, trimness and spartan lack of superfluity in the first four stanzas, features an incongruous moment of longing for its destruction: 'If only, now, the Maenads, as of right, / Came smashing crockery, with fire and sword, / We could sleep easier in our beds at night'.[47] The frenzied Greek figures that invade the poem have often been interpreted in political terms: Elmer Kennedy-Andrews has written that 'Courtyards in Delft' is a critique of the 'oppressive colonialism' of Mahon's time and place. In this analysis, the orderliness of the house is the material concomitant of the colonial desire for inhabitants of Protestant Europe to impose their form of order on peoples across the globe.[48] This reading is understandable in light of Mahon's frequent criticisms of the prevalent political attitudes of Ulster Protestant families like his own.[49] The action of the poem might also be read in terms of Mahon's artistic choices and formal development. The orderliness, rigidity and perfection that the house and the crockery symbolize are things that the poet admires: he said in an interview that he is interested in 'something being intended and achieved – purposefulness instead of randomness'. However, this sense of control and order that he so admires is also something he longs to be free from. In the same interview, he says 'I am as liable as any – and perhaps indeed more than most – to the lures of negative capability and anarchy and all those things'.[50] These competing energies are encapsulated in his representations of the

47 Mahon, 'Courtyards in Delft' in *The hunt by night* (Oxford, 1982), p. 10.   48 Elmer Kennedy-Andrews, introduction in *The poetry of Derek Mahon*, ed. Elmer Kennedy-Andrews (Gerrards Cross, 2002), p. 3.   49 Hugh Haughton quotes several interviews in which Mahon reflects on the unhealthy and introverted political climate in which he grew up (*Derek Mahon*, p. 12).   50 Eamonn Grennan, 'Derek Mahon: the art of poetry, no. 82', *Paris Review*, 154 (Spring 2000), http://www.theparisreview.org/interviews/732/the-art-of-poetry-no-82-derek-mahon, accessed 6 July 2016.

material objects in his childhood home and the destruction that he, at times, imaginatively visits upon them.

In an early poem, Mahon writes of the appeal of porcelain, with its coolness, clarity and beauty, as a model for his own work. He writes of 'my cold dream / Of a place out of time, / A palace of porcelain'.[51] The deft, spare clarity of these lines illustrates the porcelain-like qualities which his work consistently exhibited until the mid-1980s, and which it has frequently displayed ever since. His poems, with their metricality, unobtrusive rhymes and innovative use of traditional forms, have been seen as epitomizing an ideal of poetry as a well-wrought, self-contained entity. Mahon's description of his own ideal of poetry in an interview for the *Paris Review* acknowledges this, but contains an extra element. For Mahon, the best poems contain 'the hissing chemicals inside the well-wrought urn'.[52] This description supplements the idea that his poems are exemplars of masterful formal control, highlighting his attraction to what is untrammelled, Dionysian and possibly destructive. When he imagines the fragile beauty of domestic ceramics, he often imagines unconstrained forces being turned against them – the hissing chemicals that might blow the well-wrought urn apart.

In Mahon's poem 'The studio' (*Lives*, 1972), crockery is central to a vision of chaos and destruction. Written near the outset of the Troubles, the poem describes the vulnerability of interior life to broader conditions by describing the effects on an artist's studio of an unnamed event outside. The phenomena that result from this event include wailing crockery: 'You would think with so much going on outside / The deal table would make for the window, / The ranged crockery freak and wail / Remembering its dark origins'.[53] The neurotic crockery, haunted by its past, is just one of many examples of sentient domestic objects in Mahon's work.[54] The imagery of the first few lines has a more domestic feel than the title of the poem, 'The studio', a feature that perhaps offers an insight into the poem's

51 Mahon, 'The last of the fire kings' in *New collected poems*, p. 63.  52 Grennan, 'Derek Mahon'.  53 Mahon, 'The studio' in *New collected poems*, p. 37.  54 See Hanna, *Northern Irish poetry*, pp 101–4.

origins. The menaced crockery that Mahon describes has antecedents in the ceramic objects that he remembers from his childhood house.

*** 

Heaney and Mahon both have drawn on the materiality of their first houses throughout their careers. The objects, rooms and atmospheres of the houses in which they grew up remained and remain with them as reference points that inform and shape their works. Through their representations of material objects from their first houses, both poets assert the significance of these houses in shaping their respective aesthetics. In this joining of the knowledge of the adult with the experience of the child, returning to the first house is a means of asserting the continuity of the self. However, more than this, the material objects that they remember from their childhoods are far from being fixed points. Mahon's and Heaney's poetry suggests that, when the memory of a period of time is changed through the acquisition of new knowledge, the memory of the material objects associated with that time also changes. Because of this phenomenon, remembered objects and places exhibit a curious liveliness and vibrancy in the work of these poets, as their memories of things take on new associations in response to the exigencies of the present. In their poetry, memories of the first house are not fixed but are, rather, endlessly renewed resources. It is as if, as Rilke intimated, these houses and the objects in them became part of these poets' own organic beings.

# Melancholy ornaments in the house of Edna O'Brien's fiction

## Maureen O'Connor

Things matter in Edna O'Brien's fiction. Her attention to minutiae has been observed by careful readers ranging from Philip Roth, who in 1984 described his friend's work as creating a 'net of perfectly observed sensuous details', to Anne Enright, who argued in 2012 that O'Brien 'knows the precise emotional weight of objects, their seeming hopefulness and their actual indifference to those who seek to be consoled'.[1] Bill Brown, in his foundational essay, 'Thing theory', takes up the distinction made by Heidegger (in his turn, responding to Kant) between objects and things, arguing that an object requires a subject, while a thing is independent of human consciousness: 'The story of objects themselves as things, then, is the story of a changed relation to the human subject and thus the story of how the thing really names less an object than a particular subject-object relation.'[2] The distinction between the two is difficult to parse in O'Brien's early work, which features women who, as Sinéad Mooney has pointed out, manifest 'recurring anxiety' over the 'boundaries … between the I and the not-I'.[3] The emotional relationship to objects described in brief by Enright, especially the sadomasochism (S/M) hinted at in

---

1 Philip Roth, 'A conversation with Edna O'Brien: "The body contains the life story"', *New York Times*, 18 Nov. 1984; Anne Enright, review of Edna O'Brien, *Country girl: a memoir* (London, 2012), *Guardian*, 12 Oct. 2012. 2 Bill Brown, 'Thing theory', *Critical Inquiry*, 28:1 (2001), 4. 3 Sinéad Mooney, 'Sacramental sleeves: fashioning the female subject in the fiction of Edna O'Brien' in Kathryn Laing et al. (eds), *Edna O'Brien: new critical perspectives* (Dublin, 2006), p. 197.

the tension between the hopeful subject and the indifferent thing, animates representations of the ostensibly *in*animate residing in the houses of O'Brien's fiction. Other commentators have explicitly noted the sadomasochistic dynamic that characterizes many primary relationships in O'Brien's work, an observation sometimes used by critics to define her work as frivolous, drearily preoccupied with doomed heterosexual romance. This chapter will extend the S/M dynamic to include relationships between the animate and the inanimate, demonstrating the variety and complexity of the possibilities for connection in O'Brien's fiction. Such human-nonhuman entanglements distribute agency in challenging configurations and exert additional pressure on the subject-object divide – an already unstable boundary in O'Brien's representations of intra-human connection. The poignant attempts by O'Brien's abused and lonely wives and widows to vivify domestic interiors and affect what it means to dwell uncover a hidden history of small refusals to submit to patriarchal expectations of women's total self-abnegation in post-independence Ireland.

## The Irish house

Of O'Brien's sensitivity to the liveliness of things, Enright asks:

> is this the root of the (usually male, let's face it) unease about O'Brien; the worry she might become untethered from the real? It is the tension between the actual and the metaphorical that gives her sentences their enormous energy and restraint.[4]

O'Brien's 'untethered' treatment of the nonhuman material world collapses the aesthetic distance between subject and object, as well as between the real and the metaphorical, a distance necessary to the violence of figuration. There is more than one way of 'being' in O'Brien, which introduces a number of instabilities into her fiction, instabilities that expose what her biographer Amanda Greenwood

4 Enright, review.

identifies as the novelist's persistent critical target – Irish 'cultural matricide'.⁵ A constitutive linking of 'Irishness, suffering and maternity' is evident in a 'cultural ideal of maternity … threatened by the bodily functions which it struggles to deny',⁶ exemplified in the impossible model offered by the Virgin Mary, at once maternal and untainted. The irony of this unrealizable ideal, dominant in Ireland's Mariolatrous Catholic culture and reflected in the iconography of long-suffering 'Mother Ireland', is that the country must 'always be motherless'.⁷

This sadomasochistic denial of the undeniable mother fuels the homicidal rage of the killer, Michen O'Kane, in O'Brien's 2000 novel *In the forest*. A man simultaneously obsessed with and infuriated by the maternal, O'Kane murders his fantasy mother and fantasizes about being an IRA terrorist, suggesting a connection between personally and nationally self-inflicted violence. Ireland's centuries-long struggle for independence was marked by cycles of betrayal and self-destruction, evident even after independence was achieved. O'Brien often evokes this history in the self-conscious and insecure co-optation and occupation of the Irish 'big house' (as in *House of splendid isolation* and *The light of evening*), figured as reflections of the crisis of Irish male identity.⁸ The Oedipal implications of the bloody wrenching apart of the union between the kingdoms of England and Ireland, traditionally figured as a marriage between John Bull and Cathleen Ní Houlihan, make for shameful regrets and longings, insecurities and suspicions of illegitimacy (always the result of a 'sinning' mother). The forensic attention O'Brien brings to her descriptions of houses and their furnishings inevitably reveals the

---

5 Amanda Greenwood, *Edna O'Brien* (Tavistock, 2003), pp 87, 106–7.   6 Ibid., p. 87.   7 Ibid., p. 107.   8 The 'big house' was the local representation of English occupation throughout the Irish countryside. These houses, not always significantly 'big' in a literal sense, were occupied by landlords predominantly of the Protestant Anglo-Irish ascendancy. For more on O'Brien and the 'big house', see, for example, Bernice Schrank and Danine Farquharson, 'Blurring boundaries, intersecting lives: history, gender, and violence in Edna O'Brien's *House of splendid isolation*' in Lisa Colletta and Maureen O'Connor (eds), *Wild colonial girl: essays on Edna O'Brien* (Madison, WI, 2006), pp 110–42; Michael Harris, 'Outside history: relocation and dislocation in Edna O'Brien's *House of splendid isolation*' in Laing et al. (eds), *Edna O'Brien*, pp 122–37.

wounds inflicted by a damaged postcolonial masculinity, reasserting itself through the subjugation of women in post-independence Ireland.[9]

With the publication of *House of splendid isolation* in 1994, O'Brien's fiction began again to be set primarily in Ireland following a period of over twenty years (since the publication of *A pagan place* in 1972) during which none of her novels and only some short stories were set in her native country. O'Brien's earliest works are not usually recognized as belonging to the category of big house fiction, but nearly all of the rural Irish homes of her imaginings resemble in differing degrees her family home, Drewsboro, near Scarriff, Co. Clare. The early writing, in particular, draws significantly on the author's life. O'Brien opens and closes her recent memoir with descriptions and recollections of her childhood home:

> a large two-story house, with bay windows ... approached by two avenues, an old and a new. The goldish sandstone of which it was built was from the burnt ruin of a 'Big House' that had belonged to the English and that had been burnt in the Troubles, during the 1920s.[10]

The destruction was carried out by a group of rebels that reportedly included O'Brien's own father Michael, who nevertheless aspired to the elegance and status of the Protestant ascendancy, which influenced the building of his own home (a story repeated in *House of splendid isolation* and *Light of evening*). Michael O'Brien's own family came into money earned by American relations, an inheritance he drank and gambled away once in possession of it himself.

Even O'Brien's earliest texts, then, can be seen as responding in some way, however indirectly, to the big house tradition. It is useful in this context, therefore, to note what Maud Ellmann has observed of the work of a more readily recognized Irish big house novelist, Elizabeth Bowen: 'Things, in Bowen, offer none of the expected

**9** See Aidan Beatty, *Masculinity and power in Irish nationalism, 1884–1938* (Basingstoke, 2016).   **10** Edna O'Brien, *Country girl: a memoir* (London, 2012), p. 5.

comforts of solidity; they stand, like Freudian fetishes, as monuments to lack and loss. Nothing, by contrast, bears down on her imagined world with a weight more oppressive than materiality.'[11] In Bowen's fiction, objects remember and even enact loss in their uncanny liveliness. In 1984, O'Brien said of her own work, 'Loss is every child's theme because by necessity the child loses its mother and its bearings ... so my central theme is loss.'[12] The bereft women inhabiting O'Brien's early fiction, embedded deeply in the physical and emotional worlds of the author's childhood, want to believe in the power of the object to effect some kind of transformation. These magician-mothers find their ideal audience and co-conspirator in the young girl central to much of this work. Together, mother and daughter entertain assuasive visions of a vibrant domesticity. As in Bowen's fiction, in O'Brien, the object 'magnetized into being', as Ellmann describes it, externalizes some unrealized desire or painful memory.[13] For all of their personalized talismanic power, however, nearly all of the fetishized objects preserved and often hidden in the domestic spaces in O'Brien's early fiction are strikingly impersonal, anonymous, mass-produced, even things that might be considered rubbish in a more comfortable home, like empty sweet wrappers and chocolate boxes.[14] These things are further unmoored from atomized experiences and individuals by the fact that they recur with regularity across texts, as we will see.

## The sadomasochism of things

The vibrantly signifying objects under consideration wield an apotropaic power, promising escape from the evils of drudgery, poverty and domestic abuse, but the respite is temporary and contingent, when not illusory. O'Brien's interest in Ireland's pre-Christian traditions is

11 Maud Ellmann, 'Shadowing Elizabeth Bowen', *New England Review*, 24:1 (2003), 149.
12 Shusha Guppy, 'Edna O'Brien: the art of fiction, no. 82', *Paris Review*, 92 (1984), 38.
13 Ellmann, 'Shadowing', p. 148.   14 For a consideration of the status and meaning of dirt and detritus in O'Brien's work, as well as in Irish women's poetry, see Maureen O'Connor, '"The most haunting bird": unbeing and illegibility in contemporary Irish women's writing',

well documented, and her rendering of domestic detail evokes a kind of pagan animism. Nearly all the objects mimic organic forms – flowers, fruit, animals, the material bodies of saints, extensions through time of the otherwise perishable (with the possible exception of certain saints' remains), recalling Alison Landsberg's category of 'prosthetic memories', those memories that belong to no one and everyone at once.[15] Elizabeth Freeman argues, however, in her deployment of Landsberg's theory, that 'S/M may literalize the prosthetic aspect of *all* memory' (emphasis added).[16] In other words, such memories rely on props, objects used in a performance of identity and community, rendering both private and shared experiences plastic, subject to interpretation. Prosthetic memories extend beyond the personal into cultural memory, potentially transcending individual trauma, according to Freeman, by both 'bind[ing] and unbind[ing] historical subjectivity'.[17] The possible curative power of S/M, its dark promise of sharing the desire for release – including release from the trammels of self – is suggested when O'Brien says, 'All masochists are just sadists waiting to be cured', an assertion quoted by Shirley Peterson in her discussion of sadomasochistic desire in The Country Girls Trilogy.[18] According to Lynn Chancer, the hierarchical structure of the sadomasochistic relationship is erected on an unjust social arrangement, and she argues that sadomasochism inevitably emerges under conditions of patriarchy,[19] an especially oppressive version of which prevails in the mid- to late twentieth-century Ireland of O'Brien's fiction.

The psychologically immature or incomplete O'Brien protagonist, who invites and even performs self-annihilation, occupies, according to Peterson, a metonymic position vis-à-vis the 'sadomasochistic impulses that drive the mid-century Irish sociopolitical agenda', a

*Women's Studies*, 44:7 (2015), 940–55. **15** Alison Landsberg, *Prosthetic memory: the transformation of America* (New York, 2004). **16** Elizabeth Freeman, *Time binds: queer temporalities, queer histories* (Durham, NC, 2010), p. 161. **17** Ibid., p. 160. **18** Shirley Peterson, '"Meaniacs" and martyrs: sadomasochistic desire in Edna O'Brien's The Country Girls Trilogy' in Kathryn Laing et al. (eds), *Edna O'Brien: new critical perspectives* (Dublin, 2006), p. 151. **19** Lynn Chancer, *Sadomasochism in everyday life: the dynamics of power and powerlessness* (New Brunswick, NJ, 1992), p. 16.

relationship that can be extended to what Patricia Coughlan calls 'a kind of global abjection', another indication of the way in which the figure of loss in O'Brien potentially ramifies beyond the individual context.[20] Chancer also notes that the implicit S/M hierarchy is always under threat, as it is an inherently co-dependent relationship in which positions of dominance and submission can become interchangeable: the sadist needs the masochist, and so the masochist can exert a kind of paradoxical control. The subversive potential of weakness and passivity contributes to what Jack Halberstam has identified as 'shadow feminism', a practice distinguished by, among other qualities, a 'refusal of mastery'.[21] Halberstam associates this kind of feminism with 'negative forms of anticolonial knowing'.[22] Feminism under colonial/postcolonial conditions may, according to Halberstam, 'find purpose in its own failure', resorting to 'a radical form of masochistic passivity that not only offers up a critique of the organizing logic of agency and subjectivity itself, but that also opts out of certain systems built around a dialectic between colonizer and colonized', systems of especial significance in a postcolonial Irish context.[23] As Terence McSwiney, one of the leaders of the Easter Rising in Cork, famous for his martyr's death on hunger strike, is credited with saying, 'It is not those who can inflict the most but those who can suffer the most who will conquer.' If masochistic passivity can be seen as conducting a 'critique of the organizing logic of agency and subjectivity itself', a focus on 'things' or 'objects' is also necessarily, at the very least, a questioning of the distinction and distance that traditionally obtains between subject and object, a distinction on which all technologies of power are predicated.

The typical protagonist of O'Brien's early fiction to whom many critics have historically objected, is read as lacking a confident, independent 'self', a failure to comply with foundational expectations for the Western subject. For these characters, the porous, borderless 'self' of infancy is only partially repressed in adulthood. Rebecca

---

20 Peterson, "'Meaniacs'", p. 152; Patricia Coughlan, 'Killing the bats: O'Brien, abjection, and the question of agency' in Laing et al. (eds), *Edna O'Brien*, p. 178.  21 Judith Halberstam, *The queer art of failure* (Durham, NC, 2011), p. 11.  22 Ibid., p. 14.  23 Ibid., pp 28, 131.

Pelan, among others, has identified the primary 'love object' for O'Brien's protagonists as the mother, whose replacement her daughter hopelessly seeks in inevitably disappointing heterosexual partners.[24] Patricia Coughlan characterizes the mother-daughter relationship in O'Brien as 'the most intense form of attachment which the texts focus on, far deeper, more wrenching, and occasionally more ecstatic than specifically sexual woman-to-man connections'.[25] The adored and put-upon mother of O'Brien's early novels and short stories is a hard-working, self-denying country woman, usually married to a feckless alcoholic; she is, nonetheless, and perhaps unexpectedly, 'house-proud'. Bernice Schrank and Danine Farquharson have tracked a 'subtle yet dense network of echoes and anticipations' that creates a web of recurring and overlapping objects and images in O'Brien's early work'.[26] This network links several representations of the typical O'Brien mother. The particular objects produced in evidence of the 'pride' she attempts to take in her home, despite its usually decrepit state of neglect, vary little across the early fiction – ornamental mirrors hung too high to be useful, a chocolate box or paper fan in the unused fireplace, seashells, a 'whatnot' (small ornamental set of shelves), wax or paper flowers, a dust-collecting stuffed or china animal figure, as well as holy statues. That these items are often kept enshrined in a 'good' room that is never, or very rarely used – or not in a room at all, but at the landing of a stairs – heightens the poignancy of their tawdry, faded prettiness, the frailty of the private bulwark they present against the harsh reality for women of Irish rural domesticity. These precious objects, however battered, retain a kind of glamour and potency, a numinous quality that Jane Bennett refers to as 'the invisible field that surrounds and infuses the world of objects', a vibrancy emanating from the 'denied possibilities' inherent in their promise of 'non-identity', that is, evading the determining power of

24 Rebecca Pelan, 'Edna O'Brien's "love objects"' in Colletta and O'Connor (eds), *Wild colonial girl*, pp 58–76. See also, Bernice Schrank and Danine Farquharson, 'Object of love, subject to despair: Edna O'Brien's love object and the emotional logic of late romanticism', *Canadian Journal of Irish Studies*, 22:2 (1996), 22–36. 25 Coughlan, 'Killing the bats', p. 187. 26 Schrank and Farquharson, 'Blurring boundaries', 22.

dominant gender and sexual identities: 'thing power may be a starting point for thinking beyond the life-matter binary, the dominating organizational principle for adult experience'.[27] The volatile, ontologically ambiguous object in the secret world of O'Brien's rural women undermines numerous received truths about the social and domestic orders.

## Household magic

O'Brien's first novel, *The country girls* (1960), establishes the figurative and emotional patterns in home ornamentation. Many of the early chapters take place in Cait Brennan's childhood home where 'things were either broken or not used at all', including the wedding present of Doulton plates kept in a dresser: 'we never use them in case they'd get broken'. Their use as a screen against reality is literalized in their function as a hiding place for 'hundreds of bills. Bills never worried Dada, he just put them behind the plates and forgot.'[28] The 'breakfast room', never used, at least not for its ostensible purpose, serves as Cait's mother's sanctuary. Her life is a never-ending round of labour: 'She was dragged down by heavy work, working to keep the place going, and at nighttime making lampshades and fire screens to make the house prettier.'[29] The (sado)masochistically self-sacrificing mother who serves everyone else first, who eats dry toast while others breakfast on eggs and bacon, keeps a personal stash of biscuits behind a curtain in the 'breakfast room', where she also sneaks the occasional cigarette. Cait obsesses painfully over her mother's self-denial. When her mother seems to have disappeared, Cait reluctantly follows her friend Baba, who has brazenly let herself into the breakfast room in search of a treat:

> The room was dark and sad and dusty. The whatnot, with its collection of knickknacks and chocolate-box lids and statues and artificial flowers, looked silly now that Mama wasn't there.

**27** Jane Bennett, *Vibrant matter: a political ecology of things* (Durham, NC, 2010), pp 15, 20.
**28** Edna O'Brien, *The country girls* (London, 2002), pp 5, 7.   **29** Ibid., p. 8.

The crab shells that she used as ashtrays were all over the room.[30]

In the first half of the novel, before the girls begin the convent education that will spark their rebelliousness, self-satisfied, middle-class Baba adheres faithfully to the hierarchies of capital and patriarchy. Her 'masculine' gaze diminishes the beauty of the room's decorations in the eyes of Cait, who had up to now greatly admired her mother's 'taste'.

Objects lose their glamour, reclaim their thing-ness, whenever the deep mother-daughter bond is broken, to be replaced with the lone-liness of enforced normative heterosexuality, usually the daughter's pursuit of romantic relationships, consistently represented as exploitative and sterile, often ending in an unsuccessful, usually brief marriage. In a 1963 story, 'The rug', the final disappointment caused by a household object presages a future loss of just this kind, a foretaste of abandonment and isolation for the mother. The house in the story is one typical for O'Brien in this period, with its contrast between the near-derelict 'masculine' face of the house's exterior and the 'feminine' domestic interior of the home, a space of compensatory, hopeful plenitude:

> Though all outside was neglect, overgrown with ragwort and thistle; strangers were surprised when they entered the house; my father might fritter his life away watching slates slip from the outhouse roofs – but, within, that safe, square, lowland house of stone was my mother's pride and joy. It was always spotless. It was stuffed with things – furniture, china dogs. Toby mugs, tall jugs, trays, tapestries and whatnots. Each of the four bedrooms had holy pictures on the walls and a gold overmantle surrounding each fireplace. In the fireplaces there were paper fans or lids of chocolate boxes. Mantlepieces carried their own close-packed array of wax flowers, holy statues, broken alarm clocks, shells, photographs, soft rounded cushions for sticking pins in.[31]

30 Ibid., p. 31.   31 Edna O'Brien, 'The rug' in *The love object* (London, 1972), pp 63–4. First

Into this mixture of wax flowers and broken clocks, in an unmarked parcel comes a sumptuous thing, a hearthrug that is not imitation but 'real sheepskin, thick and soft and luxurious'. Mother and daughter delight in puzzling over the identity of the mysterious person who has somehow 'decided upon just the thing she needed'.[32] In this instance, it is not the rug itself that signifies independently, which may indicate that it is not a proper resident of the house – that is, a thing rather than an object. Instead, it testifies to the existence of a tasteful and thoughtful friend or relation elsewhere, evidence of connection, that the narrator's mother is actually admired, appreciated and understood as she deserves. This diverting speculation ends with the discovery that the postman has made an error. The mother's 'whole being drooped – shoulders, stomach, voice, everything'.[33] There is no escape from the domestic misery detailed earlier in the story, summarized in the narrator's observation of her mother that she 'never expected things to turn out well'. Her hopeless, familiar, mechanical gesture of constraint and submission closes the story: 'she undid her apron strings, and then retied them slowly and methodically, making a tighter knot'.[34]

As O'Brien's novels become increasingly urban and tend to be set outside of Ireland, the vibrant childhood home nevertheless still appears in some of her best-received short stories. For example, the story 'A rose in the heart', which, littered with things, provides a detailed narrative of the profound, doomed connection between mother and daughter. O'Brien's memoir reveals that the horrific birth scene opening this story is based on accounts she heard of her own birth. The room in which the birth takes place in the short story is the 'blue room', a room with 'distempered walls' in which the fireplace is fronted by 'the lid of a chocolate box with the representation of a saucy-looking lady'.[35] O'Brien's memoir describes the room in Drewsboro where she was born, also called the 'blue room':

published in the New Yorker in 1963.   32 Ibid., pp 66, 67.   33 Ibid., p. 72.   34 Ibid., pp 67, 72.   35 Edna O'Brien, 'A rose in the heart' in *Mrs Reinhardt and other stories* (London, 1986), p. 109. First published in the *New Yorker* in 1978.

walls weeping quietly away from endless damp and no fire, even though there was a fire grate, ridiculously small compared with the size of the room, in which the lid of a chocolate box had been laid as an ornament.[36]

After the difficult birth and what seems to be a period of post-partum depression, the mother and daughter in 'A rose' become intensely close:

> The food was what united them, eating off the same plate, using the same spoon, watching one another's chews, feeling the food as it went down the other's gullet. … Her mother's knuckles were her knuckles; her mother's veins were her veins … her mother's body a recess that she would wander inside for ever and ever.[37]

The two are united against a brutal father and husband who, among other cruelties, threatens his wife with a hatchet. Against the ugliness, the mother constructs oases for sharing beauty and stolen self-indulgences with her daughter:

> On the big upstairs landing, … the felt dog still lorded it, but now had an eye missing … Also on the landing there was a bowl with a bit of wire inside to hold a profusion of artificial tea roses. These tea roses were a two-toned colour, were red and yellow plastic and the point of each was seared like the point of a thorn. … In the landing at home too was the speared head of Christ. Underneath Christ was a pussy cat of black papier mâché which originally had sweets stuffed into its middle, sweets the exact image of strawberries and even a little leaf at the base, a leaf made of green glazed angelica.[38]

This promiscuous assemblage respects no boundaries, including that between the sacred and profane, as objects exchange qualities with each other and mimic other absent things. Plastic flower petals evoke

36 O'Brien, *Memoir*, pp 3–4.   37 O'Brien, 'A rose', pp 113, 114.   38 Ibid., p. 119.

the crown of thorns associated with the image of an endlessly commiserating Christ, unselfconsciously juxtaposed with an empty cat-shaped sweet container that yet retains the recollection of remarkably strawberry-shaped sweets made of 'heavenly' material. The recurrence of holy pictures and statues among such miscellanies of ornamentation in O'Brien's domestic interiors suggests the mystical 'latency' and 'excess' of all things, that which, as Brown argues, 'remains physically or metaphysically irreducible to objects … their force as a sensuous presence or as a metaphysical presence, the magic by which objects become values, fetishes, idols, and totems'.[39] The endlessly circulating economy of elusive references and referents in these scenes provides numerous instances in O'Brien of the ongoing mutual exchange described by Brown, in which the object shapes and possesses the subject, and vice versa.

In this story, this process extends to the house as a whole, which is described on the first page as having 'a strange lifelikeness as if it was not a house at all but a person observing and breathing'.[40] This uncanny domestic subjectivity, reminiscent of the watching, reproachful houses found in Bowen's fiction, will return in the final paragraph, a subjectivity entirely suffused with the memory and history of the mother-daughter bond. The grown daughter comes home after her mother's death, and longs to be in touch with her once more: 'she looked to see some sign, or hear some murmur. Instead a silence filled the room and there was a vaster silence beyond as if the house itself had died or had been carefully put down to sleep.'[41] The house and the mother have retreated into an elusive thing-ness. Having grown estranged from her mother over the years, the daughter no longer feels the human-nonhuman connection so vital to her mother's survival. According to Tim Ingold, 'Remembering is not so much a matter of calling up an internal image stored in the mind, as of engaging perpetually with an environment that is itself pregnant with the past.'[42] The daughter has lost the specific knack of

39 Brown, 'Thing theory', 5.   40 O'Brien, 'A rose', p. 108.   41 Ibid., p. 140.   42 Tim Ingold, *Perception of the environment: essay on livelihood, dwelling and skill* (London, 2000), p. 189.

engaging with environment and memory she once shared with her mother and cannot make sense of the fragments she discovers in search of her. Rifling through drawers, the daughter can only find 'bits' of the older woman's life:

> Wishes. Dreams contained in such things as a gauze rose of the darkest drenchingest red. ... Never having had the money for real style her mother had invested in imitation things – an imitation crocodile bag and an imitation fur bolero.[43]

The investment here goes beyond the monetary, so cruelly limited by the mother's unremunerated drudgery and servitude. Where, after all, was she ever likely to go carrying a crocodile bag, or, indeed, wearing a fur bolero? There is an entirely other, alternative set of experiences being 'remembered' by and through these objects, not by the daughter, but by the woman who carefully stored them away. Men are implicitly excluded from the bond between women created by a certain aesthetic, usually referred to as 'style' in O'Brien, and communicated by vividly signifying, immediately recognizable 'props' of glamorous, undomesticated femininity. The life being commemorated in the gauze rose, the crocodile bag and fur bolero never existed. Memory is, according to Freeman, 'not natural or organic at all, but depends on various prompts or even props. In turn, S/M shows us memory can prop up projects unrelated to the history it supposedly preserves.'[44] The mother's carefully archived, unused and unusable 'mementos' are the stage dressings for a lacerating yet liberating drag performance, disconnected from, indeed, alien to her own lived experience and expectation. This imagined performance of femininity at once relishes and regrets the mysterious pleasures of a denied version of womanly embodiment. From her first novel, *The country girls*, O'Brien has presented femininity as performance, inspiring both thankfulness and resentment:

43 O'Brien, 'A rose', pp 139–40.   44 Freeman, *Time binds*, p. 161.

It is the only time that I am thankful for being a woman, that time of evening when I draw the curtains, take off my old clothes, and prepare to go out. ... I shadow my eyelids with black stuff and am astonished by the look of mystery it gives my eyes. I hate being a woman. Vain and shallow and superficial.[45]

Mooney describes O'Brien's explicit deployment of drag, in the novels *Down by the river* and *August is a wicked month*, as not only highlighting the arbitrariness of the cultural order, but also offering the transgressive possibility of simultaneously articulating and eliding individuality,[46] a liberatory potential it shares with sadomasochism's painful pleasures.

## The withholding object

Objects can also be recruited to play their part in drag performance, though they are not always cooperative participants. The hallucinatory moments of transformational potential invested in selected homely objects appears to require a mother-daughter pairing to be realized, however momentarily. In another early O'Brien story, 'An outing', a three-piece suite of furniture is pressed to contribute to a staging of alternate domesticity, but withdraws its support at the last minute. This text is unlike the Irish fiction considered so far: it is set in an English city, and features English characters who are childless and leading less financially precarious lives. Every desire for connection is truncated; even the downtrodden wife's emotional relationship with objects is more cursory, more wounding. In the story, unhappily married Mrs Farley catches sight of the coveted furniture while on the bus to work cleaning other people's houses: 'Quite a good three-piece suite covered in dark-green tapestry. Second-hand, of course, but not so shabby that you'd know.'[47] She obsessively plots to raise the £9 necessary to secure the furniture, which she desires for a particular purpose – to show off her home to her 'friend', a man with

45 Edna O'Brien, *The country girls*, p. 171.   46 Mooney, 'Sacramental sleeves', p. 200.
47 Edna O'Brien, 'An outing' in *The love object* (London, 1972), p. 43.

whom she has been carrying on a furtive, though so far sexless, romance. Second-hand objects, perhaps especially furniture, have been shaped by other lives, however, and so their allegiance is suspect. Mrs Farley imagines a glowing scene built around the impulsively fetishized couch, which has not yet earned its aura of magic:

> It would be perfect. May … the sun through the windows shining on the castor oil plant, and the couch a darker shade of green with antimacassars to protect it from sun and greasy hair. There would be a cushion for behind his back, and with a bit of luck, some things would be in bloom, disguising the creosote-soaked fence.[48]

Mrs Farley is another house-proud woman who makes of her own home 'a little palace. Even her husband admitted it.' Nevertheless, her ability to determine the appearance of her own domestic interior is limited. Manifesting an interest in 'home-making' not typical of Irish husbands in O'Brien's fiction, 'Mr Farley did his own decorating and insisted on brown because it did not have to be renewed so often.' According to his wife, 'happiness was the one thing he could not abide', and his joyless, utilitarian aesthetic succeeds in smothering Mrs Farley's modest dream of demonstrating her domestic skills to advantage.[49] The second-hand suite's charms dissipate once relocated to the Farley household, where fantasies of happiness cannot be long sustained and where the furniture has established no history between thing and space, object and subject. Mrs Farley grows terrified that her friend will 'catch her out in her boasting', as the three-piece suite has failed to hit its dramatic mark: 'What he would see was a drab piece of furniture in a drab room where brown prevailed.'[50] The furniture cannot prop up the semblance of luxury and plenitude Mrs Farley has hastily attempted to erect, and the story ends with a grimly humorous image of an immortal Mr Farley and a shared yet isolated experience of comfortless domestic space, devoid of sustaining illusion:

48 Ibid.   49 Ibid., pp 44, 59, 53.   50 Ibid., p. 59.

Her husband would live forever. She and her friend were fated to walk up and down streets towards the railway bridge, and in the end they would grow tired of walking, and they would return, each to a make-shift home.[51]

In recent fiction, O'Brien has explicitly extended the unhomeliness of the 'make-shift home' to a global context. In 'Inner cowboy', a story in her 2011 collection, *Saints and sinners*, an ecological disaster is brought about by Celtic Tiger greed, fuelled by macho posturing and competition. Men are 'grabbing, buying up every perch of farm, bog and quarry', and have 'destroyed a sacred wood with its yew trees, bulldozed it in order to make pasture to fatten livestock'.[52] The massive oil spill perpetrated and then covered up by one of these men is witnessed by the childlike, sensitive male protagonist, Curly (his very name suggests aberrance),[53] who has a complex relationship to objects, as does his grandmother. Her shed, where he goes in order to hide something for his shifty cousin Donie, 'beat all for clutter':

> There was stuff in it going back hundreds of years, an old sidecar with a trap wedged over it, milk churns, milk tankards, breast slanes and foot slanes from when turf was cut by hand, and fenders and picture frames and old chairs and a horsehair sofa with the leather slashed and the coarse hair spilling out. There was a hole in the floor under the sidecar, where his great-grandfather hid his pike in Fenian times and his grandfather hid the bottles of poteen and where he [Curly] ... would hide his bag.[54]

As Brown has observed, things can gothically intervene in traditional chronology, which is collapsed and inverted here through the placement of things with no regard to hierarchical and temporal significance – farming implements, household furniture, weapons of insurrection and illicit distilling. The interior of Curly's

51 Ibid., p. 62.   52 Edna O'Brien, 'Inner cowboy' in *Saints and sinners* (London, 2011), p. 90.   53 My thanks to Professor Tadhg Foley for this observation and other helpful comments.   54 O'Brien, 'Cowboy', p. 92.

grandmother's house is similarly disrespectful of 'proper' order, as a guard who visits her home at the end of the story discovers:

> [The guard] was amazed at the amount of clobber she had accumulated, every single chair and armchair a throne of old newspapers and bags and flattened cardboard boxes. There were bits of crochet, dolls' prams, and a multitude of small china animals along the mantelpiece, above the unlit stove.[55]

Curly shares his grandmother's promiscuous love of things, her 'childlike' resistance to categorizations and priorities of aesthetic pleasure; however, his relationship to the nonhuman is ultimately tentative and destructive rather than reassuring. To protect his grandmother, Curly retrieves his cousin's bag from the shed and takes it to the bog, the place he learned in school where treasure was traditionally buried. Curly's treatment of this bag as a person/corpse makes sly reference to bog bodies, and the way in which corpses become objects when displayed in a museum setting. He places the bag into his own wardrobe and buttons it into a jacket and puts a hat on it 'so that it looked like a dead person, a dead person with the legs sawn off'.[56] The bag/body hovers in that liminal zone of 'thingness', the 'threshold between the nameable and the unnameable, the figurable and the unfigurable, the identifiable and the uniden-tifiable'.[57]

Dressing the bag in men's clothing, a kind of drag performance that crosses the human-nonhuman divide, illustrates a significant difference between Curly and the female characters discussed thus far. Unlike them, Curly struggles to conform to 'manly' expectation of behaviour and attitudes, a struggle with implications for his connection to things. Like the bag, Curly feels compelled to perform adult masculinity, but his efforts are unconvincing. Dressing up the bag recalls a child playing with dolls, and one particularly uncanny category of objects in O'Brien's fiction is toys, which often take on a life of their own, and in such a way as to voice characters' melancholy

---

55 Ibid., p. 104.   56 Ibid., p. 93.   57 Brown, 'Thing theory', 5.

dread or feelings of helplessness.[58] An Elmo doll in 'Inner cowboy' articulates the inescapability of an oppressive and compulsorily violent masculine heteronormativity, which leads to Curly's death. Curly has been bullied into acting like a 'man' and risking his own (and his grandmother's) safety for his cousin's sake by hiding the bag, which contains money and/or drugs. This act has driven Curly to despair as he hears his own voice emerging from a neighbour child's doll:

> When Curly was a young man, there was a girl two doors down that got a toy at Christmas that could talk. It was clothed in red fur, the mouth open and the tongue hanging out. It had two plastic knobs for eyes and an orange fur nose, and every so often it said 'Elmo wants you to know that Elmo loves you'. He was Elmo, only it was him saying it to himself – *I am so far in I can't get out.* It wouldn't stop.[59]

As at other times in the story, Curly struggles here with the imperative to replace an ethic of love with one of brutality. Obeying this command takes him to the brink of psychosis, which perhaps leads him to throw himself in the bog along with the bag, though whether his death is a suicide, an accident or something more sinister is never discovered. Curly's body is found by a walker who responds to a call – not a human or animal call, but the mechanical cry of a mobile phone, that, when she picks it up, feels 'alive in her hand'.[60] His last communication is through an object, an 'inappropriately' gendered light pink phone, retrieved by a woman.

Curly's tragedy emerges from his attempt to refuse the support of, and connection to, his grandmother and all of the older 'homely' values she represents. He has been bullied and shamed into rejecting the comforts of the vibrant home, filled to bursting with friendly things. He is excluded from the transcendent magic inhering in the object, not only by his gender, but also due to his positioning in

---

58 For a more developed discussion of toys in O'Brien's fiction, see O'Connor, 'Haunting bird'. 59 O'Brien, 'Cowboy', p. 102. 60 Ibid., p. 105.

twenty-first-century modernity, an era of increased disposability leading to a decrease in connection to loved objects, a notion now associated with childishness and nostalgia. A passionate relationship to things in O'Brien's domestic interiors, however, especially the impoverished interiors of mid-century rural Ireland, allowed the women trapped within to imagine revolution on a personal level as well as communally, to dare defiance and glimpse dangerous freedoms along the edges of the life-matter divide.

# A wandering to find home: *Adam & Paul* (2004)

## Tony Tracy

> Their farewell was memorable. Neary came out of one of his dead sleeps and said: 'Murphy, all life is figure and ground.'
> 'But a wandering to find home', said Murphy.
>
> —Samuel Beckett, *Murphy*

> The identities of places are inevitably unfixed. They are unfixed in part precisely because the social relations out of which they are constructed are themselves by their very nature dynamic and changing … the identity of any place, including that place called home, is in one sense forever open to contestation.
>
> —Doreen Massey, *Space, place, and gender*

What does it mean to be 'at home'? These quotations offer contrasting approaches. In the stories and dramas of Beckett, home represents a place of psychic and physical shelter from the indifferent world, a place often coterminous with death. 'In Beckett's world', writes Miller Robinson, 'one is prodded out of one's rest and one seeks rest'. 'We are not only expelled onto our personal *via dolorosa*, but we long to return to the security of darkness, to the sense of our being without consciousness, to mother, to "home".'[1] Doreen Massey,

---

1 Fred Miller Robinson, *The comedy of language: studies in modern comic literature* (Amherst, MA, 1980), p. 133.

on the other hand, exemplifies the theoretical 'turn' which under-stands space as dynamic and contested irrespective of how it may have been conceived by architects, planners or institutions. Space cannot be fixed, cannot be taken for granted because it cannot be divorced from time. As Henri Lefebvre – the writer who first conceived of space as socially produced – puts it: 'The user's space is lived – not represented (or conceived).'[2] From these two positions, home emerges as a double-edged concept: an imaginary 'lost' place, frequently identified with the maternal, to which all humans yearn to return, and the lived spaces of everyday life where we seek to be at home – generally, but not essentially, private – which are called on to meet that desire. Popular cinema has played a key cultural role in capturing both senses of home through constructions of the domestic sphere. Elizabeth Bronfen addresses the tensions within such constructions in a discussion of the 'fantasy work' done by American cinema's 'home romances'. Within a psychoanalytic framework, she argues that constructions of the home in Hollywood cinema can be identified as working to contain 'traumatic knowledge about the uncanniness that lies at the heart of all worldly emplacement'[3] – or as Dorothy in the *The wizard of Oz* puts it, 'There's no place like home.' A key strategy in re-enforcing this message is the trope of reassuring narrative conclusions, 'the return to a familiar place, to the protection of the family or the successful couple building', which on closer inspection, Bronfen argues, are often less certain than they at first appear to be.[4] Home in Hollywood is a foundational but fragile fiction. While Bronfen's study relates to mainstream American film, it is of value and wider application in its recognition that cinema operates at the intersection of representation and desire, showing things as they are *and* imagining them as they might be, enacting the place/space tensions within the concept of home itself.

In the discussion that follows I tease out these tensions in relation to *Adam & Paul*, a 2004 film dealing with a day in the life of two

2 Henri Lefevbre, *The production of space*, trans. Donald Nicholson-Smith (Oxford, 1991), p. 362.  3 Elisabeth Bronfen, *Home in Hollywood: the imaginary geography of cinema* (New York, 2004), p. 25.  4 Ibid.

male drug addicts as they cross Dublin in search of a fix.[5] Structuring this portrait are tensions in the meaning of home and homelessness. On the one hand the film is largely located in the exterior environment, faithful to the topography and spaces of contemporary Dublin where its protagonists eat, sleep and encounter others in comparable situations. On the other, *Adam & Paul* encompasses more abstract meanings of home in its portrait of lost (and undifferentiated) characters who desire a return to 'the security of darkness' and to 'being without consciousness', but who also cling to the company of each other. This essay explores these themes and tensions and argues that they come into fleeting focus in the film's central and sole domestic setting – Janine's flat – which functions as the film's 'dream house'. However, as in Bronfen's analysis (albeit in a very different register), slippages in narration problematize this as a scene of reassurance and the protagonists' displacement is reaffirmed as they re-embark upon a fated *via dolorosa*.

*Adam & Paul* begins and ends on open ground – uninhabited non-places on the edge of the city without shelter or significance. We first encounter the addicts lying alongside a dumped mattress and fridge, a tableau of abject and improvised domesticity. Placeless and perplexed, as they come to consciousness they rhetorically ask 'Where the fuck are we? … How the fuck did we end up here?' While their confusion is spatial, this opening scene, shot wide and from above, brings to mind Martin Heidegger's concept of 'thrownness' ('*Geworfenheit*'), 'the being's non-mastery of its own origin and its referential dependence on other beings', or as Michael Inwood explains it, humanity's condition of being 'thrown naked into a bare insignificant world in which it is not at home'.[6] The narrative that unfolds from this initial thrownness can therefore be read as a desire for home, a reimagining of Homer's Odyssey at the margins of modern Ireland. However, in place of a domestic destination, heroin substitutes as the driving desire and imaginary site of return,

5 Lenny Abrahamson (dir.), *Adam & Paul* (Element Pictures, 2004).  6 William J. Richardson, *Heidegger: through phenomenology to thought* (4th ed. New York, 2003), p. 37; Michael Inwood, *A Heidegger dictionary* (London, 1999), p. 38.

propelling Adam and Paul falteringly forward. Having detached themselves from the mattress and shivering in the cold morning light (a symbolic expression of birth), they encounter two unemployed youths who inform them that a dealer named Martin sells heroin in the Ballymun flats. While this setting provides a measure of social context (in 2004 the flats were a failed social project on the verge of demolition) it also develops the theme of alienation in terms of domestic demise: the youths sit on another dumped appliance, while the once-bustling high-rise homes have been abandoned and are mostly boarded up. Those that remain are occupied by male misfits like Martin, who refuses to open the door – the first of many denials to potential spaces and places of respite – and the addicts are forced to move towards the city centre.

These early scenes offer a vision of homelessness that is primarily physical; their dejection is absolute, inescapable and centred on an all-too-present body. A broader social dimension is revealed in an encounter with friends in St Stephen's Green – including Janine's brother, Wayne – in which domestic space emerges as a structuring absence. Here Adam and Paul's situation gains context – and invites sympathy – through the recovery of their past. Apparently ignorant of this history, they are told of the recent drug-related death of their friend Matthew, and we learn that as young boys, all three 'practically lived' in Marion's house (a childhood friend and sister of Wayne and Janine). From the conversation we infer that (the absent) Janine also abused heroin, but with Wayne's help she has managed to get clean and exchanged the lure of the needle for a flat of her own. The flat is evoked in idyllic terms – 'lovely' and filled with expensive 'gear'. Recognizing that Adam and Paul pose a threat to this fragile domesticity, Wayne puts them on notice to stay away: 'Lads, if I see youse near Janine – I'm not joking now – I'll kill yis.' Heroin addiction has removed them from this extended family of their childhood, leaving them without anchor or shelter. The tone of address – they are constantly scolded and talked down to – positions them as children who have not made the transition to adulthood, which is framed in terms of the attainment and maintenance of domestic independence.

The encounter produces surprisingly little recognition and no nostalgia ('a longing for home') as they stumble along their *via dolorosa*. As they do, the city unfolds as a kind of generalized domestic space with a variety of private activities (smoking hash, shooting up, defecating, sleeping, eating) and identities (criminals, drug addicts, exiles on the run) performed in public. In this collapse of public and private categories, absurdist encounters and conversations ensue. They meet homeless young men cocooned in sleeping bags sketched cheerily as self-contained homes of one. One says he has no need to wear clothes because it is so warm inside; another cheerfully opines on his favourite chocolate bar as he begs outside a shop. Collectively, these and unseen others exist below eye level and mainstream society, a fraternity known only to one another. However, while these encounters create a sense of easy commonality they do not produce a spirit of camaraderie. The taller of the two protagonists (played by Mark O'Halloran; they are undifferentiated by name throughout the film) is particularly antagonistic towards others and dismisses them as interferring and best avoided. Through these public/private encounters, Adam and Paul emerge as a vagabond version of a domestic couple whose relationship, in the absence of a conventional physical space, fulfils the function of mutual shelter and protection.

### 'Too right a free country! OUR fuckin' country!'

While the intimacy of Adam and Paul's relationship has been reinforced (if not formed) through their mutually dependent status as addicts, it is framed in somewhat different terms in an encounter with a Bulgarian immigrant that moves the narrative closer to contemporary social concerns and enlarges the film's definition of its core themes and tensions. Home here comes to refer to the 'domestic' space of the nation, while homelessness encompasses non-nationals who as refugees or migrants have recently moved into that territorial and imaginary space. Continuing the private/public motif, a public bench becomes another improvised site of domesticity as the shorter of the pair (played by Tom Murphy) arrives clutching stolen supplies of bread and milk. Noticing a well-dressed man sitting at the other end, he politely asks him to make room. However, the request is met with unexpected refusal and aggression: 'What is this – I'm sitting here first – it is public property.' While such hostility is a recurring experience for Adam and Paul, the man's foreign accent and the setting add symbolic value to the encounter. The immediate context was the relatively recent and still novel phenomenon of inward migration to Ireland. In the year of the film's production (2004), the European Union was enlarged to include ten new Eastern European countries. Following enlargement, Ireland suddenly became a desirable destination for thousands of 'new' Europeans, along with a significant number of non-EU nationals and a dramatic increase in asylum seekers. Responding to this sudden and multifaceted influx, a referendum on the Irish constitution aimed at restricting access to Irish citizenship was put before the country and passed by a large majority.[7] This so-called 'common-sense citizenship' amendment was deemed necessary to counteract alleged 'citizenship tourism' by women arriving in late-stage pregnancy. It was, in the words of Minister for Justice Brian Lenihan, a response to 'the real-life circumstances we find ourselves in', and a necessary recognition that Irish '[c]itizenship is a political right and not a human right'.[8]

Central to the referendum was a correlation between space and place: previously, one could only claim Irish citizenship – and therefore identify Ireland as home – on the basis of being born in the country; being temporarily resident did not qualify. The bench thus becomes a symbolic site within this debate – on the one hand 'open' and available to anyone who wishes to sit there, but understood as a privileged space reserved through birthright on the other:

- A fucking free country it is here. I sit where I like!
- Too right a free country! OUR fuckin' country!

7 See Iseult Honohan, 'Bounded citizenship and the meaning of citizenship laws: Ireland's *ius soli* citizenship referendum' in Linda Cardinal and Nicholas Brown (eds), *Managing diversity: practices of citizenship in Australia, Canada and Ireland* (Ottawa, 2007), pp 63–87.
8 Brian Lenihan, 'Citizenship change common sense', *Irish Times*, 28 May 2004.

- Oh, yes. Here we go.
- Yeah, here we go.

While the terms of debates such as this are as old as nationalism, their relative newness in Ireland is exposed in a highly ironic manner. In common with the young men seen in sleeping bags, the man's suitcase and appearance suggest that he is also living outside. Although the smaller protagonist has earlier expressed sympathy for Bulgarians in a tone that recalls the charitable instincts of Irish Catholicism – 'I feel sorry for them … they have nothing' – no shared sense of solidarity or circumstance is forthcoming in the 'real-life circumstances' in which they now find themselves. Indeed, their knee-jerk xenophobia quickly positions them in a Swiftian confrontation over a tiny space without any wider sense of their shared condition as homeless or Europeans. Their sense of superiority is challenged by the man's directness and worldliness: 'You are stupid person … And you are all stupid people. I am not a fucking Romanian. My whole life, I am never Romanian … I've never been in fucking Romania!'[9]

An additional irony comes from an indirect challenge to the notion of the nation as a sovereign domestic space that exists to protect its inhabitants. Although it is unacknowledged within the diegesis, the bench sits in front of the Irish Financial Services Centre (IFSC), a highly symbolic location in which to stage this scene. A pioneering instance of the post-industrial, service-based capitalism that formed the foundation of the Irish Celtic Tiger economy, the IFSC is physically present (through its office buildings and employees) but socially distant. Although located in what was once a thriving working-class community, it exemplifies what Anthony Giddens has described as the 'time-space distanciation' of late modernity. As James Arvanitakis summarizes:

9 Ironically the actor who plays this character is, in fact, Romanian. A well-known stage and screen actor and director, Ion Caramitru was Romanian minister of culture between 1996 and 2000.

In pre-modern times, societies, space and place largely coincided – the spatial dimensions of social life for the majority of the population dominated by presence of localised activities. Modernity increasingly tears space away from place by fostering relations between 'absent' others ... place becomes increasingly phantasmagorical – locales are penetrated and shaped by distant social influences.[10]

The IFSC is an expression of Giddens' notion of 'disembedding': 'the lifting out of social relations from local contexts of interaction and their restructuring across indefinite spans of time-space'.[11] Thus, while Adam and Paul squabble with another homeless European about 'OUR country', offshore companies and invisible flows of global capital do business, literally, behind their backs. Their ironic assertion that Bulgaria is a 'shithole ... in comparison to Ireland' derives from an inability to recognize their own alienation and subsequent failure to find common cause with a similarly displaced masculinity. Finally, the Bulgarian undermines their conflation of nation, identity and meaning by reasserting the primacy of a philosophical discourse over a nationalist one: 'Why am I here? Did you ever ask yourself the same question? Why are YOU here, huh? Why the fuck are YOU here?' With this, he leaves. Confounded, the two addicts move on once more, leaving the contested bench vacant.

## The oneiric house

Tired and increasingly sick, Adam and Paul now head towards the film's sole and unequivocal domestic setting. After their ceaseless wandering outdoors, Janine's flat represents a coming home that is both actual and imaginary and a scene which provides a hinge between their lost past and fated future. In his seminal work *The poetics of space*, Gaston Bachelard introduces the concept of 'an oneiric

10 James Arvanitakis, analysis and discussion of Anthony Giddens, *The consequences of modernity*, http://jamesarvanitakis.net/theorests/anthony-giddens, accessed 1 Aug. 2016.
11 Anthony Giddens, *The consequences of modernity* (Cambridge, 1991), pp 18–19.

house, a house of dream memory' to express the dual nature of the home as a physical and psychic space to which we long to return: 'Not only do we come back to [the house] but we dream of coming back to it like a bird comes back to its nest or a lamb to the fold.'[12] First mentioned during the St Stephen's Green encounter, Janine's flat enters the narrative at its midpoint (minutes 41–8) and can be read as the film's oneiric house – the 'fold' towards which Adam and Paul have been subconsciously travelling, and from which they will move towards darkness. While their motive may initially be to steal the 'lovely gear' that Wayne has rewarded Janine with, the flat functions in the film as a fleeting space of nurture and dreaming and stands as a public-housing counterpoint to the dehumanizing modernism of the Ballymun complex.[13]

As they tentatively push open the door, they cross a threshold that is more than physical. The space is 'spotless', and they are temporarily transfixed by cartoons playing on the TV. Disturbed by the sound of a child crying, they are drawn to an adjoining bedroom where their dirty and degraded condition contrasts with the cleanliness and innocence of the baby they discover. The chaos of their lives is temporarily stilled. As they pick up the child they soften ('Who's the ba-ba-ba'), then revert to customary cynicism as they check down the side of the cot for money, before resuming their baby talk. When Janine appears in the doorway the film slips free of its naturalist style to become dreamlike in tone. They look up, there is a jump cut to the three adults (and child) embracing in slow motion and the diegetic sound drops out. Then the spell is broken and a cold reality restored.

---

12 Gaston Bachelard, *The poetics of space* (Boston, 1994), pp 98–9.   13 The small complex where Janine lives is situated in Dublin's north inner city and can be identified as one of the thousands of dwellings designed by Herbert Simms, the housing architect for Dublin Corporation during the 1932–9 'slum clearance project', when a number of similar schemes were completed. These developments represent a median point in working-class housing, between the inner-city tenements depicted in the film *Pigs* (1984) and the Ballymun flats on the city's outskirts. Low-rise and scaled to their settings, the Dublin Corporation flats foster strong bonds of community and pride. Their design was derived from Simms' visit to Holland in 1925 to see the work of Michel de Klerk and Piet Kramer, key figures of the Amsterdam School and pioneering architects in working-class socialist housing. See 'Herbert Simms' in *Dictionary of Irish architects, 1720–1940*, http://www.dia.ie/architects/view/4969/Simms-HerbertGeorge, accessed 8 Apr. 2017.

We cut to a shot of Adam and Paul holding the baby from Janine's point of view:

- How the fuck did you get in?
- The door was open.
- It wasn't – I'd remember.
- It was.
- Well that's amazing that you haven't everything robbed or broken.
- Ah, no way … fuck sake.

At this point we are forced to ask who or what has generated the break in cinematic narration and how we are to understand it. Diog O'Connell describes it as an instance of 'internal focalization … the wish fulfilment and emotional need of somebody who has been ravaged by drug addiction'.[14] While this is plausible, it is important to note that the trigger for the oneiric slippage is the arrival of Janine, the return of the absent mother. Her return brings psychic completeness to the home, not only calming her infant but also producing a regressive state in Adam and Paul. Anticipating Bachelard, Freud proposed in *Civilization and its discontents* (1930) that 'the dwelling-house was a substitute for the mother's womb, the first lodging, for which in all likelihood man still longs, and in which he was safe and felt at ease'.[15] In its suspension of time through sound and picture the scene can be read within this framework of substitution, linking the sensory experience of the womb, the maternal space of home and a return to a pre-verbal state of plenitude. The scene also, of course, resembles a drug high, linking home and heroin and briefly positioning Adam and Paul's search for a score in terms of a Freudian 'lost object'. All of this is rendered in an ambivalent and almost subliminal manner, on the fringes of the narrative and outside its causal logic. The setting's status as dream house is continued in a more literal sense when the three childhood friends share a joint in the living room: 'the house shelters day-

14 Diog O'Connell, *New Irish storytellers: narrative strategies in film* (Bristol, 2010), p. 107.
15 Sigmund Freud, *Civilization and its discontents* (New York, 2010), p. 37.

dreaming, the house protects the dreamer, the house allows one to dream in peace'.[16]

Nevertheless, this dreaming is cut short by Janine, who abruptly punctures the reverie as she realizes (as Wayne had earlier) that Adam and Paul threaten the flat's function as a space of protection and nurture for her infant:

- It's good to have youse around, nice like ... you can't stay.
- Ah yea ... we know.

Sitting unaccosted, indoors and on a comfy couch – foreshadowed throughout the first half of the film – has been fleeting and Adam and Paul are expelled for the first and last time from the film's only home. As they leave, Janine refers to them as the baby's 'daddies', but any suggestion of emotional empathy on their part is immediately extinguished by their heartless mugging of a boy with Down's syndrome in search of his pocket money. The scene is traumatic but in keeping with earlier scenes, as they return to the coarsely physical and Darwinian realities of lives lived in public. To these junkies searching to score before nightfall, the intimacy and comfort of Janine's flat has made little impression, prompting neither comment nor a longing to go home in any conventional sense.

## Wandering towards darkness

Samuel Beckett's short story 'The expelled' tells of the experiences of a person thrown out of his home (the first of many Beckettian works on this theme) and bears striking parallels with the themes and structure of *Adam & Paul*: 'When I am abroad in the morning, I go to meet the sun and in the evening when I am abroad, I follow it until I am down among the dead.'[17] As the day turns to night, Adam and Paul's plight becomes both more desperate and comically chaotic

---

16 Bachelard, *Poetics of space*, p. 6.   17 Samuel Beckett, *The expelled and other novellas* (Harmondsworth, 2008), p. 25.

through a farcical series of misrecognitions and misunderstandings. After failing as lookouts for the mysterious Clank, they steal a car, crash it and come into possession of a stolen TV which they bring to a 'fence' named Kittser. In another instance of private life turned inside out, they carry the TV back to the Ballymun complex and enter a flat where they are mute bystanders to a hysterical negotiation which ends with the TV being smashed. Fleeing the building, they encounter a crowd of vigilantes attempting to break down the door of the drug dealer (Martin) they tried to score from in the opening scene. Homesickness and heroin sickness are related conditions; one is located in the body the other in the mind:

- Back where we started.
- I'm going to die.

As they sit down outside (again), two large packets of heroin fall from the sky – thrown from Martin's flat. In a short scene, their true 'coming home' takes place: we see the taller addict inject the smaller one in the leg. They visit the Bunker pub, where Janine recognizes that they are high and takes them outside. Wary of their influence, Wayne arrives, and for the final time they are told to 'fuck off'. With nothing to do, they shoot up again, outstripping their misery and entering a zone of transcendence reminiscent of Beckett's Vladimir and Estragon at the end of their day: 'We are no longer alone, waiting for the night, waiting for Godot, waiting for … waiting. All evening we have struggled, unassisted. Now it's over. It's already tomorrow.'[18]

And so it is. The soundtrack cuts to sounds of birds and the ocean over an image of bright morning. In a striking counterpoint to the dream house imagined by Bachelard and momentarily actualized in Janine's flat, Adam and Paul have slept outside again. This time their mattress has been the dunes beside the Poolbeg chimneys, first observed when they awoke on waste ground the previous morning.

**18** Samuel Beckett, *Waiting for Godot* in *The complete dramatic works of Samuel Beckett* (London, 1990), ii, p. 15.

Nothing has changed and yet everything has. Their 'epic' journey is both an echo and an inversion of the voyage undertaken in the Jim Sheridan-scripted film *Into the West* (1983), in which two young men similarly travel from the Ballymun flats to the Irish coastline. Influenced by the linking of place and identity central to the *Celtic Twilight* imaginary, the earlier film positioned Ireland's Atlantic seaboard as a mythical place of return and rebirth linked to an enduring maternal spirit. While Adam and Paul also escape the similarly imagined wasteland of the condemned flats, they move eastward towards death rather than rebirth. The camera angle reveals just one chimney: the taller, more capable addict has died in the night. Disoriented and confused, the smaller one stands up and leaves the frame, then returns to retrieve the remaining drugs from his dead friend's pocket. Without the thin thread of their relationship to sustain him, his long-term chance of survival seems slim. For the first time, he is truly without either a space or a place to call home.

## Conclusion

An early critique of *Adam & Paul* contrasted it positively with a number of contemporary Irish romantic comedies judged to be 'devoid of identifiable Irish features with which to connect', noting that:

> *Adam and Paul* turns to characterizations of the working classes, the criminal world, and the world of [the] unemployable for a glimpse at genuine Irish life … the ugly economic consequences for the working classes that counterbalance the middleclass affluence of the Celtic Tiger.[19]

But while the film undoubtedly captures a marginal milieu in a way that few – if any – contemporary Irish films have, providing 'a glimpse at genuine Irish life' in any narrowly realist sense is not its primary

19 Michael Paul Gillespie, 'The odyssey of *Adam and Paul*, a twenty-first-century Irish film', *New Hibernia Review*, 12:1 (2008), 46–7.

ambition or achievement. In tone and approach, it takes inspiration from existential rather than realist traditions, notably the work of Samuel Beckett, who, for Richard Kearney, deployed 'Irish material' to explode 'Irish Revival pretentions and particularly its claim to a fixed national identity … [which] could offer no legitimate refuge from the "filthy modern tide" of alienation'.[20] In a comparable way, *Adam & Paul* uses 'Irish material' (locations, characters, dialogue) as the basis for exploring alienation in a contemporary European context. As I have suggested, the film approaches these via a theme of homelessness focused on two characters whose domestic existence has been turned inside out as they wander Dublin in search of a fix. The material and imaginary dimensions of this theme intersect and coalesce in Janine's flat, which, through its association with mother-infant relations, becomes briefly a 'dream house' of physical and psychological shelter. This fleeting and barely registered experience of home punctuates Adam and Paul's anti-odyssey from one patch of rough ground to another, a journey that begins and ends with sleep.

20 Richard Kearney, *Navigations: collected Irish essays, 1976–2006* (Syracuse, 2006), p. 428.

# How to read a building

## Vona Groarke

Don't. You might as well say a morning convenes
in panelled reflections of itself. Or call the way
a roofline predicts its likely outcome, fate. Write 'arch',
and the word has to position itself between noun
and adjective. Put 'Lintel' as a title: see what comes of it.
I, too, may think of line endings with every quoin
or cant; of surface meaning caulked airtight;
of metaphor constructed as a tinted curtain wall.
I am alive, yes, to the notion of cantilevered sound,
open to rhymes between stone and stained glass,
sunlight and cement. Say what you like, there's a name
for every kind of window you could possibly
see through. But the room with no window
has no first line and all its stowaway fictions need
to be written in dark ink. So we deal in apertures,
we say, in the business of proportional reveal.
Twice, that I know of, it falls into place: once,
when sand in mortar is listening to rain
and again, when slate roof tiles recall small words
in a ghost hand that rubbed them clean away.

# Contributors

ANGELA BOURKE is author of the biography *Maeve Brennan: homesick at the* New Yorker (2004), *The burning of Bridget Cleary: a true story* (1999) and, most recently, the Famine Folio *Voices underfoot: memory, forgetting, and oral verbal art* (2016), along with many articles and reviews in scholarly journals and elsewhere. Joint editor of *The Field Day anthology*, iv/v: *Irish women's writing and traditions*, she writes and lectures in both Irish and English. She is professor emerita at the UCD School of Irish, Celtic Studies, Folklore and Linguistics, and a member of the Royal Irish Academy.

COLETTE BRYCE has published four poetry collections with Picador, including *The full Indian rope trick* (2004) and *Self-portrait in the dark* (2008). Her latest, *The whole & rain-domed universe* (2014), which draws on her experience of growing up in Derry during the Troubles, was given a Ewart-Biggs Award in memory of Seamus Heaney. *Selected poems*, drawing on all her books, is a Poetry Book Society Special Commendation 2017. Colette lives in Newcastle upon Tyne where she works as a freelance writer and editor. She received the Cholmondeley Award for poetry in 2010.

THEO DORGAN is a poet, novelist, prose writer, editor, essayist, translator and documentary script writer. He is also a broadcaster on radio and television. Among his recent publications are: *Liberty walks naked* (2017) and *Barefoot souls* (2015), both translations from the French of Syrian poet Maram al-Masri; *Jason and the Argonauts* (2014), a libretto; *Foundation stone: towards a constitution for a 21st century republic* (2013, editor); and the novel *Making way* (2013). His collection *Nine bright shiners*, from Dedalus Press, was awarded the Irish Times/Poetry Now Prize for the best collection published in 2014. He is a member of Aosdána.

NICHOLAS GRENE is emeritus professor of English literature at Trinity College Dublin and a member of the Royal Irish Academy. His books include *Shakespeare's tragic imagination* (Macmillan, 1992), *The politics of Irish drama* (Cambridge University Press, 1999), *Shakespeare's serial history plays* (Cambridge University Press, 2002), *Yeats's poetic codes* (Oxford University Press, 2008) and *Home on the stage* (Cambridge University Press, 2014). The *Oxford handbook of modern Irish theatre*, which he co-edited with Chris Morash, was published by Oxford University Press in 2016. *The theatre of Tom Murphy: playwright adventurer* is forthcoming from Bloomsbury in 2017.

VONA GROARKE has published seven collections of poetry with Gallery Press, the most recent being *X* (2014) and *Selected poems*, recently awarded the Pigott Prize for the best book of poetry by an Irish poet in 2016. Her book-length essay on art-frames, *Four sides full*, was also published in 2016. Her poems have recently appeared in the *New Yorker*, *Ploughshares* and the *Threepenny Review*. A former editor of *Poetry Ireland Review*, she currently teaches poetry at the University of Manchester in the UK.

ADAM HANNA is a lecturer in Irish literature in the School of English at University College Cork, where he was previously a Government of Ireland Postdoctoral Fellow (2015–17). He was brought up in Ireland, the UK and the USA. Before coming to Cork he taught in the English department of the University of Aberdeen, and before that at the University of Bristol, where he gained his doctorate (2012). He is the author of *Northern Irish poetry and domestic space* (Palgrave, 2015) and is currently writing a study of modern Irish poets' responses to legal changes.

HOWARD KEELEY directs the Center for Irish Research and Teaching at Georgia Southern University. A native of Dublin, he received his undergraduate degree from the University of Georgia and a PhD in English from Princeton University. Much of his research has focused on how nineteenth-century Irish literature reflects the ascent of the Catholic middle class. Currently, he is principal investigator on a grant-funded inquiry into the migration axis between Co. Wexford, Ireland, and Savannah, Georgia, during the 1840s and 1850s.

Lucy McDiarmid is the author or editor of eight books. Her scholarly interest in cultural politics, especially quirky, colorful, suggestive episodes, is exemplified by *Poets and the peacock dinner* (2014; paperback 2016) as well as by *The Irish art of controversy* (2005). Her most recent book is *At home in the revolution: what women said and did in 1916* (2015). The recipient of fellowships from the Guggenheim Foundation, the Cullman Center for Scholars and Writers at the New York Public Library, and the National Endowment for the Humanities, she is Marie Frazee-Baldassarre Professor of English at Montclair State University.

Mary Morrissy is the author of three novels, *Mother of pearl*, *The pretender* and *The rising of Bella Casey*, and two collections of stories, *A lazy eye* and, most recently, *Prosperity Drive*. *Mother of pearl*, her first novel, was shortlisted for the Whitbread Award (now Costa) and *The pretender* and *The rising of Bella Casey* have both been nominated for the Dublin Impac International Literary Award. Her short fiction has been anthologized widely and won her a Hennessy Award in 1984. In 1995 she was awarded the prestigious US Lannan Award, which honours writers whose work 'is of exceptional quality'. She is the associate director of creative writing at University College Cork and a member of Aosdána.

Eiléan Ní Chuilleanáin, born in 1942 in Cork, is an emeritus fellow of Trinity College Dublin, and currently Ireland Professor of Poetry (2016–19). She has published and edited academic articles and books on the literature of the English Renaissance, on translation and on Irish writing in both Irish and English. With her husband Macdara Woods she is, since 1975, a founder and co-editor of the Irish poetry journal *Cyphers*. She has published eight collections of poetry over forty-five years, and her *Selected poems* appeared in 2008. *The boys of Bluehill* was published in 2015 by Gallery Press and Wake Forest University Press.

Maureen O'Connor lectures in the School of English in University College Cork. Author of *The female and the species: the animal in Irish women's writing* (2010), she has also edited and co-edited several essay collections and special journal issues and has published widely on Irish women writers and the environment. Edited volumes include *Wild colonial girl: essays on Edna O'Brien* (2006; co-editor Lisa Colletta) and *Edna O'Brien: new critical perspectives* (2006; co-editors Kathryn Laing and Sinéad Mooney). She is currently completing a monograph on O'Brien's fiction.

RHONA RICHMAN KENNEALLY is a professor of design, architecture and the built environment, and former chair, of the department of design and computation arts at Concordia University. She is co-founder and a fellow of Concordia's School of Irish Studies, and has been the editor of the *Canadian Journal of Irish Studies* since 2010. Her research and publications on Ireland have been funded by the Social Sciences and Humanities Research Council of Canada and focus on women's work and agency in domestic space during the mid-twentieth century, with particular attention to evolving technologies in the home.

TONY TRACY lectures in film theory and history at Huston School of Film & Digital Media, NUI Galway. His research focuses on areas of Irish and Hollywood cinemas, as well as silent-film history. He has produced a number of documentaries and is founding editor of the annual review of Irish film and TV for the online journal www.estudiosirlandeses.org.

MACDARA WOODS was born in Dublin in 1942, and lived there and in Co. Meath for most of his youth. He has been publishing poems since the early 1960s, and has also collaborated internationally with composers, performers and graphic artists. He is a founder editor – since 1975 – of the Irish literary magazine *Cyphers*. His most recent collection, *Music from the big tent* (Dedalus), was shortlisted for the 2017 Irish Times Award. He is a member of Aosdána.

# Bibliography

Aalen, F.H.A. et al. (eds), *Atlas of the Irish rural landscape* (Toronto, 1997; 2nd ed. Toronto, 2011).

Abrahamson, Lenny (dir.), *Adam & Paul* (Element Pictures, 2004).

Allingham, William, *Laurence Bloomfield in Ireland: a modern poem* (London, 1864).

Arensberg, Conrad M., *The Irish countryman: an anthropological study* (New York, 1950).

Arensberg, Conrad M. & Solon T. Kimball, *Family and community in Ireland* (Gloucester, MA, 1961).

Arvanitakis, James, Analysis and discussion of Anthony Giddens, *The consequences of modernity*, http://jamesarvanitakis.net/theorests/anthony -giddens, accessed 1 Aug. 2016.

Bachelard, Gaston, *The poetics of space*, trans. Maria Jolas (Boston, 1994).

Banim, Michael, *Crohoore of the bill-hook* (1825) in *The parlour novelist: works of fiction by the most celebrated authors* (Belfast, 1846).

—, *Father Connell: a tale* (New York, 1888).

Barad, Karen, *Meeting the universe halfway: quantum physics and the entanglement of matter and meaning* (Durham, NC, 2007).

Beatty, Aidan, *Masculinity and power in Irish nationalism, 1884–1938* (Basingstoke, 2016).

Beckett, Samuel, *The expelled and other novellas* (Harmondsworth, 2008).

—, *Waiting for Godot* in *The complete dramatic works of Samuel Beckett* (London, 1990).

Bennett, Jane, *Vibrant matter: a political ecology of things* (Durham, NC, 2010).

Benson, Mary, 'Contemporary apartment living: living above place?' in Corcoran and Share (eds), *Belongings* (2008), pp 117–28.

Bew, Paul, *Ireland: the politics of enmity, 1789–2006* (Oxford, 2007).

—, *Land and the national question in Ireland, 1858–1882* (Dublin, 1978).

Blunt, Alison, *Domicile and diaspora: Anglo-Indian women and the spatial politics of home* (Oxford, 2005).

Blunt, Alison & Robyn Dowling, *Home* (London, 2006).

Bourdieu, Pierre, *The logic of practice*, trans. Richard Nice (Stanford, CA, 1990).

—, *Outline of a theory of practice* (Cambridge, 1977).

Bourke, Angela, 'Keening as theatre' in Grene (ed.), *Interpreting Synge* (2000), pp 67–79.

—, *Maeve Brennan: homesick at the* New Yorker (London & Washington, DC, 2004).

Bourke, Angela et al. (eds), *The Field Day anthology of literature*, iv/v: *Irish women's writing and traditions* (New York, 2002).

Boyce, D. George, *Nationalism in Ireland* (2nd ed. London, 1991).

Brennan, Maeve, *The rose garden* (Washington, DC, 2000).

—, *The springs of affection*, introduction by Anne Enright (Dublin, 2016).

—, *The springs of affection: stories of Dublin*, introduction by William Maxwell (New York, 1997).

Bronfen, Elisabeth, *Home in Hollywood: the imaginary geography of cinema* (New York, 2004).

Brown, Bill, 'Thing theory', *Critical Inquiry*, 28:1 (2001), 1–22.

Brown, Terence, *The life of W.B. Yeats: a critical biography* (Dublin, 2001).

Carleton, William, *Traits and stories of the Irish peasantry*, 2nd series (London, 1877).

Carpenter, Andrew (ed.), *Art and architecture of Ireland*, 5 vols (New Haven, CT, 2014).

Chancer, Lynn, *Sadomasochism in everyday life: the dynamics of power and powerlessness* (New Brunswick, NJ, 1992).

Chellar, Kevin & Carol Chellar, *300 years of Irish timekeeping* (Dublin, 2010).

Childers, Molly, 'Letters from the *Asgard*' in Martin (ed.), *Howth gun-running* (1964), pp 98–107.

Clarke, Kathleen, *Revolutionary woman: an autobiography, 1878–1972*, ed. Helen Litton (Dublin, 1990).

Clear, Caitriona, *Women of the house: women's household work in Ireland, 1922–1961, discourses, experiences, memories* (Dublin, 2000).

Coffey, Diarmaid, 'Guns for Kilcoole' in Martin (ed.), *Howth gun-running* (1964), pp 116–24.

Colletta, Lisa & Maureen O'Connor (eds), *Wild colonial girl: essays on Edna O'Brien* (Madison, WI, 2006).

Comerford, Maire, 'Alice Stopford Green' in Martin (ed.), *Howth gun-running* (1964), pp 21–4.

Comerford, R.V., *The Fenians in context: Irish politics and society, 1848–1882* (Dublin, 1985).

Corcoran, Mary P. & Perry Share (eds), *Belongings: shaping identity in modern Ireland* (Dublin, 2008).

Corcoran, Neil, *The poetry of Seamus Heaney: a critical study* (London, 1998).

Coughlan, Patricia, 'The American wedding dress', lecture at Montclair State University, Montclair, NJ, 19 Mar. 2015.

—, 'Killing the bats: O'Brien, abjection, and the question of agency' in Laing et al. (eds), *Edna O'Brien* (2006), pp 171–95.

Coulter, Carol, *The hidden tradition: feminism, women and nationalism in Ireland* (Cork, 1993).

Crowley, John et al. (eds), *Atlas of the great Irish famine* (Cork, 2012).

Dalsimer, Adele M., *Visualizing Ireland* (London, 1993).

Danaher, Kevin, *Hearth and stool and all! Irish rural households* (Cork, 1985).

—, *Ireland's traditional houses* (Dublin, 1993).

—, *Ireland's vernacular architecture* (Cork, 1975).

*Digest of evidence taken before Her Majesty's commissioners of inquiry into the state of the law and practice in respect to the occupation of land in Ireland*, part 1 (Dublin, 1847).

Dillon, Geraldine Plunkett, *All in the blood*, ed. Honor O Brolchain (Dublin, 2006).

Donoghue, Emma, *The talk of the town*, HATCH Theatre Company, Landmark Productions and Dublin Theatre Festival, 2012.

Edgeworth, Maria, *Castle Rackrent: an Hibernian tale* (3rd ed. London, 1801).

Ellmann, Maud, 'Shadowing Elizabeth Bowen', *New England Review*, 24:1 (2003), 144–69.

Enright, Anne, review of Edna O'Brien, *Country girl: a memoir* (London, 2012), *Guardian*, 12 Oct. 2012.

Evans, E. Estyn, *Irish folk ways* (London, 1957).

FitzPatrick, Elizabeth & James Kelly (eds), *Domestic life in Ireland* (Dublin, 2011).

Foster, R.F., *W.B. Yeats: a life*, ii: *The arch-poet, 1915–1939* (Oxford, 2003).

Fraser, Nancy, 'Rethinking the public sphere', *Social Text*, 25/6 (1990), 56–80.

Freeman, Elizabeth, *Time binds: queer temporalities, queer histories* (Durham, NC, 2010).

Freud, Sigmund, *Civilization and its discontents* (New York, 2010).

Fuller, Grace Pierpoint, *An introduction to the history of Connecticut as a manufacturing state* (Northhampton, MA, 1916).

Gailey, Alan, *Rural houses of the north of Ireland* (Edinburgh, 1984).

Giddens, Anthony, *The consequences of modernity* (Cambridge, 1991).

Gillespie, Michael Paul, 'The odyssey of *Adam and Paul*, a twenty-first-century Irish film', *New Hibernia Review*, 12:1 (2008), 41–53.

Glassie, Henry, 'The Irish landscape' in Rhona Richman Kenneally (ed.), 'New visual, material, and spatial perspectives in Irish studies', *Canadian Journal of Irish Studies*, 38:1/2 (2014), 27–43.

—, *Passing the time in Ballymenone: culture and history of an Ulster community* (Philadelphia, 1982).

González, Rosa, 'John McGahern' in Jacqueline Hurtley et al. (eds), *Ireland in writing: interviews with writers and academics* (Amsterdam, 1998), pp 39–50.

Greenslade, Roy, 'Morrissey on Maeve: how a house linked an author and an actor', *Guardian*, 2 Sept. 2014.

Greenwood, Amanda, *Edna O'Brien* (Tavistock, 2003).

Gregory, Lady Augusta, 'Felons of our land' in Lucy McDiarmid and Maureen Waters (eds), *Lady Gregory: selected writings* (London, 1995), pp 254–69.

Grene, Nicholas, *Home on the stage: domestic spaces in modern drama* (Cambridge, 2014).

— (ed.), *Interpreting Synge: essays from the Synge summer school, 1991–2000* (Dublin, 2000).

—, *Synge: a critical study of the plays* (Totowa, NJ, 1975).

—, 'Synge and Wicklow' in Grene (ed.), *Interpreting Synge* (2000), pp 33–7.

—, 'Synge in performance' in P.J. Mathews (ed.), *Cambridge companion to J.M. Synge* (Cambridge, 2009), pp 149–61.

—, 'Two London Playboys: before and after Druid' in Adrian Frazier (ed.), *Playboys of the Western world: production histories* (Dublin, 2004), pp 75–86.

Grennan, Eamonn, 'Derek Mahon: the art of poetry, no. 82', *Paris Review*, 154 (Spring 2000), http://www.theparisreview.org/interviews/732/the-art-of-poetry-no-82-derek-mahon, accessed 6 July 2016.

Grier, Katherine C., *Culture & comfort: people, parlors, and upholstery, 1850–1930* (Rochester, NY, 1988).

Griffin, Gerald, *The Collegians*, vol. 1 (2nd ed. London, 1829).

Guppy, Shusha, 'Edna O'Brien: the art of fiction, no. 82', *Paris Review*, 92 (1984), 22–50.

Halberstam, Judith, *The queer art of failure* (Durham, NC, 2011).

Hamilton, Mary Louisa, *The Sinn Féin rebellion as I saw it*, republished in Jeffrey (ed.), *The Sinn Féin rebellion as they saw it* (1999), pp 35–85.

Hamlett, Jane, *Material relations: domestic interiors and middle-class families in England, 1850–1910* (Manchester, 2010).

Hanna, Adam, *Northern Irish poetry and domestic space* (Basingstoke, 2015).

Harper, Margaret Mills & Catherine E. Paul (eds), *A vision: the original 1925 version* in *The collected works of W.B. Yeats*, vol. 13 (New York, 2008).

— (eds), *A vision: the revised 1937 edition* in *The collected works of W.B. Yeats*, vol. 14 (New York, 2015).

Harris, Michael, 'Outside history: relocation and dislocation in Edna O'Brien's *House of splendid isolation*' in Laing et al. (eds), *Edna O'Brien* (2006), pp 122–37.

Hart, Henry, *Seamus Heaney: poet of contrary progressions* (New York, 1993).

Haughton, Hugh, *The poetry of Derek Mahon* (Oxford, 2007).

Heaney, Seamus, *District and circle* (London, 2006).

—, *Field work* (London, 1979).

—, *Finders keepers: selected prose, 1971–2001* (London, 2002).

—, in conversation with Eleanor Wachtel, *Writers & company*, CBC Radio, 25 May 2010, http://www.cbc.ca/radio/writersandcompany/seamus-heaney-interview-1.2790940, accessed 20 Mar. 2017.

—, *New selected poems: 1988–2013* (London, 2014).

—, *Opened ground: poems, 1966–1996* (London, 1998).

—, *Seamus Heaney in conversation with Karl Miller* (London, 2000).

—, *Station Island* (London, 1984).

—, *Stations* (Belfast, 1975).

Hearn, Mona, 'How Victorian families lived' in Mary E. Daly et al., *Dublin's Victorian houses* (Dublin, 1998), pp 59–129.

'Herbert Simms' in *Dictionary of Irish architects, 1720–1940*, http://www.dia.ie/architects/view/4969/Simms-HerbertGeorge, accessed 8 Apr. 2017.

Honohan, Iseult, 'Bounded citizenship and the meaning of citizenship laws: Ireland's *ius soli* citizenship referendum' in Linda Cardinal and Nicholas Brown (eds), *Managing diversity: practices of citizenship in Australia, Canada and Ireland* (Ottawa, 2007), pp 63–87.

Hynes, Garry, 'Garry Hynes and Ann Saddlemyer in conversation', *DruidSynge*, 3 DVDs (RTÉ, Wildfire Films/Druid, 2007).

Ingold, Tim, *Perception of the environment: essay on livelihood, dwelling and skill* (London & New York, 2000).

Inwood, Michael, *A Heidegger dictionary* (London, 1999).

Jeffrey, Keith, introduction in Jeffrey (ed.), *The Sinn Féin rebellion as they saw it* (1999), pp 13–32.

— (ed.), *The Sinn Féin rebellion as they saw it* (Dublin, 1999).

Joyce, James, *Ulysses: a critical and synoptic edition*, ed. Hans Walter Gabler, 3 vols (London, 1984).

Kearney, Richard, *Navigations: collected Irish essays, 1976–2006* (Syracuse, 2006).

Kearns, K.C., *Dublin tenement life: an oral history* (Dublin, 1994).

Kelsall, Malcolm, *Literary representations of the Irish country house* (Basingstoke, 2003).

Kennedy-Andrews, Elmer, introduction in *The poetry of Derek Mahon*, ed. Elmer Kennedy-Andrews (Gerrards Cross, 2002), pp 1–28.

Kickham, Charles J., *Knocknagow; or, the homes of Tipperary* (13th ed. Dublin, 1887).

King, Linda & Elaine Sisson (eds), *Ireland, design and visual culture: negotiating modernity, 1922–1992* (Cork, 2011).

Kinmonth, Claudia, *Irish country furniture, 1700–1950* (New Haven, 1995).

—, *Irish rural interiors in art* (New Haven, 2006).

Knight of Glin & James Peill, *Irish furniture: woodwork and carving in Ireland from the earliest times to the Act of Union* (New Haven, 2007).

Kreilkamp, Vera (ed.), *Rural Ireland: the inside story* (Boston, 2012).

Laing, Kathryn, Sinéad Mooney & Maureen O'Connor (eds), *Edna O'Brien: new critical perspectives* (Dublin, 2006).

Landsberg, Alison, *Prosthetic memory: the transformation of America* (New York, 2004).

Lange, Dorothea, *Dorothea Lange's Ireland*, with Daniel Dixon and Gerry Mullins (Washington, DC, 1998).

Latour, Bruno [Jim Johnson], 'Mixing humans with non-humans: sociology of a door-closer', *Social Problems*, 35 (1988), 298–310.

Leach, Neil (ed.), *Rethinking architecture: a reader in cultural theory* (London, 1997).

Lee, Joseph J., 'The ribbonmen' in T. Desmond Williams (ed.), *Secret societies in Ireland* (Dublin, 1973), pp 25–35.

Lefevbre, Henri, *The production of space*, trans. Donald Nicholson-Smith (Oxford, 1991).

Lenihan, Brian, 'Citizenship change common sense', *Irish Times*, 28 May 2004.

Lyons, F.S.L., *Ireland since the Famine* (London, 1971).

Mac Con Iomaire, Máirtín, 'Kenneth George Besson' in James McGuire and James Quin (eds), *Dictionary of Irish biography* (Cambridge, 2009) i, pp 505–6.

Mac Laughlin, Jim & Séan Beattie (eds), *An historical, environmental and cultural atlas of County Donegal* (Cork, 2013).

*Maeve Brennan: a traveller in exile* (Araby Productions for RTÉ, 2004).

Mahaffy, Elsie, TCD, MARL, MS 2074, Mahaffy, 'The Irish rebellion'.

Mahon, Derek, *An autumn wind* (Oldcastle, Co. Meath, 2010).

—, *The hunt by night* (Oxford, 1982).

—, *New collected poems* (Loughcrew, Co. Meath, 2011).

—, *The snow party* (Oxford, 1975).

Martin, F.X. (ed.), *The Howth gun-running and the Kilcoole gun-running, 1914* (Dublin, 1964).

Matthews, Ann, *The Kimmage garrison, 1916: making billy-can bombs at Larkfield* (Dublin, 2010).

Maxwell, William, introduction in Brennan, *Springs of affection* (New York, 1997), pp 1–14.

McCarthy, Thomas, '"We could be in any city": Eiléan Ní Chuilleanáin and Cork', *Irish University Review*, 37:1 (2007), 230–43.

Mc Cormack, W.J., *Fool of the family: a life of J.M. Synge* (London, 2000).

McDiarmid, Lucy, *At home in the revolution: what women said and did in 1916* (Dublin, 2015).

— (ed.), 'Irish secular relics', *Textual Practice*, 16:2 (2002).

—, *Poets and the peacock dinner: the literary history of a meal* (Oxford, 2015).

McDonald, Peter, *Mistaken identities: poetry and Northern Ireland* (Oxford, 1997).

McManus, Ruth, 'Urban dreams – urban nightmares' in Jim Hourihane (ed.), *Engaging spaces: people, place and space from an Irish perspective* (Dublin, 2003), pp 30–44.

Miller, Daniel, *The comfort of things* (Cambridge, 2008).

Mooney, Sinéad, 'Sacramental sleeves: fashioning the female subject in the fiction of Edna O'Brien' in Laing et al. (eds), *Edna O'Brien* (2006), pp 196–218.

Moore, George, *Confessions of a young man* (New York, 1920).

—, *The untilled field* (London, 1903).

Moore, Thomas, *The poetical works of Thomas Moore, collected by himself*, vol. 4 (New York, 1853).

Morrissey, Eamon, *Maeve's house*, Abbey Theatre, Dublin, 2013.

Moynihan, Maurice (ed.), *Speeches and statements by Eamon de Valera, 1917–73* (Dublin, 1980).

Mulcahy, Catriona, 'The Honan Hostel', *Honan chapel and collection online* http://honan.ucc.ie/essays.php?essayID=6, accessed 26 Feb. 2017.

Nic Shiubhlaigh, Maire, *The splendid years* (Dublin, 1955).

Norway, Arthur Hamilton, 'Irish experiences in war' in Jeffrey (ed.), *The Sinn Féin rebellion as they saw it* (1999), pp 87–122.

O'Brien, Edna, *Country girl: a memoir* (London, 2012).

—, *The country girls* (London, 2002).

—, *The love object* (London, 1972).

—, *Mrs Reinhardt and other stories* (London, 1986).

—, *Saints and sinners* (London, 2011).

O'Brien, R. Barry, *The life of Charles Stewart Parnell, 1846–1891* (London, 1898).

O'Connell, Diog, *New Irish storytellers: narrative strategies in film* (Bristol, 2010).

O'Connor, Maureen, '"The most haunting bird": unbeing and illegibility in contemporary Irish women's writing', *Women's Studies*, 44:7 (2015), 940–55.

O'Driscoll, Dennis, *Stepping stones: interviews with Seamus Heaney* (London, 2008).

Ó Gráda, Cormac, *Ireland: a new economic history, 1780–1919* (Oxford, 1994).

Oliver Paul et al., *Dunroamin: the suburban semi and its enemies* (London, 1981).

Orlin, Lena Cowen, *Locating privacy in Tudor London* (Oxford, 2007).

—, *Private matters and public culture in post-Reformation England* (Ithaca, NY, 1994).

O'Toole, Fintan, *A history of Ireland in 100 objects* (Dublin, 2013), http://www.100objects.ie, accessed 19 June 2017.

Pelan, Rebecca, 'Edna O'Brien's "love objects"' in Colletta and O'Connor (eds), *Wild colonial girl* (2006), pp 58–76.

Pellew, George, *In castle and cabin; or, talks in Ireland in 1887* (New York & London, 1888).

Perkins, Harvey & David C. Thorns, *Place, identity and everyday life in a globalizing world* (Basingstoke, 2011).

Peters, Ann, 'A traveler in residence: Maeve Brennan and the last days of New York', *Women's Studies Quarterly*, 33:3/4 (2005), 66–89.

Peterson, Shirley, '"Meaniacs" and martyrs: sadomasochistic desire in Edna O'Brien's The Country Girls Trilogy' in Laing et al. (eds), *Edna O'Brien* (2006), pp 151–70.

Pike, Michael & Emmett Scanlon, '*Habitus*: a social anthropology of the contemporary house extension' in Elizabeth FitzPatrick and James Kelly (eds), *Domestic life in Ireland* (Dublin, 2011), pp 311–36.

Pine, Emilie, 'Coming clean? Remembering the Magdalen laundries' in Oona Frawley (ed.), *Memory Ireland, 1: History and modernity* (Syracuse, NY, 2011), pp 151–71

Quinlan, Christina, 'Discourse and identity: a study of women in prison in Ireland' (PhD, Dublin City University, 2006).

—, 'Home and belonging: a study of women in prison in Ireland' in Corcoran and Share (eds), *Belongings* (2008), pp 129–35.

Quinn, Antoinette, 'Staging the Irish peasant woman: Maud Gonne versus Synge' in Grene (ed.), *Interpreting Synge* (2000), pp 117–34.

*Report of the commissioners appointed to take the census for the year 1841* (Dublin, 1841).

*Report of the trial of the queen, at the prosecution of the rt. hon. the attorney general against Charles Stewart Parnell (et al.) for conspiracy in inciting tenants not to pay rents contracted for and deterring tenants from payment of rent, commencing Tuesday, December 28, 1880, and terminating Tuesday, January 25, 1881* (Dublin, 1881).

Reynolds, Paige (ed.), 'Irish things', *Éire-Ireland*, 46:1/2 (2011).

Richardson, William J., *Heidegger: through phenomenology to thought* (4th ed. New York, 2003).

Richman Kenneally, Rhona, 'Cooking at the hearth: the "Irish cottage" and women's lived experience' in Oona Frawley (ed.), *Memory Ireland, ii: Diaspora and memory practices* (Syracuse, NY, 2012), pp 224–41.

—, 'The elusive landscape of history: food and empowerment in Sebastian Barry's "Annie Dunne"' in Máirtín Mac Con Iomaire and Eamon Maher (eds), '*Tickling the palate': gastronomy in Irish literature and culture* (New York, 2014), pp 79–98.

—, 'Tastes of home in mid-twentieth-century Ireland: food, design, and the refrigerator', *Food and Foodways*, 23 (2015), 80–123.

—, 'Towards a new domestic architecture: homes, kitchens and food in rural Ireland during the long 1950s' in Elizabeth FitzPatrick and James Kelly (eds), *Food and drink in Ireland* (Dublin, 2016), pp 325–47.

—, 'Memory as food performance: the cookbooks of Maura Laverty' in Michael Kenneally and Margaret Kelleher (eds), *Ireland and Quebec: multidisciplinary perspectives on history, culture and society* (Dublin, 2016), pp 166–82.

Robinson, Fred Miller, *The comedy of language: studies in modern comic literature* (Amherst, MA, 1980).

Roche, Nessa M., *The legacy of light: a history of Irish windows* (Dublin, 1999).

Roth, Philip, 'A conversation with Edna O'Brien: "The body contains the life story"', *New York Times*, 18 Nov. 1984.

Royal Institute of the Architects of Ireland, *Building on the edge of Europe/ Construire à la frange de l'Europe: a survey of contemporary architecture in Ireland embracing history, town and country* (Dublin, 1996).

Ruskin, John, *Sesame and lilies* (1865).

Schrank, Bernice & Danine Farquharson, 'Blurring boundaries, intersecting lives: history, gender, and violence in Edna O'Brien's *House of splendid isolation*' in Colletta and O'Connor (eds), *Wild colonial girl* (2006), pp 110–42.

—, 'Object of love, subject to despair: Edna O'Brien's love object and the emotional logic of late romanticism', *Canadian Journal of Irish Studies*, 22:2 (1996), 22–36.

Simmons, James, 'The trouble with Seamus Heaney' in Elmer Kennedy-Andrews (ed.), *Seamus Heaney: a collection of critical essays* (New York, 1992), pp 39–66.

Smith, James M., *Ireland's Magdalen laundries and the nation's architecture of containment* (Notre Dame, IN, 2007).

Smyth, Gerry, *Space and the Irish cultural imagination* (Basingstoke, 2001).

Spring Rice, Mary, 'Diary of the *Asgard*, July 1914' in Martin (ed.), *Howth gun-running* (1964), pp 68–97.

Stevens, Wallace, *The collected poems* (New York, 1954).

Sullivan, Margaret F., *Ireland of today: the causes and aims of Irish agitation* (Philadelphia, 1881).

Synge, J.M., *Collected letters*, i: *1871–1907*, ed. Ann Saddlemyer (Oxford, 1983).

—, *Collected works*, i: *Poems*, ed. Robin Skelton (London, 1962).

—, *Collected works*, ii: *Prose*, ed. Alan Price (London, 1966).

—, *Collected works*, iii: *Plays 1*, ed. Ann Saddlemyer (London, 1968).

—, *Collected works*, iv: *Plays 2*, ed. Ann Saddlemyer (London, 1968).

—, *Travelling Ireland: essays, 1898–1908*, ed. Nicholas Grene (Dublin, 2009).

Tange, Andrea Kaston, *Architectural identities: domesticity, literature and the Victorian middle classes* (Toronto, 2010).

Thuente, Mary Helen, *The harp re-strung: the United Irishmen and the rise of Irish literary nationalism* (Syracuse, 1994).

*United Irishman*, 24 Oct. 1903.

Unwin, Raymond, and Barry Parker, *The art of building a home: a collection of lectures and illustrations* (London, New York & Bombay, 1901).

Wincott Heckett, Elizabeth, 'The part played by women in the making of the Honan Chapel', *Honan Chapel and collection online*, http://honan. ucc.ie/essays.php?essayID=8, accessed 26 Feb. 2017.

Yeats, W.B., *Collected poems*, ed. Augustine Martin (London, 1992).

—, *The letters of W.B. Yeats*, ed. Allen Wade (London, 1954).

— (ed.), *Representative Irish tales* (Atlantic Highlands, NJ, 1979).

— (ed.), *Stories from Carleton, with an introduction by W.B. Yeats* (London, 1889).

# Index